Adobe®
PageMaker®

Library of Congress Catalog No.: 95-77726

ISBN: 1-56830-235-5

10 9 8 7 6 5 4 3 2   First Printing: August 1995

The information in this book is furnished for informational use only, is subject to change without notice, and should not be construed as a commitment by Adobe Systems Incorporated. Adobe Systems Incorporated assumes no responsibility for any errors or inaccuracies that may appear in this book. The software and typefaces mentioned in this book are furnished under license and may only be used or copied in accordance with the terms of such license.

PANTONE ® Computer video simulations used in this product may not match PANTONE-identified solid color standards. All trademarks noted herein are either the property of Pantone, Inc. or their respective companies. PANTONE Open Color Environment™ (POCE™) © Pantone, Inc. 1994.

Pantone, Inc. is the copyright owner of PANTONE Open Color Environment™ (POCE™) and Software which are licensed to Adobe to distribute for use only in combinations with Adobe PageMaker. PANTONE Open Color Environment™ (POCE™) and Software shall not be copied onto another diskette or into memory unless as part of the execution of Adobe PageMaker.

PostScript® is a trademark of Adobe Systems Incorporated ("Adobe"), registered in the United States and elsewhere. PostScript can refer both to the PostScript language as specified by Adobe and to Adobe's implementation of its PostScript language interpreter.

Any references to "PostScript printers," "PostScript files," or "PostScript drivers" refer, respectively, to printers, files, and driver programs written in or supporting the PostScript language. References in this book to the "PostScript language" are intended to emphasize Adobe's standard definition of that language.

Adobe, the Adobe Press logo, Acrobat, Acrobat Exchange, Adobe Dimensions, Adobe Illustrator, PageMaker, Adobe Photoshop, Adobe Teach, Adobe Type Manager, Adobe Garamond, Birch, Madrone, Minion, Myriad, Poplar, Trajan, Classroom in a Book, Classroom in a Box, and PostScript are trademarks of Adobe Systems Incorporated which. Macintosh is a registered trademark of Apple Computer, Inc., Windows is a registered trademark of Microsoft Corporation. All other trademarks are the property of their respective owners.

Printed in the United States of America by Shepard Poorman Communications, Indianapolis, Indiana.

Published simultaneously in Canada.

Adobe Press books are published and distributed by Hayden Books, a division of Macmillan Computer Publishing. For individual orders, or for educational, corporate, or retail sales accounts, call 1-800-428-5331. For information, address Hayden Books, 201 W. 103rd Street, Indianapolis, IN 46290.

Part Number: 0197 1662 (8/95)

CONTENTS

Featuring the first full-color commercial printing press job in the book, this jewelcase booklet incorporates color photographs, illustrations, and other graphics that you will manipulate and refine using the tools offered with the Adobe PageMaker application, including the Image Control command.

Offering maximum precision and control, Adobe PageMaker makes it possible to integrate text and graphics from many sources into virtually any kind of printed document. Assembling this full-color book cover design gives you further opportunity to explore these possibilities.

Using the new multiple master pages feature, it is possible for your multipage publications to employ a virtually unlimited number of master pages. To assemble the three-color magazine article, you will assemble two master pages, and then apply them to individual double-page spreads.

With the electronic distribution of publications becoming more prevalent, see how you can use Adobe Acrobat™ to convert your Adobe PageMaker files to Portable Document Format (PDF). Retaining the page layout, color, graphics, and typography of the original document, PDF files can be viewed on-screen or printed using Adobe Reader™ or Adobe Exchange™.

Adobe® PageMaker® 6.0 offers tools for each person in the publishing cycle: graphic artists and designers; writers, editors, and typesetters; production artists and prepress professionals. With Adobe PageMaker it is possible to integrate text

WHAT YOU NEED TO KNOW

and graphics from many sources into virtually any kind of publication, from newsletters and brochures to color catalogs and magazines, with maximum precision and control.

PREREQUISITES

Before beginning to use Adobe PageMaker *Classroom in a Book™*, you should have a working knowledge of the Macintosh® and its operating conventions. You should know how to use the mouse and standard Macintosh menus and commands. You should also know how to open, save, and close files. If you need to review these techniques, see the documentation that came with your Macintosh.

ABOUT CLASSROOM IN A BOOK

Classroom in a Book teaches you all the basics (as well as many advanced techniques) that you need to know to get the most out of Adobe PageMaker. The lessons in this book center around an international theme of architecture. The publications you will assemble include a flyer, newletter, poster, compact disc jewelcase booklet, book cover design, magazine article, and a catalog that can be converted to a PDF (Portable Document Format) file to be distributed electronically.

Unlike a real work environment, *Classroom in a Book* is designed to let you move at your own pace, and even make mistakes! Although the lessons are designed with a specific publication in mind, and provide step-by-step instruction to help you achieve those results, there is room for exploration and experimentation. You may follow the book from start to finish, or pick which ever lesson interests you the most.

Classroom in a Book is not meant to replace documentation that comes with Adobe PageMaker. Only the commands and options used in the lessons are explained in this book. For comprehensive information about all of the program's features, refer to the *Adobe PageMaker 6.0 User Guide.*

HOW TO GET STARTED

Before you begin using Adobe PageMaker *Classroom in a Book*, you need to make sure that your system is set up correctly, and that you have installed the required software and hardware. The following list summarizes what you need to do.

- Check the system requirements

- Install the Adobe PageMaker application

- Install the fonts included on the Adobe PageMaker *Classroom in a Book* CD-ROM disc

- Copy the files (included on the Adobe PageMaker *Classroom in a Book* CD-ROM disc) to your hard drive.

Checking system requirements

To access the *Classroom in a Book* CD-ROM disc, you need a double-speed or higher CD-ROM drive. To execute the lessons in *Classroom in a Book*, your system must include the hardware and software described in the *Adobe PageMaker 6.0 Getting Started* booklet.

To watch Adobe Teach™ movies, your system must meet or exceed the following requirements:

- 8 MB of free RAM
- System 7 or higher
- Double-speed or higher CD-ROM player
- QuickTime™ installed on your system

Note: To install QuickTime, place the QuickTime extension from the QuickTime 1.6.1 folder in your system folder.

Installing the Adobe PageMaker program

This book does not include the Adobe PageMaker software. You must purchase the software separately. Use the *Adobe PageMaker 6.0 Getting Started* booklet that comes with the Adobe PageMaker software to install the Adobe PageMaker application.

Installing the fonts

In addition to using some commonly-used fonts, all lessons included in this book feature Adobe Originals® fonts. These fonts are found on the *Classroom in a Book* CD-ROM disc in the *Fonts* folder. For information on how to install these fonts, refer to the *PM CIB Readme* file on the *Classroom in a Book* CD-ROM disc.

Copying the Classroom in a Book files

The Adobe PageMaker *Classroom in a Book* CD-ROM disc includes files for all lessons. You may copy all or one lesson to your system.

Important: Since the files on the Classroom in a Book *CD-ROM disc are not locked, it is possible to make and save changes to them. If you inadvertently make changes to a file installed on your system, make sure it is selected and choose Revert from the File menu to restore it. If you inadvertently save any changes to a file, you must re-copy the file from the* Classroom in a Book *CD-ROM disc to view an uncorrupted file.*

To install the CD-ROM folders, create a folder on your computer and name it *Adobe PageMaker CIB*, and then copy the folders for the lessons from the CD-ROM disc into the *Adobe PageMaker CIB* folder to access the files for each lesson. To save room, copy the files for each lesson as needed.

The *Classroom in a Book* CD-ROM disc includes a *Projects* folder, so that you can save the Adobe PageMaker files that you will create as you're working through *Classroom in a Book*.

USING INTERIM FILES

An interim file is a file that contains portions of the final artwork file. We have included interim files for several reasons. For example, you may not want to do everything in a long lesson. Or maybe you completed part of a lesson and accidentally lost your working file.

To use the interim file, open the interim file at the specified point in the lesson. Since the interim file contains the artwork for all steps in the lesson up to that point, you can continue the lesson from that point.

WATCHING ADOBE TEACH MOVIES

Adobe Teach movies are QuickTime movies included with *Classroom in a Book*. You can watch a movie to see a preview of what's to come in a lesson, or your can go back and review the movie after you've tried a new technique. You can even watch a movie right now. You will see the Adobe Teach movie icon whenever it's time to watch a movie.

Note: To get the best results playing Adobe Teach movies, set your monitor to 256 colors or thousands of colors.

1 Quit (or exit) the Adobe PageMaker application.

2 Double-click the *Adobe Teach™ movies* folder on the *Classroom in a Book* CD-ROM disc to open it.

3 If Adobe ATM® 3.8.2 or higher is not installed on your system, double-click the *AcroRead.mac* icon to install Adobe ATM and Adobe Acrobat Reader®.

Note: For information about installing Adobe Acrobat Reader, double-click the Read-me-Reader 2.0.1 *file on the* Classroom in a Book *CD-ROM disc.*

4 Double-click the *Adobe Teach™ movie menu* icon to launch Adobe Acrobat Reader and open the Movie menu screen.

The Movie menu screen is a PDF (Portable Document Format) file.

5 In the Movie menu screen click a camera icon above the desired movie title to open a movie.

6 To play the movie, click the arrow button in the lower-left corner of the display window.

Note: To adjust the volume, choose the desired volume level from the speaker pop-up menu in the lower-left corner of the display window. To replay a movie (or a portion of a movie), drag the progress indicator to the left.

7 To close a movie, click the close box in the upper-left corner of the display window to display the Movie menu screen.

8 To exit the Movie menu screen, hold down the Command key and press period (.), and to exit Adobe Acrobat Reader, hold down the Command key and press Q.

Home Review

Spacious **three bedroom, two bath Victorian located in the historic city of Cambridge.**

Freshly **painted exterior and interior detail.**

Modern **renovations boast the finest electronic appliances, and highest quality fixtures.**

Landscaped **by a premiere Boston architect.**

Close to the beautiful Charles River, this home shares the historic charm of its Cambridge neighborhood.

In the heart of the Boston area lies a true architectural gem. This Victorian dwelling exemplifies turn-of-the-century New England architecture at its best. In addition to its prime location just minutes from downtown Boston, this home enjoys spectacular views of the Charles River and the downtown Boston skyline. Completely restored with attention to historic detail, this three-story, three-bedroom residence has incorporated all of the functional requirements of today's home. The magnificent interior boasts all original oak finishing, including a breathtaking spiral bannister, and built-in bookcases in the library. The kitchen has been fully modernized with state of the art appliances, yet retains the houses original charm with its high ceilings, ornate moldings, and fully operational wood-stove. The original bay windows, refinished hardwood floors, and ornate paint trim make this home's interior complete and as spectacular as its proud exterior. Consistent with the practical charm of Victorian architecture, no space is wasted. The most spectacular room of all is the converted attic. It clearly takes full advantage of its immense size and high ceiling with skylights, windows, and a stairway leading out to a small widow's walk.

This Cambridge residence bestows the colonial charm of New England's past upon this quaint neighborhood. It resides just two blocks from the historic house used as George Washington's headquarters in 1775, and later occupied by poet Henry Wadsworth Longfellow. A stroll north on Lyon Street past a hilly intersection looks out over the pine and maple woods of a nearby park, a dramatic contrast with the blue Massachusetts bay beyond. These stunning views must have inspired architects to execute their best work. For more information about this property please contact Joan Rutherford at Harbor Realty.

The first lesson involves assembling a single-page, black-and-white flyer from start to finish. Since importing text and graphics elements from many different sources is one of the

HOME REVIEW FLYER

specialties of Adobe PageMaker, the photograph and most of the text featured in this flyer were generated and edited elsewhere, and are ready for you to import into Adobe PageMaker. ■ In addition to importing text and graphics into an Adobe PageMaker publication, this lesson shows you how to create text and graphic elements. Using some of the tools that are included in the Adobe PageMaker application, you will draw several graphics elements (square, circle, and line) that are included in the flyer design. To demonstrate how to type text directly into a publication, you will generate two text elements (headline and address) yourself.

Before assembling any publication in this book, each lesson instructs you to open and view the final version of the publication. For this lesson, you will open the final version of the flyer publication, and follow the step-by-step instructions

HOME REVIEW FLYER

that introduce some of the basic features and tools of the Adobe PageMaker program. Even if you have experience using the Adobe PageMaker application, this introduction may reveal some useful tips and techniques.

This project covers:
- Throwing away the *Adobe PageMaker 6.0 Prefs* file
- Launching the Adobe PageMaker program
- Adjusting the view of a publication
- Opening a new and existing publication
- Setting up the horizontal and vertical rulers
- Displaying and hiding guides
- Positioning the zero point
- Using the pointer tool, the text tool, and the magnifying glass
- Specifying multiple columns
- Locking the guides
- Creating, placing, formatting, and positioning text and graphics elements
- Creating a drop cap
- Applying a tint to text
- Specifyng a hanging indent
- Creating ruler guides
- Drawing circles, rectangles, and lines
- Adjusting the stacking order

- Range kerning text
- Deactivating the Snap to Guides option
- Printing the flyer on a desktop laser printer.

BEFORE YOU BEGIN

All files and fonts needed for this lesson are found on the Adobc PageMaker *Classroom in a Book* CD-ROM disc in the folders *01Lesson* and *Fonts*, respectively.

If this is your first time to use Adobe PageMaker, it should take about 2 hours to complete this lesson. If you have some experience using Adobe PageMaker, it should take about 90 minutes to complete this lesson.

Throwing away the Adobe PageMaker 6.0 Prefs file

Before launching the Adobe PageMaker program, throw away the *Adobe PageMaker 6.0Prefs* file to ensure all settings are returned to their default values.

1 Open the System folder on your hard disk, and double-click the *Preferences* folder in the System folder.

2 Drag the *Adobe PageMaker 6.0 Prefs* file in the *Preferences* folder to the Trash, and choose Empty Trash from the Special menu.

Adobe® PageMaker® 6.0 Prefs   Trash

3 Close the System folder.

The Adobe PageMaker preferences settings are returned to their default values.

Launching the Adobe PageMaker application

After verifying the correct fonts are installed on your system, you will launch the Adobe PageMaker application.

Note: All files on the Adobe PageMaker Classroom in a Book CD-ROM disc have been locked for your protection.

1 Make sure the fonts Minion Display Regular, Minion Display Italic, Myriad MM 700 Bold 600 Normal, and Myriad MM 215 Light 600 Normal are in-stalled on your system.

Minion is a 1990 Adobe Originals typeface by Robert Slimbach. Minion is inspired by classical, old-style typefaces of the late Renaissance, a period of elegant, beautiful, and highly readable type designs. Created primarily for text setting, Minion combines the aesthetic qualities that make text type highly readable with the versatility of digi-tal technology. The Minion family contains black weight, display, and swash fonts, expert sets, and a full range of ornaments, for uses that range from limited-edition books to newsletters to packaging.

Myriad is an Adobe Originals typeface designed by Carol Twombly and Robert Slimbach in 1992. Myriad, a multiple master typeface, is a sans serif design that allows the generation of thousands of individual fonts from one master typeface by interactively varying the design attributes of weight and width. Myriad makes a good text face as well as providing flexibility for filling display needs in all sizes and mediums.

2 Double-click the *Adobe® PageMaker® 6.0* icon to launch the Adobe PageMaker program.

Adobe® PageMaker® 6.0

Once launched, Adobe PageMaker displays the pull-down menus across the top of your monitor display.

Opening an existing document

Before assembling the publication featured in this lesson, you will open the final version of the publication, and follow the step-by-step instructions to become aquainted with the Adobe PageMaker application.

Time out for a movie

If your system is capable of running Adobe Teach movies, play the movie *Toolbox Tour* to see a preview of the introduction to the Adobe PageMaker program that is covered in this lesson. For information on how to play Adobe Teach movies, see the section What You Need To Know at the beginning of this book.

1 Choose Open from the File menu (Command-O), and in the Open Publication dialog box double-click the *01Final* file in the *01Lesson* folder.

Adobe PageMaker opens the final version of the publication you will assemble in this lesson, with horizontal and vertical rulers extending along the top and left edges of the publication window.

TIP: TO TOGGLE
BETWEEN THE DISPLAY
SIZES FIT IN WINDOW
AND ACTUAL SIZE, HOLD
DOWN THE COMMAND
AND OPTION KEYS
AND CLICK THE PAGE
OR THE PASTEBOARD.

Notice the toolbox displayed in the upper-left corner of the publication window. The toolbox displays tools that you click to select. In addition to offering positioning, sizing, and formatting information about the selected text or graphic element.

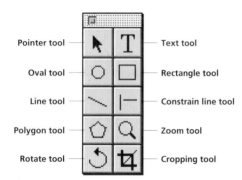

Notice how the Control palette spans the lower portion of the publication window. The Control palette provides quick access to many of the commands and options available in the pull-down menus. By default, the Adobe PageMaker application opens an existing publication with the palettes that were open when it was last saved.

The grayed-out text and graphics elements are arranged within a rectangular boundary known as a page. Whenever creating a new publication, you define the dimensions of the page. By definition, only text or graphics elements positioned within the bounds of the page will be printed.

The white area surrounding the page is known as the pasteboard. The term pasteboard, like many of the terms you will encounter in this course, originates from pre-electronic publishing technology, where layout artists assembled text and graphics elements on a physical pasteboard, using the extra space around a page as a work space. Much the same now as then, you can use the pasteboard in Adobe PageMaker as a work space, allowing you to view, organize, and manipulate text and graphics elements before positioning them on the page.

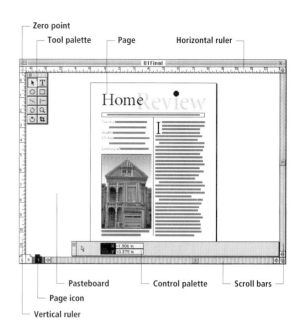

The page icon 1 in the lower-left corner of your publication window indicates the *01Final* publication consists of a single page.

Adjusting the view of a publication

By default, Adobe PageMaker opens a publication in the display size that was selected when it was last saved. For this reason, this publication is displayed in the display size Fit in Window.

Note: When the size of this page is reduced to fit within a 13-inch (or smaller) monitor, the 10-point text is displayed as gray bars (greeked). By default, Adobe PageMaker displays 9-point text or smaller as gray bars.

1 Choose View from the Layout menu and Actual Size from the submenu (Command-1) to select it, making sure the option is checked.

The view of this publication is magnified to its actual size (its size when printed), making it possible to read the text.

2 Click or drag the scroll bars on the right and bottom edges of the display window to scroll the view of the page.

For whatever reason, you may wish to use the following method to scroll in your publication.

3 Hold down the Option key, position the cursor on the page or pasteboard, hold down the mouse button until the cursor is displayed as a grabber hand, drag in any direction, and release the mouse button to scroll the view of the page.

4 Click the magnifying glass in the toolbox to select it.

The cursor is displayed as a magnifying glass. The magnifying glass makes it easy to magnify and reduce the view of selected portions of the page. With the magnifying glass selected, you can magnify the view of a specific portion of the page by clicking it, or dragging to marquee select it.

5 With the magnifying glass selected in the toolbox, hold down the Option key.

The magnifying glass icon is displayed with a minus (-) sign.

6 Click the page to reduce the view of the page to display size Fit in Window.

7 With the magnifying glass still selected in the toolbox, drag to marquee select any portion of the page.

The view of the selected portion of the page fills the publication window.

8 Hold down the Option key, and double-click the magnifying glass in the toolbox to display the entire page at the display size Fit in Window.

Note: Double-click the magnifying glass to view the page in display size Actual Size.

Using the rulers

Extending along the top and left borders of your publication window, the horizontal and vertical rulers serve to help you position text and graphics elements on a page.

1 Click the pointer tool in the toolbox (black arrow in the palette in the upper-left corner of the publication window) to select it.

In addition to selecting the pointer tool, clicking the pointer tool in the toolbox will deselect all objects in a publication and remove an existing insertion point.

2 Without clicking in your publication, move the cursor around the publication window, and notice how the hairline indicators in the vertical and horizontal rulers correspond to the position of the cursor.

Also notice how when no text or graphics elements are selected in your publication, the Control palette displays the horizontal and vertical alignments of the cursor as X and Y coordinates, respectively.

Note: Since inches is the measurement system established for this publication, the Control palette and the horizontal and vertical rulers reflect inches as the unit of measure.

Positioning the zero point

By default the zero points on the horizontal and vertical rulers are positioned at the upper-left corner of a single-sided page.

1 Without clicking in your publication, move the cursor to the upper-left edge of the page, noticing how the zeros on the horizontal and vertical rulers are aligned with the upper-left edge of the page.

TIP: TO SELECT THE
MAGNIFYING GLASS,
HOLD DOWN THE
SHIFT KEY AND
PRESS THE F8 KEY.

2 If necessary, click the scroll bars along the right and bottom edges of the publication window to view the upper-left corner of the page.

This intersection of zeros is known as the zero point. By default, the zero point of single publications is positioned at the intersection of the upper-left edge of the page. To measure distances from specific areas of your page, you can move the zero point to any location.

3 With the pointer tool selected, position the cursor on the crosshair of the zero point (at the intersection of the rulers in the upper-left corner of your publication window), and hold down the mouse button.

When you select the zero point, horizontal and vertical guides indicate the position of the zero point.

4 With the mouse button still held down, drag the zero point down and right until the horizontal and vertical guides are roughly aligned with the upper-left edge of the letter H in the headline text Home Review, and release the mouse button.

Zero point

The horizontal and vertical rulers indicate the new location of the zero point.

5 Double-click the crosshair of the zero point to restore the zero point to its default location at the upper-left edge of the page.

Setting up the rulers

You can set the horizontal and vertical rulers to the measurement system you prefer. In general, it's a good idea to choose a measurement system before you assemble a publication.

1 Choose Preferences from the File menu.

The Preferences dialog box displays the available options for customizing your publication window. If a publication is open, the options you select in the Preferences dialog box apply to that publication only. If no publication is open, the options you choose apply to all new publications you create.

2 In the Preferences dialog box notice how Inches is selected from the Measurements in pop-up menu and the Vertical ruler pop-up menu.

Adobe PageMaker makes it possible to work with the horizontal and vertical rulers set to different units of measure.

3 In the Preferences dialog box choose Picas from the Vertical ruler pop-up menu, and click OK.

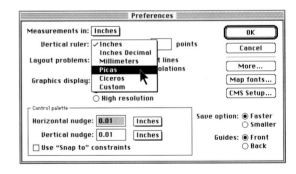

The horizontal ruler reflects the unit of measure (Inches) originally selected in the Measurements in pop-up menu. The vertical ruler indicates picas as the unit of measure.

TIP: TO VIEW AN OPEN PUBLICATION, CHOOSE THE PUBLICATION FROM THE WINDOW MENU OR CLICK THE TITLE BAR OF THE PUBLICATION.

Note: Derived from an old term for metal type of that size, a pica is a measure of type (approximately equal to 1/6 of an inch), divided into 12 points (each point equal to .0138 (1/72) of an inch).

Notice how the text and graphics elements remain in the same position on the page. Even though you usually work with one unit of measure throughout a publication, you can see it is possible to change to another unit of measure at any time, without altering the positioning of elements.

4 Choose Preferences from the File menu, and in the Preferences dialog box choose Inches from the Vertical ruler pop-up menu, and click OK to restore the original measurement system.

5 Choose Guides and Rulers from the Layout menu and Show Rulers from the submenu (Command-R) to deselect it, making sure it is unchecked.

The rulers are hidden, providing more room on the screen.

6 Once again, choose Guides and Rulers from the Layout menu and Show Rulers from the submenu to select it, displaying the rulers.

Displaying guides

It's a good time to look at some of the nonprinting guides we used to assemble this publication.

1 Choose View from the Layout menu and Fit in Window from the submenu (Command-0) to view the entire page.

2 Choose Guides and Rulers from the Layout menu and Show Guides from the submenu (Command-J) to select it, making sure it is checked.

The *01Final* publication is displayed with all nonprinting guides.

Notice the light blue (dotted on black and white monitors) horizontal and vertical ruler guides positioned at various locations on the page. These ruler guides are used to position text and graphics on the page accurately. It is possible to have as many as 120 ruler guides on the page, in any combination of horizontal and vertical.

The pink horizontal lines at the top and bottom of the columns are the top and bottom margins guides. The darker blue vertical lines indicate the columns. Column guides help define areas for text to flow into automatically. All of these lines are displayed as dotted lines on a black and white monitor.

Note: Column guides overlap the left and right margin guides.

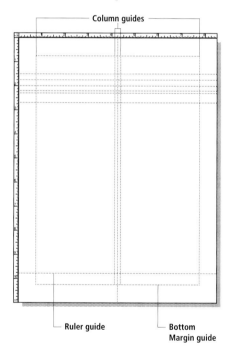

3 If you have altered the *01Final* file, choose Revert from the File menu, and when prompted, click the OK button to revert to the original version of the file.

TIP: TO VIEW ON-LINE HELP, CHOOSE USING PAGEMAKER HELP FROM THE HELP MENU (QUESTION MARK ICON IN THE RIGHT PORTION OF THE MENU BAR), AND CLICK THE TOPIC ON WHICH YOU WANT HELP.

Note: If you have saved any changes made to the 01Final *file, copy the original* 01Final *file from the* 01Lesson *folder on the Adobe PageMaker* Classroom in a Book *CD-ROM disc.*

Planning to print this flyer

Now that you have seen the publication you will assemble, it's a good idea to gather all printing requirements before you start to work. Designed to be printed on a 300 dpi (dots per inch) desktop laser printer, this flyer (including the grayscale TIFF image scanned at 100 dpi), can print successfully on a wide variety of PostScript and non-PostScript printers.

Since most printers do not print to the very edge of the page, you will need to determine the maximum printable area of a page, and adapt your design accordingly. If the documentation that came with your printer does not provide the specific dimensions of the maximum printable area, you can manually determine it. To do so, use Adobe PageMaker to draw a shaded box that covers an entire page, and print the page on the target printer to verify the imageable area.

ASSEMBLING A TWO-COLUMN FLYER

After opening a new publication, you will place and format text and graphics elements to assemble this two-column flyer.

Since Adobe PageMaker makes it possible to open more than one publication at a time, allow the final version to remain open as you assemble the flyer. When necessary, use the *01Final* publication as a reference.

Opening a new publication

After setting the options in the Document Setup dialog box, you will name and save your publication.

1 Choose New from the File menu (Command-N).

The Document Setup dialog box prompts you to establish some of the specifications for the flyer publication. To override the Adobe PageMaker defaults applied to all new publications, choose Document Setup from the File menu when no publication is open. For this example, you will select options that will apply to this publication alone.

2 In the Document Setup dialog box click the Double-sided check box to deselect it, type .75 inch in the Left box and make sure the Right, Top, and Bottom boxes indicate a value of .75 inch (to establish a .75-inch margin around the entire page), and click OK.

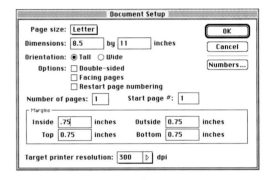

Note: If you plan to resize monochrome bitmap images (the photograph in this flyer is a grayscale TIFF image), you need to specify the resolution of the target printer, since Adobe PageMaker uses the printer resolution to adjust the resolution of monochrome bitmap images to match the resolution of the printing device.

The dimensions of the untitled publication reflect the Letter page size of 8.5 inches by 11 inches. The rectangle formed by solid lines of different colors (displayed as dotted lines on a black and white monitor) indicates the position of your margin guides. Margin guides are nonprinting lines to help you with the placement of text and graphics.

TIP: TO SELECT THE POINTER TOOL, HOLD DOWN THE SHIFT KEY AND PRESS THE F1 KEY.

By default, every publication has at least one column that spans the image area between the left and right margin guides. For this reason, the dark blue vertical column guides overlap the pink left and right margin guides. Again, all guides are displayed as dotted lines on a black and white monitor.

3 With the pointer tool selected, position the cursor on either vertical dark blue (or dotted) column guide, hold down the mouse button until the cursor is displayed as a double-headed arrow, and drag left or right, to view the pink (or dotted) margin guide behind it.

Adobe PageMaker makes it possible to adjust the size of a single column to be a different width than the image area between the left and right margin guides.

4 Drag the column guide until it is aligned with its original position over the margin guide.

Note: Unlike most word-processing applications, Adobe PageMaker makes it possible to print text and graphics elements positioned in the margins.

5 If you do not have a *Projects* folder, create one now.

6 Choose Save As from the File menu, and in the Save Publication As dialog box type **01Work** in the Name box, make sure the Publication option is selected, select the *Projects* folder, and click OK.

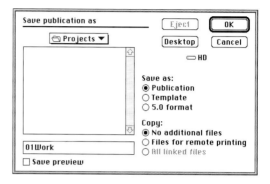

Adobe PageMaker saves the *01Work* publication.

Specifying column guides

With the .75-inch margins already established using the Document Setup dialog box, you are ready to add column guides and ruler guides, two additional types of nonprinting lines. Column guides serve as text boundaries and help you to position text and graphics. Unlike column guides, ruler guides do not control the flow of text; they help you align text and graphics precisely.

As you have already seen, every publication has at least one column, the image area between the left and right margin guides. For this flyer, you will divide the image area into two columns.

1 Choose Column Guides from the Layout menu, and in the Column Guides dialog box type **2** columns in the Number of columns box and **.25** inch in the Space between columns box, and click OK.

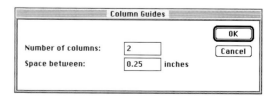

When you specify two or more (up to twenty) columns, Adobe PageMaker automatically creates columns of equal width, filling the entire image area between the left and right margin guides. The vertical space between the columns is called the gutter.

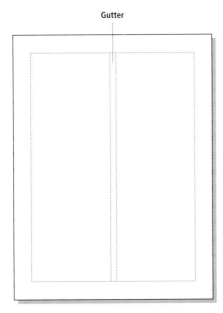

To create columns of varying width, you can drag the column guides, manually resizing the columns.

2 With the pointer tool selected, position the cursor on any column guide, and drag the column guide to the left or right.

3 Choose Column Guides from the Layout menu, and in the Column Guides dialog box notice how the Numbers of columns box displays the option Custom, type 2 columns in the Number of columns box to restore the two columns of equal width, and click OK.

4 Choose Save from the File menu (Command-S).

Locking the guides

Once you have established the final design grid, it is a good idea to lock the guides, preventing column and ruler guides being moved accidentally.

1 Choose Guides and Rulers from the Layout menu and Lock Guides from the submenu.

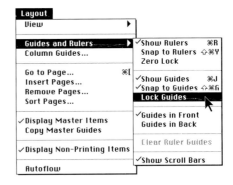

2 Attempt to move the column guides.

Note: If you want to move or delete a guide (margin, column, or ruler) when the guides are locked, choose Guides and Rulers from the Layout menu and Lock Guides from the submenu to de-select the option. After you move or delete a guide, re-lock the guides.

Placing a graphic

You will use the Place command to import a photograph into the flyer publication. Adobe PageMaker provides the ability to import, link, and export text and graphics elements that are saved in an Adobe PageMaker-compatible format. For more information on placing graphics, refer to the *Adobe PageMaker 6.0 User Guide.*

After scanning this particular photograph on a flatbed scanner, it was imported into Adobe Photoshop® to be sized for the flyer, and saved as a grayscale image in tag image file format (TIFF) at a resolution of 100 dpi.

Note: A desktop image design and production tool, Adobe Photoshop allows you to create original artwork, correct color, retouch and composite scanned images, and prepare professional-quality separations and output.

1 Choose Place from the File menu (Command-D), and in the Place Document dialog box double-click the *01GraphicA* file in the *01Lesson* folder.

The cursor is displayed as a graphics icon. You will position the graphics icon where you want the upper-left corner of the graphic to be, and then click.

2 With the graphics icon displayed, click anywhere on the page to place the photograph.

Adobe PageMaker positions the photograph so that its upper-left corner is aligned with the position of the upper-left corner of the graphics icon when you clicked to place the photograph.

The eight square graphics handles displayed at the corners and edges of the photograph indicate the graphic is selected, and make it possible to resize a graphic vertically, horizontally, or both. The Control palette reflects the attributes of the selected graphic, and offers an alternative to manipulating objects manually. This means it is possible to enter precise values in the Control palette to move and resize objects.

Now that the photograph is placed in the flyer publication, you will position the photograph in the lower-left portion of the page, reduce the size of the photograph, and then undo the resizing operation.

3 With the pointer tool selected, position the cursor in the center of the photograph, and hold down the mouse button until the cursor is displayed as a four-headed arrow.

4 With the mouse button still held down, drag the photograph beyond the bottom edge of the page.

Adobe PageMaker automatically scrolls the page as you drag an object.

5 With the mouse button still held down, drag the photograph until its left and bottom edges are aligned with the left and bottom margin guides, respectively, and release the mouse button.

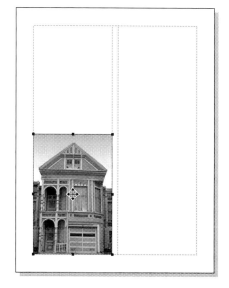

After placing and aligning text in the right column, you will reposition the photograph to be aligned with the text. For now, take this opportunity to experiment with resizing the photograph.

6 With the pointer tool still selected, position the cursor on one of the corner handles, and drag toward the center of the photograph, reducing its size.

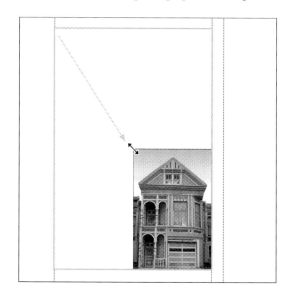

TIP: TO SELECT THE

TEXT TOOL, HOLD

DOWN THE SHIFT

KEY AND PRESS

THE F2 KEY.

Even though it is possible to resize bitmap images (formed by a rectangular grid of pixels) in Adobe PageMaker, you will get the best printing results if your images are accurately sized before you import them into Adobe PageMaker.

Note: When you hold down the Command key as you resize a monochrome bitmap image, Adobe PageMaker adjusts the resolution of that image to match the resolution of your target printer, giving you the best possible printing results. This technique, called magic stretch, neither improves nor harms color or grayscale TIFF images, EPS (Encapsulated PostScript) graphics, or draw-type graphics, and it does not benefit monochrome bitmap images contained in EPS or draw-type graphics. For more information on this technique, refer to the Adobe PageMaker 6.0 User Guide.

7 Choose Undo from the Edit menu (Command-Z) to restore the photograph to its original size.

Important: Adobe PageMaker provides the ability to undo a single level of modification.

8 If you are unable to restore the photograph to its original size, click the photograph with the pointer tool to select it, press the Delete key, and re-import the *01GraphicA* file.

9 Choose Save from the File menu.

Note: Choosing the Save command deselects all objects in a publication.

Placing text in the right column

It is possible to insert text into a publication created in other word-processing applications. Some of these outside sources can include word processors (such as WordPerfect™, Word™, Microsoft Works™, etc.), text or table editors, and spreadsheet files in Excel™ and Lotus 1-2-3™ format, or other Adobe PageMaker 4.x, 5.0, or 6.0 publications. For more information on importing and managing text, refer to the *Adobe PageMaker 6.0 User Guide.*

1 Choose Place from the File menu, and in the Place Document dialog box double-click the *01TextA* file in the *01Lesson* folder.

 The cursor is displayed as a loaded text icon.

2 With the loaded text icon positioned in the right column below the top margin guide, click to place the text, taking care to avoid clicking outside of the column.

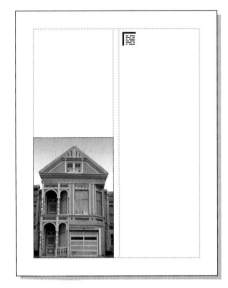

The text flows into the column automatically.

Note: If you click outside of the column, the text will not flow into the column. If this is the case, make sure the pointer tool is selected, click the placed text, press the Delete key, and import the 01TextA *file again.*

The windowshades that stretch horizontally across the top and bottom borders of the text indicate the text is selected as a text block. A text block, like a graphic, is an object that you can move, resize, and reshape. In addition to the loops in the center, there are square corner handles at each end of the windowshade. With the pointer tool selected, you can drag a corner handle to manually adjust the size, shape, or location of a text block.

Top windowshade handle
Corner handle

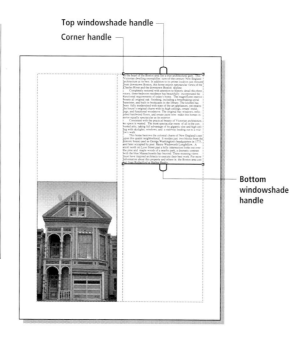

Bottom windowshade handle

The empty windowshade handle at the top of a text block indicates the beginning of a story. The empty windowshade handle at the bottom of a text block indicates the end of a story. Recognized by Adobe PageMaker as a single unit, a story can be one letter or several hundred pages of text, and can be contained in a single text block or threaded through many different ones.

3 Position the cursor on the bottom window-shade handle (bottom loop), and drag up to reduce the size of the text block.

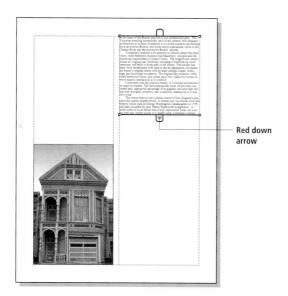

Red down arrow

The red down arrow in the bottom windowshade handle indicates the end of the story is not displayed.

4 Position the cursor on the bottom window-shade handle (bottom loop), and drag down, making sure the entire story is displayed.

Note: Clicking the red down arrow will load the remaining text, causing the cursor to be displayed as a loaded text icon. If you want to unload the text when the loaded text icon is displayed, click any tool in the toolbox.

Much like adjusting the height and width of a graphic element, you can adjust the height and width of a text block by dragging a corner handle. Corner handles are positioned at the left and right edges of the top and bottom windowshade handles.

5 With the pointer tool selected, position the cursor on the lower-left corner handle of the text block in the right column, hold down the mouse button until the cursor is displayed as a double-headed arrow, drag it in any direction, and release the mouse button, adjusting the width and the height of the text block.

Adobe PageMaker automatically reflows the text within the text block. Depending on the size of the text block, the red down arrow in the bottom windowshade handle may indicate the entire story is not displayed.

6 Choose Undo from the Edit menu to restore the text block to its original size.

7 If you are unable to restore the text block to its original size, click the text block with the pointer tool to select it, press the Delete key, and import the *01TextA* file again.

8 Choose Save from the File menu.

Formatting the text in the right column

You will enter precise values in the Control palette to apply type specifications (such as size, typeface, and type style) to the text in the right column.

Note: To create, edit, or format text, the text tool must be selected.

1 Click the text tool in the toolbox to select it.

The cursor is displayed as an I-beam, and the Control palette displays frequently used type specification options, providing quick access to most of the options that are available from the pull-down menus.

2 With the text tool selected, click the text in the right column to establish an insertion point, and choose Select All from the Edit menu (Command-A) to select the entire story.

The type specifications you select in the Control palette will apply to the selected text only. To select a word, double-click it with the text tool. To select a paragraph, triple-click it with the text tool. To select a single character or the entire contents of a text block, drag to select the target text with the text tool.

3 In the Control palette choose Myriad MM 215 Light 600 Normal from the Font pop-up menu, type **10** points in the Size box and **17** points in the Leading box, and click the Apply button.

Font pop-up menu   Size box

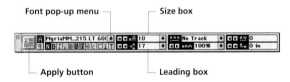

Apply button   Leading box

When formatting text using the Control palette, it is possible to apply the specification by pressing the Return key (rather than clicking the Apply button), provided the Control palette is activated when you press the Return key. If you press the Return key while the text is selected, you will replace the text with a hard-carriage return.

The point size of a font is the height of the font from the bottom of the descenders (such as p) to the top of the ascenders (such as h), but does not indicate the height of each letter. For example, a lowercase "a" set in 12-point type is not 12 points high.

Entering a value in the Leading box in the Control palette sets the height of the vertical space in which the text is placed. You will find this vertical space is referred to as the leading, the slug, or the leading slug. Like type size, the leading is measured in points. Unlike type size, leading is an exact measurement. 12-point leading is always 12 points high.

Note: In the days when letter forms were carved into blocks, the term slug referred to the height of the block.

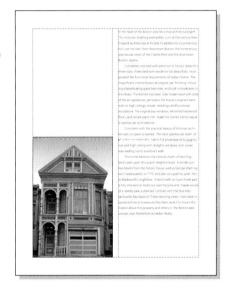

4 Choose Save from the File menu.

TIP: TO VIEW A PAGE IN DISPLAY SIZE FIT IN WINDOW, HOLD DOWN THE OPTION KEY, AND DOUBLE-CLICK THE MAGNIFYING GLASS IN THE TOOLBOX.

Creating a drop cap

When selecting a letter to be a drop cap, you cause the letter to be enlarged over a specified number of lines.

1 With the magnifying glass selected in the toolbox, drag to marquee select the first paragraph in the right column, magnifying its view.

2 With the text tool selected, drag to select the first letter of the first paragraph in the right column.

3 In the Control palette choose Minion Display Regular from the Font pop-up menu.

When choosing any selection from a pop-up menu (or clicking a button) in the Control palette, the selection is automatically applied to the text, without having to click the Apply button.

> In the heart of the Boston area lies a true arch
> This Victorian dwelling exemplifies turn-of-th
> England architecture at its best. In addition to
> tion just minutes from downtown Boston, th

4 Choose PageMaker Plug–ins from the Utilities menu and Drop Cap from the submenu, and in the Drop Cap dialog box type **4** lines in the Size box, and click OK.

5 Click the zoom box in the upper-right corner of the publication window once or twice to force the Adobe PageMaker program to redraw the screen at the current screen view.

6 Choose View from the Layout menu and Fit in Window from the submenu to view the entire page.

7 Choose Save from the File menu.

Positioning the text block in the right column

You will manually position the text block in the right column, aligning the baseline of the last line of text with the bottom margin guide. The baseline is the imaginary line on which the text (letters) rest. Descenders (such as y) fall below the baseline.

1 Magnify the view of the lower-half portion of the page.

2 With the pointer tool selected, click the text in the right column to select it as a text block.

Note: In addition to moving, rotating, resizing, and reshaping a text block, it is possible to connect to or separate from other text blocks while keeping the flow of text (the story) intact from text block to text block.

3 With the text still selected as a text block, hold down the Shift key (to constrain the movement to 45°), and drag the text block until the baseline of the last line of text is aligned with the bottom margin guide, with its left and right edges aligned with the right column guides.

4 Choose Save from the File menu.

Positioning the graphic

To allow for a 2-line caption under the photograph, you will align the bottom of the photograph with the text in the adjacent (right) column. Aligning text and graphics elements within a publication is one of the keys to successful page layout.

1 Position the cursor on the horizontal ruler, hold down the mouse button until the cursor is displayed as a double-headed arrow, drag down to create a horizontal ruler guide that is aligned with the baseline of the third from the bottom line of text in the right column, and release the mouse button.

2 With the pointer tool selected, drag the photograph until its bottom edge is aligned with the horizontal ruler guide (that you just created), with its left and right edges aligned with the left column guides.

Note: When you drag an object (text or graphic) over a guide, it is possible to view the portions of the guide overlapped by the object as red (white on a black and white monitor).

The photograph is aligned with the text in the right column, and you are ready to create the caption text for the photograph.

3 Choose Save from the File menu.

Creating the caption text

Rather than importing existing text into Adobe PageMaker, you will type the two-line caption, and position it below the photograph, aligning the baseline of the second line of text with the bottom margin guide.

Adobe PageMaker has all the word-processing capabilities you need to type and format your text from scratch. While it is possible to create and edit text in layout view, you may find many advantages to using Story Editor, the full-featured word processor included with the Adobe PageMaker program. For more information about the Story Editor, refer to the *Adobe PageMaker 6.0 User Guide.*

Just as with formatting text, the text tool must be selected when you create or edit text.

1 With the text tool selected, click in the left column below the photograph to establish an insertion point.

The blinking cursor on the left margin guide indicates the position of the insertion point.

2 Type the following in uppercase and lowercase letters: **Close to the beautiful Charles River, this home shares the historic charm of its Cambridge neighborhood.**

Because you established an insertion point within the left column, the width of the text block automatically equals the width of the column.

3 With the text tool still selected, triple-click the caption text to select it.

Triple-clicking text selects a single paragraph. By definition, a paragraph ends with a hard-carriage return.

4 In the Control palette choose Minion Display Italic from the Font pop-up menu, type **11** points in the Size box and **17** points in the Leading box, and click the Apply button.

5 With the pointer tool selected, click the caption text to select it as a text block, hold down the Shift key (to constrain the movement to 45°), and drag the text block until the second line of caption text is aligned with the bottom margin guide, with its left and right edges aligned with the left column guides.

The caption text in the left column is aligned with the text in the right column.

6 Choose Save from the File menu.

Placing text in the left column

Again, you will place text created and saved with a word-processing application, automatically flowing it into the left column.

1 Choose View from the Layout menu and Fit in Window from the submenu.

2 Choose Place from the File menu, and in the Place Document dialog box double-click the *01TextB* file in the *01Lesson* folder.

The cursor is displayed as a loaded text icon.

3 With the loaded text icon displayed, click in the left column just below the top margin guide to place the text.

The text flows into the column automatically.

4 With the magnifying glass selected in the toolbox, drag to marquee select the entire left column above the photograph.

5 With the text tool selected, click anywhere in the left column text block to establish an insertion point, and choose Select All from the Edit menu to select the entire story.

6 In the Control palette choose Myriad MM 700 Bold 600 Normal from the Font pop-up menu, type **10** points in the Size box and **27** points in the Leading box, and click the Apply button.

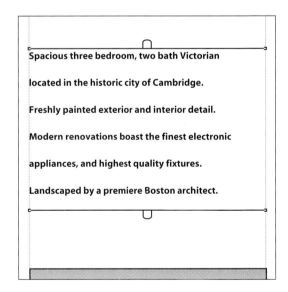

7 Choose Save from the File menu.

Applying a tint to text

A tint is a lightened color. For this lesson, you will use the Colors palette to apply a 40% tint of black (gray) to the first word in each paragraph above the photograph.

In addition to applying colors and tints to text, it is possible to apply colors and tints to lines, rectangles, ellipses, text, and monochrome or grayscale bitmapped images (such as TIFF images) that you import into Adobe PageMaker.

1 Choose Colors from the Window menu (Command-K) to open the Colors palette.

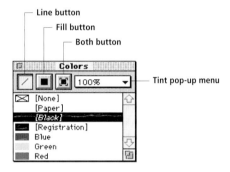

The Colors palette displays a list of available colors, including the Line, Fill, and Both buttons in the upper-left corner of the palette. You select one of these buttons when you want to apply color or tint to a line, a fill, or both (the line and fill on a rectangle or ellipse).

Note: To apply color (or a tint of a color) to text, the text must be selected with the text tool.

2 With the text tool selected, double-click the first word (in the first paragraph) in the left column to select it.

Double-clicking text with the text tool selects an entire word.

3 In the Colors palette make sure Black is selected in the list of colors, and choose 40% from the Tint pop-up menu to apply a 40% tint of black to the text.

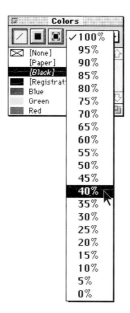

In addition to applying a tint, you will format the first word of each paragraph to display a 20-point italic font.

4 With the first word still selected, in the Control palette choose Minion Display Italic from the Font pop-up menu, type **20** points in the Size box, and click the Apply button.

5 Repeat the previous three steps for the first word in each paragraph (in the text block above the photograph), applying the 40% tint of black and the 20-point italic font to the first word in each paragraph.

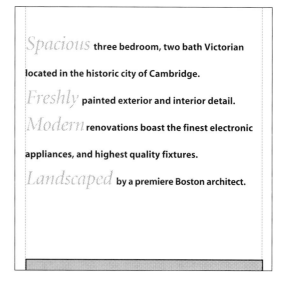

6 Choose Save from the File menu.

Indenting the text

Use the Indents/tabs command to set tab stops (up to 40 per column), the indent levels of paragraphs, and the leader style, such as dots or dashes, for the spaces between tab stops. In this example, you will indent all lines that follow the first line of each paragraph by setting a hanging indent.

Note: Indents move text inward from the left and right edges of a text block, and tabs position text at specific locations in a text block.

TIP: TO VIEW A PAGE IN DISPLAY SIZE ACTUAL SIZE, DOUBLE-CLICK THE MAGNIFYING GLASS IN THE TOOLBOX.

Time out for a movie

If your system is capable of running Adobe Teach movies, play the movie *Using Indents* to see a preview of this section that demonstrates using the Indents/tabs dialog box. For information on how to play Adobe Teach movies, see the section What You Need To Know at the beginning of this book.

1 With the text tool selected, click the text in the left column to establish an insertion point, and choose Select All from the Edit menu to select the text.

2 Choose Indents/tabs from the Type menu (Command-I).

The Indents/tabs dialog box displays a ruler with increments that match the current rulers in the publication window. Depending on your monitor and the selected display size, the ruler may be aligned with the left edge of the selected text.

3 In the Indents/tabs dialog box position the cursor on the bottom black triangle at the zero point on the ruler, and drag until the Position box indicates .5 inch.

The top triangle moves with the bottom triangle.

4 Drag the top black triangle back to its original position (aligned with the zero point on the ruler), and click OK to set a ½-inch hanging indent.

The text in the left column displays the hanging indent.

Spacious **three bedroom, two bath Victorian located in the historic city of Cambridge.**

Freshly **painted exterior and interior detail.**

Modern **renovations boast the finest electronic appliances, and highest quality fixtures.**

Landscaped **by a premiere Boston architect.**

5 Choose Save from the File menu.

Creating a ruler guide

Now that the text in the left column is placed and formatted, you are ready to align it with the text in the right column.

You may recall aligning the baseline of the last line of text in the right column with the bottom margin guide. Since the text block just placed and formatted in the left column does not extend to the bottom margin guide, you will create a horizontal ruler guide. This ruler guide will help you align the text in the left column with the text in the right column.

1 Choose View from the Layout menu and Actual Size from the submenu.

2 From the horizontal ruler, drag to create a horizontal ruler guide that is aligned with the baseline of the first line of text in the right column.

As you drag down from the horizontal ruler, the Y indicator in the Control palette displays precise vertical positioning information.

Note: As was mentioned before, it is possible to position up to 120 ruler guides anywhere on a page.

3 With the pointer tool selected, click the text in the top portion of the left column to select it as a text block.

4 Position the cursor on the text block, hold down the Shift key (to constrain the movement to 45°), and drag the text block until the baseline of the first line of text is aligned with the horizontal ruler guide you just created, with its left and right edges aligned with the left column guides.

The text in the left column is aligned with the text in the right column.

5 Choose Save from the File menu.

Creating the display text

You will create the display text (heading) that is positioned above the columns of text. Display text, by its size or weight, is used to attract attention. After typing the heading and assigning text attributes, you will align the heading text on a ruler guide.

1 Click the text tool in the toolbox.

The cursor is displayed as an I-beam.

2 Click the pasteboard above the page to establish an insertion point.

Before typing the text, you will establish the type specifications.

3 In the Control palette drag to select Minion Display Regular from the Font pop-up menu, and type **82** points in the Size box, and click the Apply button.

Font pop-up menu ⎯⎤   ⎡⎯ Size box

4 Type **Home Review** in uppercase and lower-case letters.

Note: When you create or place text on any part of the pasteboard (except the pasteboard to the left of the page), the width of the text block automatically equals the width of the image area between the left and right margin guides.

5 From the horizontal ruler, drag to create a horizontal ruler guide at 1.5 inches.

You will align the baseline of the text with this horizontal ruler guide.

6 With the pointer tool selected, click the text Home Review to select it as a text block, position the cursor on one of the right corner handles, hold down the mouse button until the cursor is displayed as a diagonal double-headed arrow, drag it until it is roughly aligned with the right edge of the text, and release the mouse button, reducing the width of the text block.

7 With the text Home Review still selected as a text block, position the cursor on the text block, and hold down the mouse button until the cursor is displayed as a four-headed arrow.

If you click on the object and hold the mouse button down until the cursor is displayed as a four-headed arrow, Adobe PageMaker displays an image of the object while you are dragging it.

8 With the mouse button still held down, drag the text block until the baseline of the display text is aligned with the 1.5-inch horizontal ruler guide, with the left edge of the text aligned with the left margin guide, and release the mouse button.

Note: If you select a text or graphic object and move it immediately, Adobe PageMaker displays the bounding box that contains the object. Known as the quick-drag method, it is useful when you want to align an object by one of its edges.

9 Choose Save from the File menu.

Cutting and pasting text

You will cut the word Review from the display text Home Review, and paste it into your publication, creating another text block.

1 With the text tool selected, double-click the word Review to select it.

TIP: TO SELECT THE
RECTANGLE TOOL, HOLD
DOWN THE SHIFT KEY
AND PRESS THE F4 KEY.

2 Choose Cut from the Edit menu (Command–X) to cut the selected text.

3 With the pointer tool selected, click the word Home to select it as a text block, and drag a right corner handle until it is roughly aligned with the right edge of the text, reducing the width of the text block to better organize your work space.

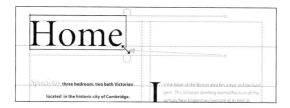

4 With the text tool selected, choose Paste from the Edit menu (Command–V).

The pasted text is displayed to be selected as an individual text block.

5 With the text tool still selected, double-click the word Review to select it.

6 In the Control palette type **122** points in the Size box, and click the Apply button.

The text Review is set in a larger point size than the text Home.

7 Choose Save from the File menu.

Applying a tint to the display text

You will apply a 20% tint of black to the display text Review.

1 If the Colors palette is not displayed, choose Colors palette from the Window menu to open the Colors palette.

2 In the Colors palette make sure Black is selected in the list of colors, and choose 20% from the Tint pop-up menu.

Now that you have applied a tint of black to the text, reduce the size of the text block and position it.

3 From the horizontal ruler, drag to create a horizontal ruler guide at 1.75 inches.

4 With the pointer tool selected, click the word Review to select it as a text block, and drag a right corner handle until it is roughly aligned with the right edge of the text, reducing the size of the text block.

5 With the text still selected as a text block, drag the text block until the baseline of the text is aligned with the 1.75-inch horizontal ruler guide, with the stem of the uppercase "R" in the word Review intersecting the lowercase "e" in the word Home.

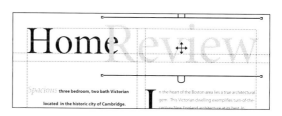

6 Choose Save from the File menu.

Adjusting the stacking order

To begin, notice how the word Review overlaps the word Home. Since you just pasted the word Review to the publication, the text object Review is positioned at the top of the stack.

As you place, paste, draw, or create text or graphics elements, Adobe PageMaker assigns each object the top position in the stacking order. The stacking order is the order in which objects overlap one another on the page. Moving or modifying an object does not affect the stacking order.

1 With the pointer tool selected, click the word Review to select it as a text block.

2 Choose Send to Back from the Arrange menu (Command-B) to stack the word Review behind the word Home, at the bottom of the stack.

Since the Send to Back command sends the selected text or graphic element to the bottom of the stack, the word Home overlaps the word Review.

3 Choose Save from the File menu.

Drawing a circle

Adobe PageMaker offers a variety of drawing tools, giving you more options for creating graphics. You will use the ellipse tool to draw a circle, accentuating the dot above the letter i in the word Review.

1 With the magnifying glass selected in the toolbox, drag to marquee select the letter i in the word Review.

2 Click the ellipse tool in the toolbox to select it.

The cursor is displayed as a crosshair icon.

3 Hold down the Shift key (to constrain the ellipse to be a circle), hold down the mouse button, drag to draw a circle approximately twice the size of the dot above the letter i, and release the mouse button.

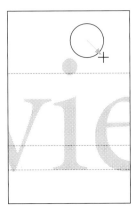

4 If you are not satisfied with the size of the circle, make sure the graphics handles are displayed around the circle (indicating it is selected), press the Delete key, and draw another circle.

5 In the Colors palette make sure the Both button is selected, and click Black to apply the color black to the line and fill of the circle.

6 With the pointer tool selected, click the circle to select it, and drag it until it is centered on the dot above the letter i.

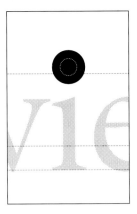

7 Choose Save from the File menu.

Drawing a box

After drawing a box, you will assign a width to the line around the box, and manually position it below the display text Home Review.

1 Choose View from the Layout menu and Actual Size from the submenu, and scroll to view the page just below the display text Home Review.

2 From the horizontal ruler, drag to create two horizontal ruler guides at 2 inches and approximately 2.3 inches.

3 Click the rectangle tool in the toolbox to select it.

The cursor is displayed as a crosshair icon. Using the rectangle tool, you can draw rectangles or squares of any size.

4 Position the cursor on the intersection of the left margin guide and the 2-inch horizontal ruler guide, hold down the mouse button, drag to the intersection of the right margin guide and the 2.3-inch horizontal ruler guide, and release the mouse button to draw a box.

5 If you are not satisfied with the rectangle, make sure the graphics handles are displayed around the rectangle, press the Delete key, and draw another rectangle.

6 Choose Line from the Element menu and Hairline from the submenu to assign a line style and weight to the line of the box.

Note: Even though you will not perceive a difference in line width on most monitors, the line will print correctly. This is because most monitors are set to display 72 pixels per inch with one pixel corresponding to one point. Because the width of a hairline equals .25 point, the monitor is not capable of displaying that fractional width. Any printer capable of 300-dot-per-inch resolution will have no trouble printing the line.

Notice how after you release the mouse button, part of the box is obscured by the ruler guide. By default, the ruler guides are displayed in front of all text and graphics elements.

7 Choose Guides and Rulers from the Layout menu and Guides in Back from the submenu to display the guides behind the text and graphics elements.

The hairline is displayed on the page.

8 Choose Save from the File menu.

Dragging to define a text block

After creating the address text, you will center the text in the hairline box using the paragraph view of the Control palette.

To create the display text Home Review, you may recall selecting the text tool, clicking the pasteboard to establish an insertion point, and typing the display text. Now, to create the address text, you will use a different approach that involves selecting the text tool, dragging to define a text block (rather than just clicking), and then typing the address text.

1 With the text tool selected, position the cursor on the left margin guide, hold down the mouse button, drag to draw a box that extends to the right margin guide (exact height is not important), and release the mouse button, defining a text block that spans the image area between the margin guides.

When you release the mouse button, the blinking cursor is displayed on the left margin guide, indicating the text insertion point.

2 In the Control palette choose Myriad MM 700 Bold 600 Normal from the Font pop-up menu, type **10** points in the Size box and choose 130% from the Scaling pop-up menu to establish the type specifications for the text you are about to create.

Horizontal Scale box ⌐

3 Type **322 Harvard Street, Cambridge** in uppercase and lowercase letters.

You are ready to use the Control palette to apply the paragraph specifications to the address text.

Note: When applying one or more paragraph specifications to a single paragraph, you must establish an insertion point in the paragraph. When applying paragraph specifications to multiple contiguous paragraphs, you must ensure some text in each target paragraph is selected.

4 With an insertion point still established in the address text, in the Control palette click the Paragraph-view button to view the paragraph view of the Control palette.

As with type specification options, the paragraph view of the Control palette provides quick access to frequently used paragraph specification options available in the pull-down menus.

5 With the address text still selected, in the Control palette click the Center-align button to center the text in the text block.

Center-align button

Paragraph-view button

Since you defined the text block to outline the hairline box, the text is centered in the hairline box.

6 Choose Save from the File menu.

Range kerning the address text

In addition to the fonts you use, the spacing between letters, words, and lines can have tremendous impact on a publication. Range kerning is one of the available techniques for increasing or decreasing the space between letters.

To range kern the address text, you will select the entire range of address text, and enter a precise value in the Control palette to increase the original letter spacing (tracking) of the text.

Note: Range kerning can be applied to a selected range of text only.

1 With the text tool selected, triple-click the address text to select it.

Triple-clicking text with the text tool selects an entire paragraph. Also, notice how the Control palette still displays the options for formatting paragraphs.

2 In the Control palette click the Character-view button, and in the character view of the Control palette type .75 em space in the Kerning box, and click the Apply button to apply range kerning to the address text.

Character-view button　　　Kerning box

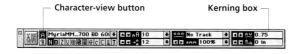

Adobe PageMaker accepts kerning values between -1 and 1 (1 equals 1 em space), accurate to .01 em space. Negative values move characters closer together, and positive values move characters further apart.

Note: An em space is a horizontal space equal to the width of one em. Unlike absolute units of measure (inches and picas), an em is a relative unit of measure. This means that if you insert an em space into 12-point type, the em space is 12 points wide.

3 From the horizontal ruler, drag to create a horizontal ruler guide at approximately 2.2 inches.

The baseline for the address text is established.

4 With the pointer tool selected, click the address text to select it as a text block, hold down the Shift key (to constrain the movement to 45°), and drag the text block until the baseline of the text is aligned with the 2.2-inch horizontal ruler guide.

5 Choose Save from the File menu.

Drawing a vertical line

As a finishing touch to the flyer publication, you will use the constrained-line tool to draw a vertical line that will be centered in the gutter (the vertical space between the columns). The constrained-line tool makes it possible to draw straight lines that are constrained to 45° angles.

1 Choose Guides and Rulers from the Layout menu and Snap to Guides from the submenu to deselect it, making sure it is unchecked.

Activated when you create a publication, the Snap to Guides option causes the guides to exert a magnetic-like pull on text and graphics objects.

2 From the vertical ruler, drag to create a vertical ruler guide at 4.25 inches.

The vertical ruler guide is displayed in the center of the gutter.

3 Choose View from the Layout menu and Fit in Window from the submenu.

4 Click the constrained-line tool in the toolbox to select it.

The cursor is displayed as a crosshair icon.

5 Align the crosshair cursor with the intersection of the bottom edge of the address box and the 4.25-inch vertical ruler guide, and drag down to the bottom margin guide to draw the line.

6 With the vertical line still selected, choose Line from the Element menu and Hairline from the submenu to apply a line style and weight to the line.

You have completed assembling the flyer, so take a moment to view your work.

7 Choose Guides and Rulers from the Layout menu and Show Guides from the submenu to hide the view of the rulers.

8 Choose Save from the File menu to save the *01Work* publication.

PRODUCING THE FLYER

Given the specifications and requirements of this black-and-white publication, it can be printed successfully on any 300 dpi desktop laser printing device, and then photocopied for on-demand (the desired amount, when you need it) distribution.

1 Before choosing the Print command, select Chooser from the Apple menu, and in the Chooser dialog box select the target printing device. For information on setting up your printer and selecting the appropriate printer driver, see the *Adobe PageMaker 6.0 Getting Started* booklet.

2 Choose Print from the File menu (Command-P) to open the Print: Document dialog box for the type of printer you selected.

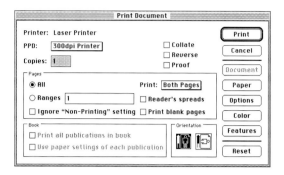

In addition to displaying the most frequently adjusted settings, the Print: Document dialog box displays buttons that you select to open additional printing dialog boxes. For more information on these options, refer to the *Adobe PageMaker 6.0 User Guide.*

3 If you have a PostScript printer, be sure to select a PostScript Printer Description (PPD) from the PPD pop-up menu in the Print: Document dialog box that matches your printer type.

You are ready to specify some additional printing options.

4 In the Print: Document dialog box click the Color button, and in the Print: Color dialog box make sure the Grayscale radio button is selected.

5 In the Print: Color dialog box click the Options button, and in the Print: Options dialog box choose Optimized from the Send Image data pop-up menu.

The Optimized setting makes it possible to print high-resolution images on a low-resolution device.

5 Click the Print button to print the flyer.

6 Click the close boxes in the title bars of *01Work* and *01Final* to close the publications.

Since you will throw away the *Adobe PageMaker 6.0 Prefs* file at the beginning of every lesson, quit the Adobe PageMaker application.

7 Choose Quit from the File menu (Command-Q) to exit the Adobe PageMaker application.

14 Calle Libertade
28004 Madrid,
España

BRAGA + BRAGA *Arquitectos*

14 Ca
28004 Madrid,
España

BRAGA + BRAGA *Arquitectos*

Sr. and Sra. Pérez
Alcalá, 18
Madrid, España
2P4 N47

Estimados Esperanza y Rodrigo,

Realmente disfruté la visita a su casa y estoy muy interesada en trabajar con ustedes para desarrollar al máximo su potencial. La videocinta de Esperanza, en conjunto con la visita y su lista de requisitos, han plasmado sus metas arquitectónicas y paisajistas. El diseño actual de la casa y el de sus alrededores están bien integrados, así que creo que se pueden lograr esas metas. La casa, especialmente desde el exterior, es fuerte y puede beneficiarse con un tratamiento más uniforme de las ventanas y las puertas. El interior requiere un poco más de trabajo, pero definitivamente el potencial está allí.

Estamos orgullosos de informarles que la Doña Calderón, la directora de la renovación del Museo del Prado, ha pasado a formar parte de nuestro distinguido grupo de arquitectos y diseñadores de nuestra oficina en Madrid. Nuestros diseñadores tienen acceso a las mejores telas, muebles Europeos y del Mediterráneo así como a baldosas pintadas a mano. Por favor refiéranse a la lista incluída respecto a costos.

Creo que su casa tiene un gran potencial y que juntos podemos compartir buenos momentos diseñando un hogar que cumpla con las necesidades estéticas y funcionales, aprovechando al máximo el bello sitio que ustedes han escogido para ello. Esperamos poder ayudarles a convertir en realidad sus sueños.

Atentamente,

Marie Esperanza Braga
e mail: mbraga@bb.com

14 Calle Libertade
28004 Madrid,
España

BRAGA + BRAGA *Arquitectos*

• S P A I N •

2

It's possible to conceive and create part or all of your letterhead design yourself. You will see how ficticious Madrid architects Braga+Braga used Adobe PageMaker to arrange text

ARCHITECT'S LETTERHEAD

and graphics for a simple yet striking letterhead design, incorporating the use of two spot colors. Spot colors are printed on a commercial printing press using premixed inks. With hundreds of spot colors to choose from, you can use them to achieve an exact color match or to add visual impact to a publication at a nominal cost. ■ In addition to using spot colors, the letterhead design incorporates the use of tints of spot colors. Where a spot color printed at 100% is a solid color and has no dot pattern, a tint of a spot color is a lightened spot color that is created by printing smaller halftone dots of the spot color.

This lesson also shows you how to save the letterhead design as a custom template. Of course, once the letterhead is printed, it's easy to use the custom template to assemble text to be printed on your own printer. To demonstrate the entire

ARCHITECT'S LETTERHEAD

process, you will create the Braga+Braga letterhead template, and then assemble a letter that is meant to be printed on the letterhead stationary. The text featured in the lesson is in Spanish, since Marie Braga is addressing a Spanish-speaking client in her letter.

This lesson covers:

• Establishing an application default measurement system

• Creating, saving, and opening a custom template

• Selecting and applying spot colors

• Creating a tint of a spot color

• Resizing, reflecting, and rotating a text block

• Grouping and ungrouping objects

• Adjusting the stacking order

• Using the Tile command

• Dragging objects from one publication to another

• Using the Lock Position and Non-Printing commands

• Printing on a commercial printing press.

BEFORE YOU BEGIN

All the files and fonts needed to assemble the letterhead are found on the Adobe PageMaker *Classroom in a Book* CD-ROM disc in the folders *02Lesson* and *Fonts*, respectively. In addition, the *Extras* folder on the *Classroom in a Book* CD-ROM disc includes the file *02Intl*, an interim file of artwork that you may wish to use.

It should take you approximately 2 hours to complete this lesson.

Launching the Adobe PageMaker application

Before beginning to assemble the publication for this lesson, you will use the Preferences dialog box to establish application defaults, and then you will open the final version of the letterhead you will create.

1 Before launching the Adobe PageMaker program, throw away the *Adobe PageMaker 6.0 Prefs* file to ensure all settings are returned to their default values.

2 Make sure the fonts Adobe Garamond, Adobe Garamond Italic, Adobe Garamond Semibold Italic, and Myriad MM 830 Black 600 Normal are installed.

Like the Myriad typeface used in the previous lesson, Adobe Garamond is an Adobe Originals typeface. Some of the most popular typefaces in history are those based on the types of the sixteenth-century printer, publisher, and type designer Claude Garamond, whose sixteenth-century types were modeled on those of the Venetian printers from the end of the previous century. Adobe designer Robert Slimbach went to the Plantin-Moretus museum in Antwerp to study the original Garamond typefaces. This served as the basis for the design of the Adobe Garamond romans; the italics are based on types by Robert Granjon, a contemporary of Garamond's. This elegant, versatile design, the first Adobe Originals typeface, was released in 1989, and includes three weights, plus a titling font, alternate characters, and an Expert Collection to provide a flexible family of text types.

3 Double-click the *Adobe® PageMaker® 6.0* icon in the Adobe PageMaker folder to launch the Adobe PageMaker program.

Setting an application default

Before opening a publication, open the Preferences dialog box to establish picas as the measurement system.

1 Choose Preferences from the File menu.

The Preferences dialog box displays some of the application defaults that will be applied to any new publication you create. You may recall from the previous lesson that the horizontal and vertical rulers reflect the units of measure selected in the Measurements in and Vertical ruler pop-up menus, respectively.

2 In the Preferences dialog box choose Picas from the Measurements in pop-up menu and Picas from the Vertical ruler pop-up menu, and click OK.

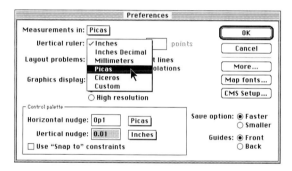

Since no publication is open, this application default will be applied to any new publication you create. Application defaults can be overridden at any time for the particular publication you are working on, setting a publication (temporary) default. Unlike application defaults, publication defaults will not be applied to the new publications you create.

Opening an existing document

1 Choose Open from the File menu (Command-O), and in the Open Publication dialog box double-click the *02FinalA* file in the *02Lesson* folder.

The full view of the page displays a single column of text framed on the top and left edges with a letterhead design. The letterhead design features a variety of text and graphics elements, incorporating the use of two spot colors. Spot colors are printed on a printing press using premixed inks. With hundreds of spot colors to choose from, you can use them to achieve an exact color match or to add visual impact to a publication at a nominal cost.

2 Choose Guides and Rulers from the Layout menu and Show Guides from the submenu (Command-J) to display all guides (column, ruler, and margin) used to assemble this publication.

Notice how all guides are displayed behind the text and graphics elements. Even though you just accepted the application default to show the guides in front of text and graphics in the Preferences dialog box, this previously created publication retains the publication defaults that were set when it was last saved. Again, the application defaults you just set in the Preferences dialog box will be applied only to new publications you create.

3 Choose Guides and Ruler from the Layout menu and Guides in Front from the submenu.

Now the guides are displayed over the text and graphics.

4 Choose Open from the File menu, and in the Open Publication dialog box double-click the *02FinalB* file in the *02Lesson* folder.

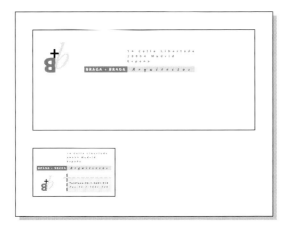

The *02FinalB* publication displays the envelope and business card you will assemble as well.

Talk with your printer

Printing these letterhead publications on a commercial printing press involves delivering files to your prepress service provider (who can perform prepress tasks, and who will ultimately create film separations of your publication on a image-setter), and then delivering film separations to your printer.

Well in advance of delivering publications to be printed, be sure to review the design with your printer and your prepress service provider. Based on the design, your skills, time, and equipment, your printer and your service provider can evaluate the requirements of the project and the services you require. If you would like a referral for an Adobe Authorized Service Provider in your area, contact Adobe Customer Service at 1-800-833-6687.

Note: In some cases, imagesetting and printing services are provided at the same facility.

In this example, expect a service provider to point out how the adjacent colors featured in the letterhead will require trapping (before creating film separations). Art that has not been trapped can easily misregister on the press, causing gaps to appear between adjacent colored elements. Trapping compensates for misregistration by slightly overlapping adjacent colors. For more information on trapping, refer to the *Adobe Print Publishing Guide.*

It is crucial to anticipate this sort of issue, since it will determine how you prepare files to be delivered to your service provider. Even though it may be possible for your service provider to edit a PostScript file, it is recommended to deliver a publication as an Adobe PageMaker file, (provided your service provider has the Adobe PageMaker program). For more information on preparing files, refer to the *Adobe PageMaker 6.0 User Guide.*

ASSEMBLING A CUSTOM TEMPLATE

Before assembling the letter you see in the final publication, you will create and save a custom template that can be opened whenever you want to assemble a letter.

Opening a new publication

Whenever you create a new publication, the Document Setup dialog box prompts you to specify the page size, orientation, page numbering, margins, and printer type resolution.

1 Choose New from the File menu (Command-N), and in the Document Setup dialog box notice how Letter is selected from the Page pop-up menu.

By default, when you create a new publication, the Document Setup dialog box displays the page-size Letter to be selected, with the corresponding page dimensions in picas (51 picas by 66 picas equals 8.5 inches by 11 inches) displayed.

2 In the Document Setup dialog box choose Legal from the Page size pop-up menu, and notice how the corresponding page dimensions in picas (51 picas by 84 picas equals 8.5 inches by 14 inches) are displayed.

The Legal page size is one of the preset page sizes available in the Page pop-up menu. If the page size you want is not available in the Page pop-up menu, it is possible to enter precise values in the Dimensions boxes to customize the page size. For this lesson, however, you will use the Letter page size.

3 In the Document Setup dialog box choose Letter from the Page size pop-up menu, click the Double-sided check box to deselect it; and pressing the Tab key to move from box to box, type **10** picas in the Left box, **4p6** in the Right box, **4p6** in the Top box, and **4p6** in the Bottom box to set the Margins in picas option, and click OK.

Note: 4p6 indicates 4 picas and 6 points (where 1 pica equals 12 points).

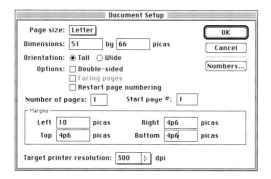

The margin guides form a rectangle enclosing the image area, which is where you will put most of your text and graphics. The horizontal and vertical rulers reflect the currently selected unit of measure, picas.

Saving the publication as a template

Even though the template is not assembled, you will name it and save it as a template. Saving a publication as a template means that when you open this template, Adobe PageMaker opens an untitled copy of the template, not the original document.

1 If you do not have a *Projects* folder, create one now.

2 Choose Save As from the File menu, and in the Save Publication dialog box type **02WorkA** in the Name box, select the *Projects* folder, click the Template radio button (ensuring the file will be saved as a template, not as a publication), and click OK.

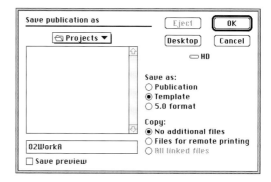

Establishing a design grid

Continuing to assemble your letterhead template, place the horizontal and vertical ruler guides that will allow you to align text and graphics precisely, without printing or restricting the flow of text.

1 Make sure the entire page in displayed. If necessary, choose View from the Layout menu and Fit in Window from the submenu (Command-0).

Adobe PageMaker will scroll automatically to undisplayed portions of a page when you drag text or graphics elements only.

2 Position the cursor on the vertical ruler that extends along the left edge of the publication window, and drag to create a vertical ruler guide at 2p (2 picas), using X coordinate value in the Control palette if necessary.

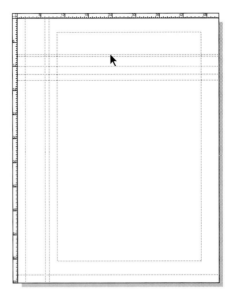

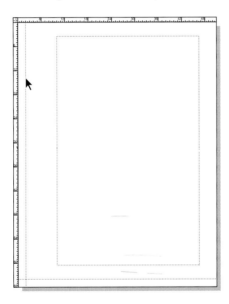

3 Using the same procedure, create two additional vertical ruler guides at 7p and 8p.

4 From the horizontal ruler, drag to create horizontal ruler guides at 64p, 15p6, 14p, 12p, 9p6, and 9p.

5 Choose Save from the File menu (Command-S) to save the template.

Locking the ruler guides

Now that you have positioned the ruler guides, you will use the Lock Guides command to lock them in place. The Lock Guides command locks ruler guides and column guides in place, preventing you from moving them accidentally.

1 Choose Guides and Rulers from the Layout menu and Lock Guides from the submenu.

Note: To reposition or delete a ruler guide, choose the Lock Guides command again to unlock the guides.

2 Choose Save from the File menu.

Creating the display text

With imagination you can use Adobe PageMaker to create display text elements that go a long way toward enhancing your publications. Display text, usually 14 points or larger, is used to attract attention.

1 Magnify the view of the pasteboard above the page, making it possible to assemble the letterhead on an uncluttered work space.

2 With the text tool selected in the toolbox, click above the page to establish an insertion point.

Notice how the cursor is displayed as an I-beam, and the Control palette displays the default type specifications (font: Times, size: 12 points).

3 With the insertion point already established, type an uppercase letter **B**.

4 With the text tool selected, double-click the uppercase B to select it.

5 In the Control palette choose Myriad MM 830 Black 600 Normal from the Font pop-up menu, type **65** points in the Size box, and click the Apply button to apply the type specifications to the selected text.

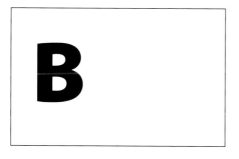

6 With the text tool still selected, click the pasteboard above the page (away from the uppercase B), and type + (a plus sign).

7 Double-click the plus sign to select it, and in the Control palette choose Myriad MM 830 Black 600 Normal from the Font pop-up menu, type **50** points in the Size box, and click the Apply button.

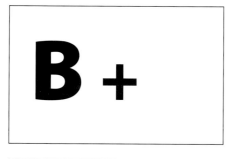

8 With the text tool still selected, click the pasteboard above the page (away from the uppercase B and plus sign), and type a lowercase letter **b**.

9 Double-click the lowercase b to select it, and in the Control palette choose Adobe Garamond Italic from the Font pop-up menu, type **110** points in the Size box, and click the Apply button.

10 Choose Save from the File menu.

Resizing text blocks

Since you did not define the text block size of the three text objects just created, take a moment to resize each one.

1 With the pointer tool selected, click the uppercase B to select it as a text block.

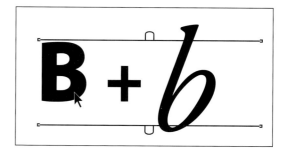

Once a text element is selected as a text block (with the pointer tool), the text block can be resized, positioned, or transformed.

Notice how the windowshades extend well beyond the bounds of the uppercase B. Since you did not define the dimensions of this text block, Adobe PageMaker defined the width of the text block to equal the image area between the left and right margin guides. Even though it is possible to manipulate an oversized text block, reducing its width to a more manageable size is advised.

Note: If you create or place text within a column (without defining the dimensions of the text block), Adobe PageMaker defines the width of the text block to equal the width of the column. On the other hand, if you create or place text on the pasteboard to the left of the page (without defining dimensions of the text block), Adobe PageMaker restricts the width of the text block to extend no further than the left edge of the page.

2 With the uppercase B still selected as a text block, drag a right corner handle until it is roughly aligned with the right edge of the uppercase B, reducing the width of the text block.

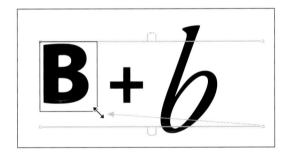

3 Following the same procedure, reduce the width of the text blocks for the plus sign and the lowercase b.

With the width of the text blocks reduced, it is easier to select, view, and manipulate these text blocks.

4 Choose Save from the File menu.

Defining spot colors

Before applying colors to the display text you just created, you will select two predefined spot colors from one of the libraries of color-matching systems included with Adobe PageMaker.

As was mentioned before, spot colors are printed on a printing press using premixed inks. Use spot colors when you have something like a corporate logo that requires an exact color match, or if you want to add impact to a publication at a nominal cost.

Note: Incorporating spot and process colors into a publication created in Adobe PageMaker is simple, but to get the best printed results, you need to understand how spot and process colors are printed. Refer to the Adobe Print Publishing Guide *for more information.*

1 Choose Define Colors from the Element menu, and in the Define Colors dialog box click the New button.

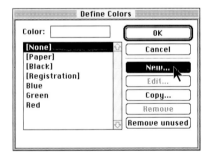

The Edit Color dialog box prompts you to select a color. You can specify a spot or process color as RGB (red, green, and blue), HLS (hue, lightness, saturation), or CMYK (cyan, magenta, yellow, and black). Each model represents a different approach to describe color.

2 In the Edit Color dialog box choose PANTONE®
Uncoated from the Libraries pop-up menu.

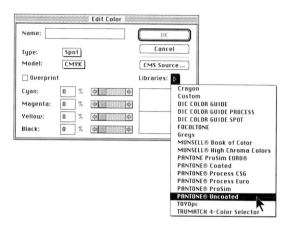

3 In the Library: PANTONE® Uncoated dialog
box scroll through the colors.

PANTONE offers 736 spot colors that set the
industry standard for reproducible spot-color
inks, and 3,006 process colors organized chro-
matically, including process-color simulations
of the spot-color library.

4 Even though it is possible to click a color to
select it, type **660** in the PANTONE CVU box,
and click OK.

Note: CVU stands for Computer Video Uncoated.

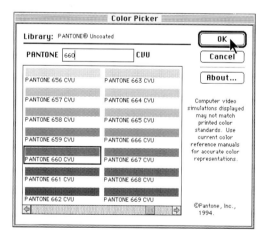

5 In the Edit Color dialog box click OK to accept
the default color name displayed in the Name
box.

The Define Colors dialog box displays the color
you have just selected and prompts you to select
or create another color.

6 In the Define Colors dialog box click the
New button.

7 In the Edit Color dialog box make sure the
Spot and CMYK options are selected, and choose
PANTONE ® Uncoated from the Libraries pop-
up menu.

8 In the Library: PANTONE Uncoated dialog
box type **5595** in the PANTONE CVU box, and
click OK.

9 In the Edit Color dialog box click OK to accept
the default color name displayed in the Name
box.

10 In the Define Colors dialog box click OK to
close it.

11 Choose Save from the File menu.

Applying spot colors

After opening the Colors palette, you will apply
the spot colors you just selected to the display
text. In addition to text, you can apply colors to
lines, rectangles, ellipses, and monochrome and
grayscale bitmapped images.

1 Choose Colors from the Window menu (Command-K) to open the Colors palette.

In addition to displaying the two spot colors you
selected, the Colors palette displays three spot
colors, Blue, Green, and Red, and four items you
cannot remove, [None], [Paper], [Black], and
[Registration].

The three buttons Line, Fill, and Both in the upper-left corner of the Colors palette allow you to apply or change the color of a line, a fill, or the line and fill on a rectangle or ellipse. It is possible to apply a color to text regardless of which of these buttons is selected.

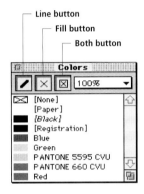

2 With the text tool selected, double-click the uppercase B to select it, and in the Colors palette click PANTONE 660 CVU to apply the spot color to the uppercase B.

Note: To apply color to text, the text must be selected with the text tool. After applying a color, the text must be deselected to display the applied color.

3 With the text tool still selected, double-click the lowercase b to select it, and in the Colors palette click PANTONE 5595 CVU.

4 Choose Save from the File menu.

Reflecting a text block

You can reflect any object (text or graphic element) vertically or horizontally, using the Reflecting options in the Control palette.

1 With the pointer tool selected, click the uppercase B to select it as a text block.

2 In the Control palette click the Horizontal reflecting button.

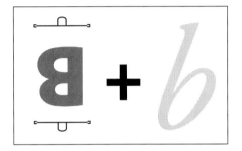

Vertical reflecting button
Horizontal reflecting button

The uppercase B is displayed to be horizontally reflected.

3 With the uppercase B still selected as a text block, in the Control palette click the Vertical reflecting button.

The uppercase B is displayed to be vertically reflected.

4 Choose Save from the File menu.

Positioning text blocks

In order to compose a logo design using the display text, you manually position the text blocks, allowing text to overlap text.

1 With the magnifying glass selected in the toolbox, drag to marquee select the three text objects, magnifying the view of them.

To align these text elements, you will use the slow-drag method of positioning objects, displaying text as you drag a text block. When you use the quick-drag method, a bounding box indicates the dimensions of the text block as you drag, but no text is displayed.

2 With the pointer tool selected, click the uppercase B to select it as a text block, position the cursor on the text block, and hold down the mouse button until the cursor is displayed as a four-headed arrow.

3 With the mouse button still held down, drag the text block until the vertical stem of the plus sign is aligned with the vertical stem of the uppercase B as shown in the illustration below, and release the mouse button.

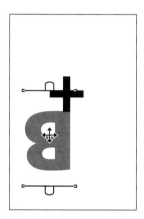

4 With the pointer tool still selected, click the lowercase b to select it as a text block, and drag the text block until the stem of the lowercase b overlaps the uppercase B as shown in the following illustration.

5 Choose Save from the File menu.

Adjusting the stacking order of text objects

Notice how the lowercase b overlaps the uppercase B and the plus sign. Since the lowercase b was created last, it is positioned at the top of the stack, and since the uppercase B was created first, it is positioned at the bottom of the stack. Even though you have modified and moved each text block, Adobe PageMaker maintains the original stacking order, where each newly created element is added to the top of the stack.

You will use the Send Backward command to move the lowercase b from the top of the stack to the middle of the stack. Unlike the Send to Back command that moves an object to the bottom of the stack, the Send Backward command moves an object back in the stack in single-position increments.

1 With the pointer tool selected, click the lowercase b to select it as a text block.

2 Choose Send Backward from the Arrange menu (Command-9).

With the lowercase b positioned in the middle of the stack, it is overlapped by the plus sign, now positioned at the top of the stack.

3 Choose Save from the File menu.

Grouping text objects

Now that the three text objects are positioned, grouping them together will allow you to position them as a single entity on the page.

1 Choose Select All from the Edit menu (Command-A) to select all text and graphics elements in your publication.

2 Choose Group from the Arrange menu (Command-G).

The text objects are joined together as a single entity, with handles indicating the group is selected.

3 Position the cursor in the center of the group, and drag to position the logo design in the upper-left corner of the page.

4 Click the pointer tool to deselect all objects, and choose Views from the Layout menu and Fit in Window from the submenu.

5 Find the intersection of the 9p6 horizontal ruler guide and the 8p vertical ruler guide, using the X and Y indicators in the Control palette as you move (not drag) the cursor in the page.

6 Once again, position the cursor in the center of the group, and drag it until the bottom edge of the logo design is aligned with the 9p6 horizontal ruler guide, with the left edge (the bowls, not the stem) of the uppercase B aligned with the 8p vertical ruler guide.

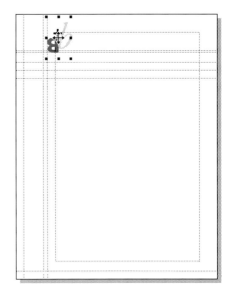

7 Choose Save from the File menu.

Using the Control palette to resize a rectangle

After using the rectangle tool to draw a box, you will enter precise values in the Control palette to resize it.

1 Select the rectangle tool in the toolbox, and drag to draw a box of any dimension near the top of the page.

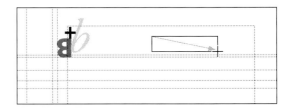

TIP: TO SCROLL THE VIEW OF THE PAGE, HOLD DOWN THE OPTION KEY, AND DRAG IN ANY DIRECTION.

2 With the box still selected, in the Control palette make sure a corner reference point or the center reference point in the Proxy icon is selected (to make it possible to resize both dimensions of an object), type **11p** in the Width box and **1p6** in the Height box, and press the Return key.

Once an object is selected, you can click a graphics handle (or one of the reference points in the Proxy icon) to select it as the reference point. You can use the Control palette to resize, move, crop, rotate, skew, or reflect an object based on the selected reference point.

Note: When you select a reference point in the Proxy icon, the corresponding point on the object remains stationary when you modify the object. If you double-click an unselected reference point, or single-click a selected reference point (box), it becomes a two-way arrow (or a four-way arrow if you click the center point). Rather than remaining stationary, the corresponding point on the object changes position when you modify the object. When a middle-edge reference point is selected, Adobe PageMaker restricts the modification to the selected (single) dimension.

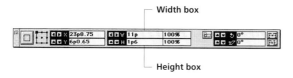

— Width box

— Height box

To create another box that will be flush with the first box, you will copy and paste the first box, and then use the Control palette to resize the pasted box.

3 With the box still selected, choose Copy from the Edit menu (Command-C) to copy the box to the Clipboard.

4 Choose Paste from the Edit menu (Command-V) to paste a second box to be slightly offset from the first box.

5 With the second box selected, in the Control palette type **17p4** in the Width box, and press the Return key to increase the width of the second box.

Note: Depending on where you drew the boxes, your artwork may look different than the following illustration.

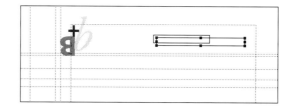

6 Choose Save from the File menu.

Applying spot colors to the boxes

Using the Colors palette, you will apply spot colors to the line and fill of the two boxes. As was mentioned before, the three buttons Line, Fill, and Both allow you to apply or change the color of a line, a fill, or both on a rectangle or ellipse. In this example, you want to apply color to the line and fill of both boxes.

1 In the Colors palette click an unselected button (Line, Fill, or Both) to select it, noticing how one button can be selected at a time

— Line button

— Fill button

— Both button

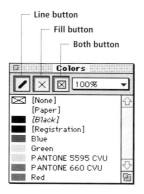

2 With the pointer tool selected, click the line of the first (smaller) box to select it.

3 In the Colors palette click the Both button, and click PANTONE 660 CVU to apply a spot color to the line and fill of the box.

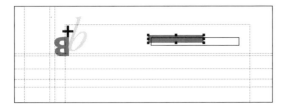

4 With the pointer tool selected, click the line of the second (larger) box to select it, and in the Colors palette click PANTONE 5595 CVU.

5 Choose Save from the File menu.

Positioning graphics

You will manually position the boxes to be aligned with existing ruler guides.

1 With the pointer tool selected, click the second (larger) box to select it, and drag it until its left edge is aligned with the right edge of the first (smaller) box.

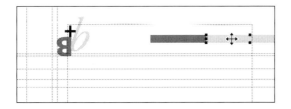

2 Magnify the view of the boxes to make it possible to ensure the edges of the boxes are precisely aligned.

3 Press the arrow keys (or clicking the nudge buttons in the Control palette) to move the selected box in 1-pixel increments.

4 Choose View from the Layout menu and Fit in Window from the submenu to view the entire page.

5 With one of the boxes still selected, hold down the Shift key (to select multiple objects), click the unselected box to select both boxes

6 Drag the boxes until their bottom edges are aligned with the 9p6 horizontal ruler guide, with the right edge aligned with the right margin guide.

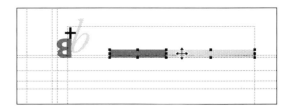

7 Choose Group from the Arrange menu to group the objects into a single entity.

8 Choose Save from the File menu.

Placing, formatting, and positioning the text Braga+Braga

After placing text, you will cut and paste portions of the placed text to format it, and then position it in the leftmost box.

1 Choose Place from the File menu (Command-D), and in the Place Document dialog box double-click the *02TextA* file in the *02Lesson* folder.

2 With the loaded text icon displayed, scroll to view the pasteboard above the page, and click the pasteboard to place the text.

3 Magnify the view of the placed text on the pasteboard.

4 With the text tool selected, drag to select the text Braga+Braga in the first line.

5 In the Control palette choose Myriad MM 830 Black 600 Normal from the Font pop-up menu, type **12** points in the Size box, type **.2** em space in the Kerning box, and click the All caps button.

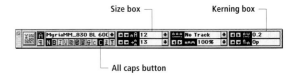
Size box —   Kerning box —

— All caps button

6 With the text Braga+Braga still selected, choose Cut from the Edit menu (Command-X).

Before pasting the text you just cut, you will drag to define a text block that spans the width of the leftmost box, making it easier to center the text in the leftmost box.

7 With the text tool still selected, drag to define a text block in the leftmost box, spanning the width of the leftmost box without attempting to select an exact vertical dimension.

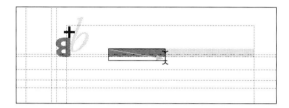

8 Choose Paste from the Edit menu to paste the text Braga+Braga in the text block you just defined.

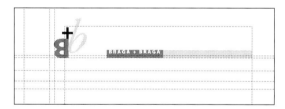

By default, the text is left-aligned in the text block.

9 With the insertion point still established in the text Braga+Braga, in the Control palette click the Paragraph-view button, and in the paragraph view of the Control palette click the Center-align button to center the text in the text block.

Center-align button
Paragraph-view button

Since you defined the text block to span the width of the leftmost box, the text is centered horizontally in the leftmost box.

10 With the text tool selected, drag to select the text Braga+Braga, and in the Colors palette click Paper to apply the color paper to the text.

Applying the color paper to text or graphics elements causes the color of the paper on which you print to show through the selected object.

Before aligning the text Braga+Braga, you will turn off the Snap to Guides option.

11 Choose Guides and Rulers from the Layout menu and Snap to Guides from the submenu (Shift, Command-G) to deselect it, making sure it is unchecked.

12 With the pointer tool selected, click the text Braga+Braga to select it as a text block, hold down the Shift key (to constrain the movement to 45°), and drag the text block until the baseline of the text is aligned with the 9p horizontal ruler guide.

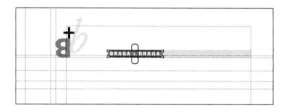

13 Choose Save from the File menu.

Formatting and positioning the text Arquitectos

You will follow a similar procedure for the text Arquitectos (meaning architects in Spanish) that fills the rightmost box of the double box.

1 If necessary, scroll to view the placed text on the pasteboard.

2 With the text tool selected, click to the immediate left of the first line of the placed text Arquitectos to establish an insertion point, and press the Delete key to delete the character space at the beginning of the line.

3 With the text tool still selected, double-click the text Arquitectos to select it.

4 In the Control palette click the Character-view button, and in the character view of the Control palette choose Adobe Garamond Semibold Italic from the Font pop-up menu, type **13** points in the Size box, and click the Apply button.

Character-view button

5 With the text Arquitectos still selected, choose Cut from the Edit menu.

6 With the text tool still selected, drag to define a text block just above the rightmost box, spanning the width of the rightmost box (exact height is not important).

Note: Dragging directly in the rightmost box could possibly select the text in the adjacent box.

7 Choose Paste from the Edit menu to paste the text Arquitectos in the text block you just defined.

8 With the insertion point still established in the text Arquitectos, in the Control palette click the Paragraph-view button, and in the paragraph view of the Control palette type **1p2** in the Left indent box and the Right indent box, and click the Force-justify button.

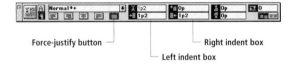

Force-justify button
Right indent box
Left indent box

In force-justified text, Adobe PageMaker justifies (aligns) the text with the left and right edges of the text block even if it contains only a few characters, spacing them so that the text fits exactly between the vertical edges of the text block. Since you set 1p2 left and right indents, the text is force-justified 1p2 away from the vertical edges of the text block.

9 With the pointer tool selected, click the text Arquitectos to select it as a text block, hold down the Shift key (to constrain the movement to 45°), and drag the text block until the baseline of the text is aligned with the 9p horizontal ruler guide.

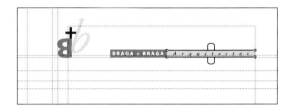

10 Choose Save from the File menu.

Formatting and positioning the address text

After cutting the address text from the placed text on the pasteboard, you will position it in the upper-right portion of the page.

1 If necessary, scroll to view the placed text on the pasteboard.

2 With the text tool selected, drag to select the first three lines of the remaining placed text (the address) on the pasteboard.

3 In the Control palette click the Character-view button, and in the character view of the Control palette drag to select Myriad MM 830 Black 600 Normal from the Font pop-up menu, type **10** points in the Size box, **15** points in the Leading box, **.73** em space in the Kerning box, and click the Apply button.

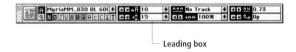

Leading box

4 With the address text still selected, choose Cut from the Edit menu.

5 From the vertical ruler guide, drag to create a vertical ruler guide at 29p2.

6 With the text tool still selected, drag to define a text block that spans from the 29p2 vertical ruler guide to the right margin guide, above the text Arquitectos (exact height is not important).

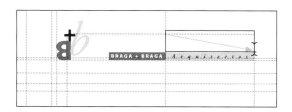

7 Choose Paste from the Edit menu to paste the address text into the text block you just defined.

8 From the horizontal ruler, drag to create a horizontal ruler guide at 7p.

9 With the pointer tool selected, click the address text to select it as a text block, and drag the text block until the baseline of the last line of text is aligned with the 7p horizontal ruler guide, with the right edge of text aligned with the right margin guide.

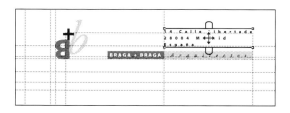

A portion of the address text is positioned within the top margin.

10 With the text tool selected, drag to select the address text, and in the Colors palette click PANTONE 660 CVU to apply a spot color to the text.

11 Choose Save from the File menu.

Drawing lines

The letterhead design includes two dashed lines that you will create using the constrained-line tool. The constrained-line tool makes it possible to draw straight lines that are constrained to 45° angles on the page.

1 Choose View from the Layout menu and Fit in Window from the submenu.

The first line you will draw is a horizontal line that is aligned with the 14p horizontal ruler guide.

2 With the constrained-line tool selected in the toolbox, position the cursor on the intersection of the 14p horizontal ruler guide and the 2p vertical ruler guide, and drag to draw a horizontal line that extends to the right margin guide.

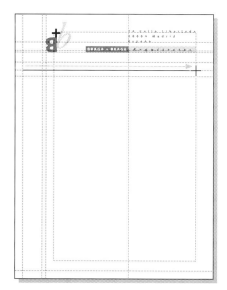

Since the guides (margin, column, and ruler) are in front of the text and graphics, the 14p horizontal ruler guide overlaps the line you just drew.

3 Choose Guides and Rulers from the Layout menu and Guides in Back from the submenu to display the horizontal line over the horizontal ruler guide.

4 With the line still selected, choose Line from the Element menu and 1-point dashed line from the submenu to apply a line style and weight to the line.

5 In the Colors palette make sure the Line button is selected, and click PANTONE 5595 CVU to apply a spot color to the line.

The second line you will draw is a vertical line that is aligned with the 8p vertical ruler guide.

6 With the constrained-line tool still selected, position the cursor on the intersection of the 12p horizontal ruler guide and the 8p vertical ruler guide, and drag to draw a vertical line that extends to the 64p horizontal ruler guide.

7 With the second line still selected, choose Line from the Element menu and 1-point dashed line from the submenu, and in the Colors palette click PANTONE 660 CVU.

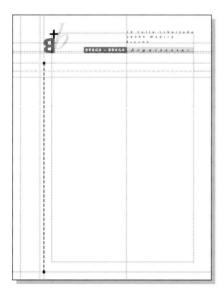

8 Choose Save from the File menu.

Applying a tint of a spot color to a box

After drawing a box in the left margin, you will use the Colors palette to fill the box with a 30% tint of a spot color, a lightened version of the spot color.

1 With the rectangle tool selected in the toolbox, position the cursor on the intersection of the dashed lines, and drag to the intersection of the 64p horizontal ruler guide and the 2p vertical ruler guide to draw a box.

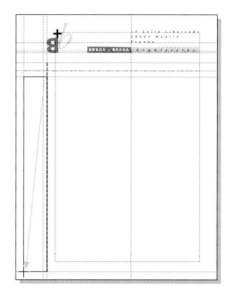

2 With the box still selected, in the Colors palette make sure the Both button is selected, click PANTONE 5595 CVU, and choose 30% from the Tint pop-up menu.

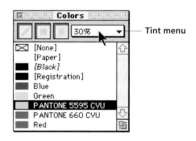

3 Choose Save from the File menu.

Rotating a text block

After using the Control palette to rotate a text block, you will format the rotated text, and then position it in the tinted box.

1 With the pointer tool selected, click the remaining line of placed text (telephone and fax numbers) to select it as a text block.

2 In the Control palette type **90°** in the Rotate box, and press the Return key.

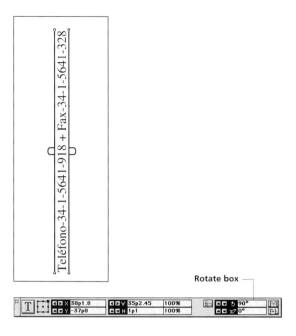

Rotate box

The windowshade handles of the rotated text are vertically aligned with the text.

4 Choose Save from the File menu.

Formatting the rotated text

You will format the text before positioning it in the tinted box, since formatting text after positioning it can alter its alignment.

1 With the magnifying glass selected in the tool-box, drag to marquee select the rotated text.

2 Drag to select the first portion of the rotated text that includes the telephone number (Tele-fono-34-1-5641-918).

3 In the Control palette choose Myriad MM 830 Black 600 Normal from the Font pop-up menu, type **9** points in the Size box, type **.6** em space in the Kerning box, and click the Apply button.

4 Drag to select the remaining rotated text (+ Fax-34-1-5641-328), and in the Control palette choose Adobe Garamond Semibold Italic from the Font pop-up menu, type **11** points in the Size box, type **.6** em space in the Kerning box, and click the Apply button.

5 Choose View from the Layout menu and Fit in Window from the submenu.

6 Choose Guides and Rulers from the Layout menu and Guides in Front from the submenu.

7 With the pointer tool selected, click the rotated text to select it as a text block, and drag the text block until the baseline of the rotated text is aligned with the 7p vertical ruler guide, with the left corner handles (at the bottom) aligned with the bottom edge of the tinted box.

Since the tinted box overlaps the rotated text, you will adjust the stacking, making it easier to check the alignment of the rotated text.

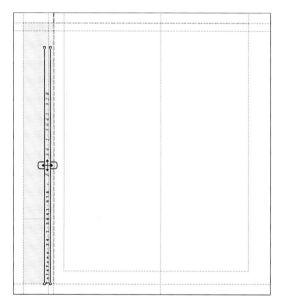

8 Choose Save from the File menu.

Adjusting the stacking order

Since you created the box after placing (importing) the rotated text, the box is positioned at the top of the stack, with the rotated text retaining the stacking position assigned to it when it was imported.

1 With the pointer tool selected, click the rotated text to select it as a text block, and choose Bring Forward from the Arrange menu (Command-8) to move the rotated text forward one position in the stack.

Notice how the box still overlaps the rotated text. Since Adobe PageMaker assigns each created, pasted, or placed object the top position in the stack, several pasted text objects (cut from the imported text) and two lines are positioned above the rotated text in the stack.

Note: Moving and modifying a text or graphic element does not alter its position in the stack.

Rather than repeatedly selecting the Bring Forward command to move the rotated text forward in one-position increments, you will use the Bring to Front command.

2 With the box still selected, choose Bring to Front from the Arrange menu (Command-F) to position the rotated text at the top of the stack.

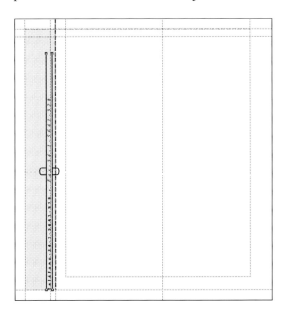

The rotated text is displayed over the box.

3 Make sure the baseline of the rotated text is aligned with the 7p vertical ruler guide, with the left corner handles (at the bottom) aligned with the bottom edge of the tinted box.

4 Choose Save from the File menu.

Resizing a text block

To center the rotated text between the top and bottom edges of the tinted box, you will manually resize the text block to span the vertical length of the box, and then you will use the Control palette to center the text in the text block.

1 Choose View from the Layout menu and Fit in Window from the submenu.

2 With the pointer tool selected, click the rotated text to select it as a text block.

3 Position the cursor on a right corner handle, and drag the handle up until it is aligned with the top edge of the tinted box, resizing the text block.

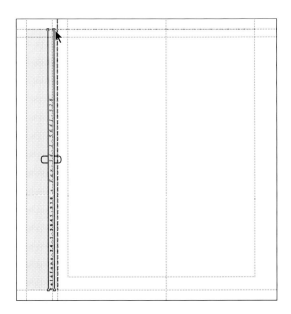

The text block spans the vertical length of the tinted box, and you are ready to apply the paragraph specification that centers the rotated text in the text block.

4 With the text tool selected, click the rotated text to establish an insertion point.

Note: To apply paragraph specifications to a single paragraph, you must establish an insertion point in the paragraph. To apply paragraph specifications to multiple contiguous paragraphs, you must select some text in each of the target paragraphs.

5 In the Control palette click the Paragraph-view button, and in the paragraph view of the Control palette click the Center-align button to center the text in the text block.

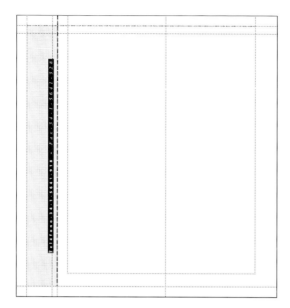

Since the text block spans the vertical length of the tinted box, the text is horizontally centered in the vertical box, and the letterhead template is completely assembled.

6 Choose Guides and Rulers from the Layout menu and Show Guides from the submenu to hide the view of the guides used to assemble this template.

7 Choose Save from the File menu to save the *02WorkA* template.

You are ready to assemble the envelope and business card.

Note: Interim file 02Int1 *was saved at this point. To open it, double-click the* 02Int1 *file in the* Extras *folder.*

ASSEMBLING THE ENVELOPE

Using the text and graphics elements from the *02WorkA* template, you will create the design for an envelope.

Tiling the publication window

After opening a custom template that includes outlines of a business-sized envelope and a business card, you will use the Tile command to display all open publications within the publication window.

1 Without closing the open publications, choose Open from the File menu, and in the Open Publication dialog box double-click the *02Template* file in the *02Lesson* folder.

The untitled copy of the template displays outlines of a business-sized envelope and a standard-sized business card.

2 Choose Save As from the File menu, and in the Save publication as dialog box type **02WorkB** in the Name box, select the *Projects* folder, and click OK.

3 Choose Tile from the Window menu to tile the publication window with all open publications and templates.

The publication window displays the publications *02FinalA*, *02FinalB*, *02WorkA*, and *02WorkB*.

4 Click the close boxes in the title bar of the *02FinalA* and *02FinalB* publications to close them.

Since the publication window displays two un-tiled publications, you will use the Tile command again.

5 Choose Tile from the Window menu to tile the publication window with two publications.

It will be easier to assemble the envelope with a large view of the publications.

Dragging a group from one publication to another

Adobe PageMaker makes it possible to drag text, graphics, and groups from publication to publication. Before you drag and drop a portion of the letterhead design from the *02WorkA* publication to the *02WorkB* publication, you will group the required text and graphics elements into a single entity.

1 Click the title bar of the *02WorkA* publication to make it the active publication.

2 With the pointer tool selected, drag to mar-quee select all letterhead elements (B + b logo, double box, and address) above the letter text in the *02Lesson* publication (without selecting the dashed lines, the tinted box, or the letter text).

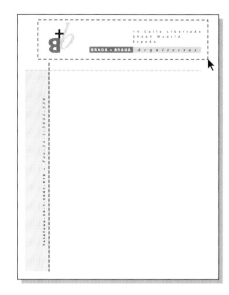

3 If necessary, hold down the Shift key, and click individual elements to be included or excluded from the selection.

4 Choose Group from the Arrange menu (Com-mand-G) to group the text and graphics elements into a single entity.

5 Position the cursor in the center of the group in the *02WorkA* publication, hold down the mouse button, drag the group to the center of the *02WorkB* publication, and release the mouse button.

The group is still selected in the *02WorkA* publication (because it's the active publication), and the Control palette displays the available options for modifying a group.

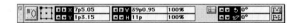

6 With the pointer tool selected, click the group in the *02WorkB* publication to select it, activating the *02WorkB* publication.

7 With the pointer tool selected, drag to align the text in the upper-left corner of the envelope, approximately 3p from the top and left edges of the envelope outline as shown in the illustration below.

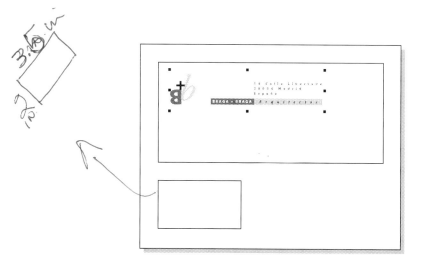

The envelope design is complete.

8 Choose Save from the File menu to save the *02WorkB* publication.

ASSEMBLING A BUSINESS CARD
In addition to creating text and graphics elements, assembling the business card involves copying and pasting existing elements, and applying new type specifications to the pasted text elements.

Creating a tinted box
After drawing a box, you will use the Control palette to resize the box, and the Colors palette to fill the box with a 30% tint of a spot color.

1 With the magnifying glass selected in the toolbox, drag to marquee select the business-card outline, magnifying its view.

2 With the rectangle tool selected in the toolbox, drag to draw a box of any dimension.

3 With the box still selected, in the Control palette type **11p2.5** in the Width box and **3p7.5** in the Height box, and press the Return key.

4 With the box still selected, in the Colors palette make sure the Both button is selected, click PANTONE 5595 CVU, and choose 30% from the Tint pop-up menu.

5 From the vertical ruler, drag to create a vertical ruler guide at 13p3.

6 With the pointer tool selected, click the tinted box to select it, and drag the box until its left edge is aligned with the 13p3 vertical ruler guide, about one point (p1) above the bottom edge of the business card as shown in the illustration below.

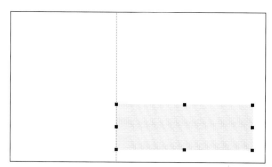

7 Choose Save from the File menu.

Drawing lines
Like the letterhead design, the business card design includes two dashed lines that you will create using the constrained-line tool.

The first line you will draw is a horizontal line that is aligned with the top edge of the tinted box.

1 With the constrained-line tool selected in the toolbox, position the cursor on the upper-right corner of the tinted box, and drag left to draw a horizontal line that extends about one pica (1p) beyond the left edge of the tinted box.

2 With the line still selected, choose Line from the Element menu and 1-point dashed line from the submenu.

3 In the Colors palette make sure the Line button is selected, and click PANTONE 5595 CVU to apply a spot color to the line.

TIP: TO SCROLL THE VIEW OF THE PAGE, HOLD DOWN THE OPTION KEY, AND DRAG THE PAGE IN ANY DIRECTION.

The second line you will draw is a vertical line that is aligned with the left edge of the tinted box.

4 With the constrained-line tool still selected, position the cursor on the lower-left corner of the tinted box, and drag up to draw a vertical line that extends about 1p beyond the top edge of the tinted box.

5 With the second line still selected, choose Line from the Element menu and 1-point dashed line from the submenu, and in the Colors palette click PANTONE 660 CVU.

6 Choose Guides and Rulers from the Layout menu and Guides in Back from the submenu.

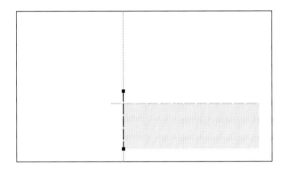

7 Choose Save from the File menu.

Copying text from one publication to another

Since the business card includes some text not found on the envelope, you will copy the telephone/fax text in the *02WorkA* template, and paste it to the *02WorkB* publication.

1 Click the title bar of the *02WorkA* template to make it the active publication.

2 With the text tool selected, triple-click the telephone/fax text in the tinted box to select it, and choose Copy from the Edit menu.

3 Click the title bar of the *02WorkB* publication to make it the active publication.

4 With the text tool still selected, drag to define a text block that spans the width of the tinted box (exact height is not important).

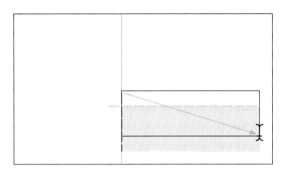

5 Choose Paste from the Edit menu, and magnify the view of the business-card outline.

The pasted text is not rotated like the copied text, because you copied the text only, not the rotated text block.

6 With the text tool selected, drag to select the plus sign (in between the two numbers), and press the Return key, replacing the plus sign with a hard carriage return.

Inserting a hard carriage return into a paragraph creates two paragraphs from a single paragraph.

7 Triple-click the first paragraph (telephone number) in the pasted text to select it.

8 In the Control palette click the Character-view button, and in the character view of the Control palette choose Myriad MM 830 Black 600 Normal from the Font pop-up menu, type **6** points in the Size box, **11.5** points in the Leading box, and **.2** em space in the Kerning box, and click the Apply button.

9 Triple-click the second paragraph (fax number) in the pasted text to select it, and in the Control palette type **7** points in the Size box, **11.5** points in the Leading box, and **.35** em space in the Kerning box, and click the Apply button.

10 With the insertion point still established in the text block, choose Select All from the Edit menu to select the entire story.

11 In the Control palette click the Paragraph-view button, and in the paragraph view of the Control palette type **p8** in the Left indent box and **p8** in the Right indent box, and click the Force-justify button.

12 With the pointer tool selected, click the text in the tinted box to select it as a text block, hold down the Shift key (to constrain the movement to 45°), and drag the text block until the text is vertically centered in the tinted box.

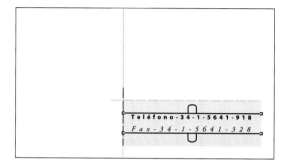

13 Choose Save from the File menu.

Copying, pasting, and formatting the address text

After ungrouping the text and graphics elements in the envelope, you will copy the address text and drag it to the business-card outline, applying new type specifications and aligning it in the upper-right portion of the business card.

1 Scroll to view the envelope design in the *02WorkB* publication.

2 With the pointer tool selected, click the group in the envelope outline to select it.

3 Choose Ungroup from the Arrange menu (Command-U) to ungroup all elements, making it possible to move the text and graphics elements independently.

4 Click the pasteboard (or an empty portion of the page) to deselect all objects.

5 With the pointer tool selected, click the address text to select it as a text block, and choose Copy from the Edit menu.

As with text, it is also possible to copy and paste a text block.

6 Choose Paste from the Edit menu to paste a copy of the address text block to be slightly offset from the original address text block.

7 With the pasted address text selected as a text block, drag the text block just to the right of the business-card outline.

You are ready to apply new type specifications to the pasted address text.

8 With the text tool selected, click the pasted address text to establish an insertion point, and choose Select All from the Edit menu to select all text in the text block.

9 In the Control palette click the Character-view button, and in the character view of the Control palette type 7 points in the Size box, 12 points in the Leading box, and .55 em space in the Kerning box, and click the Apply button to apply the new type specifications to the pasted address text.

10 With the pointer tool selected, click the pasted address text to select it as a text block, and drag the upper-right corner handle until it is roughly aligned with the right edge of the first line of address text, reducing the width of the text block.

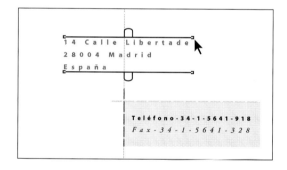

The bottom windowshade handle may display a red down arrow, indicating the entire story is not displayed.

11 If the red down arrow is displayed in the bottom windowshade handle, drag the bottom windowshade down to display the entire story.

12 With the pasted address text still selected as a text block, drag the text block until the left edge of the text is aligned with the 13p3 vertical ruler guide in the upper-right portion of the business card as shown in the illustration below.

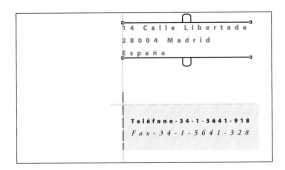

13 Choose Save from the File menu.

Creating the double boxes

After drawing the boxes, you will use the Control palette to resize the boxes, and the Colors palette to fill each box with a spot color.

1 With the rectangle tool selected in the toolbox, drag to draw a box of any dimension to the right of the business card.

2 With the box still selected, in the Control palette type **7p9** in the Width box and **1p2** in the Height box, and press the Return key.

3 In the Colors palette make sure the Both button is selected, and click PANTONE 660 CVU.

4 With the rectangle tool still selected, drag to draw another box of any dimension to the right of the first box.

5 In the Control palette type **11p3** in the Width box and **1p2** in the Height box, and press the Return key.

6 In the Colors palette click PANTONE 5595 CVU.

7 With the pointer tool selected, drag the second box until its left edge is flush with the right edge of the first box, magnifying the view of the edges to check for precise alignment.

8 With one of the boxes still selected, hold down the Shift key (to select multiple objects), click the adjacent box to select it, and choose Group from the Arrange menu.

You will slow drag this group to the business-card outline to view the objects as you drag. If you fast drag a group, the bounding box of the group is displayed as you drag.

9 With the group still selected, position the cursor in the center of the group, and hold down the mouse button until the cursor is displayed as a four-headed arrow.

10 With the mouse button still held down, drag the group until the vertical edge (where the boxes are joined) is aligned with the 13p3 vertical ruler guide, with the box vertically centered between the address text and the tinted box, and release the mouse button.

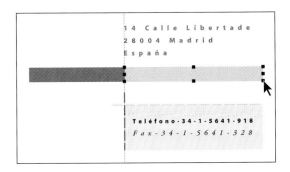

11 Choose Save from the File menu.

Copying, pasting, and formatting the text Braga+Braga

After copying the text Braga+Braga (in the leftmost box of the double boxes in the envelope design), you will drag to define a text block in the leftmost box in the business-card design, applying new type specifications and aligning it in the leftmost box.

1 Scroll to view the envelope design.

2 With the text tool selected, triple-click the text Braga+Braga in the envelope design to select it, and choose Copy from the Edit menu.

3 Scroll to view the business-card outline.

4 With the text tool selected, drag to define a text block that spans the width of the leftmost box of the double boxes (exact height is not important), and choose Paste from the Edit menu to paste the text Braga+Braga into the text block.

You are ready to apply new type specifications to the pasted text.

5 With the insertion point still established in the pasted text, choose Select All from the Edit menu, and in the Control palette type **8** points in the Size box and **.3** em space in the Kerning box, and click the Apply button to apply the new type specifications.

6 With the pointer tool selected, click the text Braga+Braga to select it as a text block, hold down the Shift key (to constrain the movement to 45º), and drag the text block until the text is vertically centered in the leftmost box.

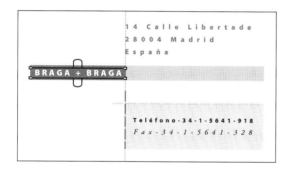

7 Choose Save from the File menu.

Copying, pasting, and formatting the text Arquitectos

You will format and position the text Arquitectos in the rightmost box of the double boxes using a similar procedure used to format and position the text Braga+Braga in the leftmost box.

1 Scroll to view the envelope design.

2 With the text tool selected, triple-click the text Arquitectos in the rightmost box (of the double boxes) in the envelope design to select it, and choose Copy from the Edit menu.

3 Scroll to view the business-card outline.

4 With the text tool selected, drag to define a text block that spans the width of the rightmost box of the double boxes (exact height is not important), and choose Paste from the Edit menu to paste the text Arquitectos into the text block.

You are ready to apply new type specifications to the pasted text.

5 With the insertion point still established in the pasted text, choose Select All from the Edit menu to select it, and in the Control palette type **10** points in the Size box, and click the Apply button to apply the new type specification.

6 In the Control palette click the Paragraph-view button, and in the paragraph view of the Control palette type **p10** in the Left indent box and **p10** in the Right indent box, and press the Return key.

7 With the pointer tool selected, click the text Arquitectos to select it as a text block, hold down the Shift key (to constrain the movement to 45º), and drag the text block until the text is vertically centered in the rightmost box.

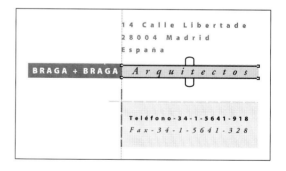

8 Choose Save from the File menu.

Applying new type specifications to the B+b logo

After copying and pasting the three text elements in the B+b logo design, you will apply new type specifications to each text object, and realign the text objects into the logo design.

1 Scroll to view the envelope design; and with the pointer tool selected, drag to marquee select the B+b logo design in the envelope.

2 Choose Group from the Arrange menu to group the three text objects, choose Copy from the Edit menu, and then choose Paste from the Edit menu to paste a copy of the grouped B+b logo.

3 With the pasted group still selected, drag the group to the right of the business-card outline.

After ungrouping the three text objects, you will apply type specifications to each text object.

4 With the B+b logo still selected, choose Ungroup from the Arrange menu.

5 Magnify the view of the B+b logo.

6 With the text tool selected, double-click the lowercase b to select it.

7 In the Control palette click the Character-view button, and in the character view of the Control palette type **55** points in the Size box, and click the Apply button.

8 Double-click the uppercase B to select it, and in the Control palette type **32** points in the Size box, and click the Apply button.

9 With the text tool still selected, double-click the plus sign to select it, and in the Control palette type **25** points in the Size box, and click the Apply button.

Applying new type specifications to the text objects has forced them out of alignment.

10 With the pointer tool selected, align the three text objects of the B+b logo, clicking individual text objects to select them as text blocks, and dragging the text blocks until the B+b logo looks like the original logo on the envelope.

Since Adobe PageMaker maintains the original stacking order of objects, including when they are moved or modified, you do not need to adjust the stacking order of the text objects.

11 With the pointer tool selected, drag to marquee select the three B+b logo text objects, and choose Group from the Arrange menu to group the text objects into a single entity.

12 With the group selected, position the cursor on the B+b logo group, and drag it until it is positioned in the lower-left portion of the business-card outline as shown in the illustration below.

You are finished assembling the business card design.

TIP: TO ACTIVATE AN OPEN PUBLICATION, CLICK ITS TITLE BAR.

13 Choose View from the Layout menu and Fit in Window from the submenu.

14 Choose Guides and Rulers from the Layout menu and Show Guides from the submenu to hide the view of the guides.

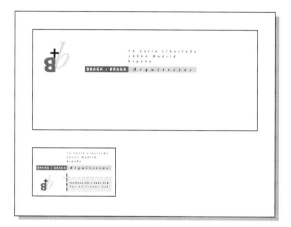

15 Choose Save from the File menu to save the *02WorkB* publication.

PRINTING THE LETTERHEAD

Now that you have assembled all elements for the letterhead (stationary, envelope, and business card), you are ready to prepare these publications to be sent to a service provider. In addition to performing trapping and various prepress tasks, your service provider will create the spot color film separations on an imagesetter that will be delivered to your commercial printer.

Using the Lock Position command

To prepare the individual letterhead publications (letterhead, envelope, and business card) to be sent to your service provider, you will use the Group command to group all text and graphics elements in each publication into a single entity, and then apply the Lock Position command to each publication to lock all text and graphics elements, protecting your work from any accidental changes.

1 With the *02WorkB* publication still activated, choose Select All from the Edit menu to select all text and graphics elements in the publication.

2 Choose Group from the Arrange menu to group all elements into a single entity.

3 With the group still selected, choose Lock Position from the Arrange menu (Command-L) to lock the group.

4 Choose Save from the File menu to save the *02WorkB* publication.

5 Choose *02WorkA* from the Window menu to activate the template you assembled.

6 With the *02WorkA* publication displayed, click the pointer tool in the toolbox, and choose Select All from the Edit menu.

7 Choose Group from the Arrange menu to group all elements into a single entity.

8 With the group still selected, choose Lock Position from the Arrange menu to lock the group.

9 Choose Save from the File menu to save the *02WorkA* template as an Adobe PageMaker file.

You are ready to deliver these letterhead publications to your service provider. In addition to verifying the correct trapping specification with the printer, your service provider will expect you to verify the line screen frequency with the printer. For this example, a suitable line screen frequency could range from 80 lpi (lines per inch) to 150 lpi. Knowing the line screen frequency, your service provider will create film separations that range from 1200 dpi (dots per inch) to 2400 dpi. Once the film separations are complete, you are ready to deliver them to your printer.

ASSEMBLING A LETTER

Using the *02WorkA* template you assembled, you will place and align the letter text, and prepare the letter publication to be printed on a desktop laser printer.

Using the Non-Printing command

Since the letterhead stationary includes the text and graphics for the letterhead design, you will use the Non-Printing command to designate all text and graphics in the letterhead template to be nonprinting.

1 With the *02WorkA* publication activated, choose Select All from the Edit menu to select all text and graphics in the newly opened publication.

2 Choose Non-Printing from the Element menu to select it, making sure it is checked.

All text and graphics elements are still displayed, allowing you to view them as you assemble the letter. The cyan-colored handles (white on black and white monitors) indicate the elements that will not be printed.

3 Choose Guides and Rulers from the Layout menu and Show Guides from the submenu to select it, making sure it is checked.

Opening the letterhead template

Now that all text and graphics in the *02WorkA* template have been designated to be non-printing, you are ready to open a copy of the template.

1 With *02WorkA* template activated, click the close box in the title bar to close the letterhead template.

Closing the *02WorkA* template before you reopen it better demonstrates how you would use a custom template.

2 Choose Open from the File menu, and in the Open Publication dialog box single-click the *02WorkA* file in the *Projects* folder.

The Open Publication dialog box indicates a copy of the template will be opened. Even though you will open a copy of the template, it is possible to open the original template by clicking the Original radio button.

3 In the Open Publications dialog box click OK.

Because you have saved *02WorkA* as a template, Adobe PageMaker opens an untitled copy of the template, preserving the contents of the template.

4 Choose Save As from the File menu, and in the Save Publication As dialog box type **02WorkC** in the name box, make sure the *Projects* folder is selected, and click OK.

Placing the letter text

After placing the letter text in this single-column publication, you will align it with an existing horizontal ruler guide.

1 Choose Place from the File menu, and in the Place Document dialog box double-click the *02TextB* file in the *02Lesson* folder.

2 With the loaded text icon displayed, click between the margin guides, below the letterhead design, to place the text.

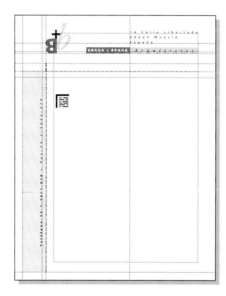

The left-aligned text flows between the margins of the page. Since the desired type specifications have been applied to the letter text already, you are ready to position the letter text on the page.

Note: The empty top and bottom windowshade handles indicate the entire story is displayed.

3 With the letter text still selected as a text block, drag it until the baseline of the first line of text is aligned with the 15p6 horizontal ruler guide, with the left edge of the text aligned with the left margin guide.

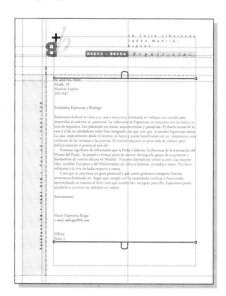

The letter publication is completed.

4 Choose Guides and Rulers from the Layout menu and Show Guides from the submenu to hide the view of the guides.

5 Choose Save from the File menu to save the *02WorkC* publication.

If the preprinted letterhead stationary were available, you could print the *02WorkC* publication on a desktop laser printer.

6 Load the letterhead stationary in a 300 dpi desktop printer, choose Print from the File menu (Command-P), select the desired options in the printing dialog boxes, and click the Print button to print the letter.

7 Close all open publications, and choose Quit from the File menu (Command-Q) to quit the Adobe PageMaker application.

Preservation of thirty-one
major trees identified in the
northeast corner of the site
would significantly reduce the
total...

BELLA COOLA

The Bella Coola Development Study
merges community requirements for the
envisioned facility and the alternative
approaches to building on the Bella

Coola Northern Pointe site. Consultants' re-
ports regarding structural considerations and
tree evaluation are included for their continued application to the problem. An effort
has been made to work with the full extent of
space requirements currently voiced by the
Western Division Management Center and the
Bella Coola Village Organization. Other organizations were queried to form the basis of
judgment in determining the overall need. This
recognizes that as the program development
progresses, tenant requirements may change,
but the essential square footage and cubi
c limitations for a below grade structure will
remain. In addition, it has been envisioned that
jointly required facilities would be available for
all organizations to use on a shared basis, utilizing movable walls for privacy.

In utilizing the Northern Pointe site, it is
initially assumed that the envisioned facilities would be largely accommodated below
grade, and that above grade structures would
be intended to accommodate those func-
tions demanding particular visibility and identity, such as a community recreation center.

It is very possible that significant heat-
ing and cooling economies would be
achieved by virtue of underground construction and the application of appropriate solar
collection techniques. The southern face of
proposed structures along Grant Road offer
optimum orientation for collection of solar
energy. Additionally, natural illumination of
below grade spaces would significantly improve the quality of the indoor environment
and has been recognized as an important
component of the project.

AVAILABLE SPACE ANALYSIS

On the schematic site plan of the Northern
Pointe site, a total area of some 200 feet by
450 feet is indicated as the proposed maximum extent of below grade development. In
addition, we believe that a 345 feet by 475
feet area to the north of the community center may be considered for future inclusion in
Northern Pointe development plans, although
it is not under consideration in this study.

Spectacular solar site: the southern face along
Grant Road will provide enough solar energy
for the entire three level structure.

• CANADA •

For this lesson you assemble a 3-page, black-and-white publication. This project proposal presents an architect's plan for the development of a community facility within the coast-

PROJECT PROPOSAL

al town of Bella Coola. Located in British Columbia, the western-most province of Canada, Bella Coola is named for the people who have inhabited the region for uncounted generations. ■ To establish a base for this multipage publication, you will assembled a master page. Once assembled, this master page will make it possible to place text and graphics elements, column guides, and page-number markers (for automatic page numbering) on every page within the proposal publication automatically.

In addition to assembling a master page, this lesson introduces you to using styles to apply character and paragraph formatting attributes to paragraphs. More than ensuring consistency in a publication, styles free you from repeatedly se-

PROJECT PROPOSAL

lecting and applying individual formatting attributes to each paragraph in a publication. Even though the Adobe PageMaker application provides a collection of styles (style sheet), you will create and edit styles to build a style sheet specific to this publication.

This lesson covers:

- Establishing a master page

- Adding tints to the Colors palette

- Using the Control palette to resize objects proportionally and move objects

- Specifying automatic page numbering

- Establishing a publication default line style and weight

- Moving ruler guides

- Displaying and hiding master-page elements

- Overriding the default leading method

- Autoflowing text

- Adjusting the tracking (the spacing between words and letters)

- Varying the number of columns on a page

- Deactivating hyphenation for a paragraph

- Overriding type and paragraph specifications

- Creating, editing, and applying styles

- Creating a custom text wrap

- Using the quick-drag technique to move a graphic.

BEFORE YOU BEGIN

All files and fonts needed for this lesson are found on the Adobe PageMaker *Classroom in a Book* CD-ROM disc in the folders *03Lesson* and *Fonts*, respectively. In addition, the *Extras* folder on the Adobe PageMaker *Classroom in a Book* CD-ROM disc includes the files *03Int1* and *03Int2*, interim files of artwork that you may wish to use.

It should take you approximately 2 hours to complete this lesson.

Opening an existing document

Let's take a look at the final version of the proposal you will create in this lesson.

1 Before launching the Adobe PageMaker program, throw away the *Adobe PageMaker 6.0 Prefs* file to ensure all settings are returned to their default values.

2 Make sure the fonts Birch, Minion Display, Minion Semibold, Minion Semibold Italic, Myriad MM 700 Bold 600 Normal, and Myriad MM 215 Light 600 Normal are installed.

All fonts used in this publication are Adobe Originals fonts. Birch, designed in 1990 by Adobe Designer Kim Buker, is modeled after a Latin Condensed wood type found in an 1879 William Page specimen book. A particularly legible condensed display typeface, Birch is notable for its angled serifs.

Note: Serifs are the little feet at the tops and bottoms of letters. Typefaces without serifs are generally called sans (without) serifs.

3 Double-click the *Adobe® PageMaker® 6.0* icon to launch the Adobe PageMaker program.

4 Choose Open from the File menu (Command-O), and in the Open Publication dialog box double-click the *03Final* file in the *03Lesson* folder to view the proposal you will create.

TIP: TO MOVE FOR-
WARD ONE PAGE,
HOLD DOWN THE
COMMAND KEY, AND
PRESS THE TAB KEY.
TO MOVE BACK ONE
PAGE, HOLD DOWN
THE COMMAND AND
SHIFT KEYS, AND
PRESS THE TAB KEY.

The full view of the first page displays a variety of text and graphics elements, where a single column of text is positioned above two columns of text. The page icons in the lower-left corner of the publication window indicate this document consists of three pages.

5 Click page icon 2 in the lower-left corner of the publication window to view the second page.

The left margin of the second page displays the rotated display text, page number, and graphics that appear on each page of this document.

6 Click page icon 3 to view the third page.

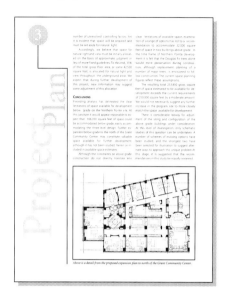

Again, the left margin displays the graphics and rotated display text.

7 Click page icon 1 to return to the first page.

8 Choose Guides and Rulers from the Layout menu and Show Guides from the submenu (Command-J) to display the guides used to assemble this proposal.

Defining printing requirements

This project proposal was designed to be printed on a 300 dpi or 600 dpi desktop laser printing device. As was mentioned in the first lesson, you need to determine the maximum printable area of the target printing device before assembling a publication. When printed on a 300 dpi or 600 dpi desktop laser printing device, images scanned at a resolution of 100 dpi will meet the print quality requirements of this publication.

ASSEMBLING A MASTER PAGE

To produce a more cohesive design for this multi-page publication, you will establish a master page that will contain a variety of design elements such as, repeating text, page numbering, and graphics elements that will be common to all pages in this publication. Column guides and ruler guides can also be placed on a master page.

Creating a new publication

To create a master page, open a new or existing publication, and then display the master page itself.

1 Choose New from the File menu (Command-N), and in the Document Setup dialog box click the Double-sided check box to deselect it, type 2.5 inches in the Left box, .75 inch in the Right box, .75 inch in the Top box, and .75 inch in the Bottom box to set the margin guides, and click OK.

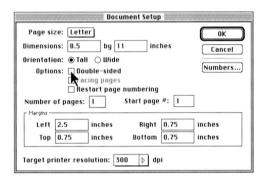

The publication window displays the untitled publication with the specified page dimensions and margin guides.

2 If you do not have a *Projects* folder, create one now.

3 Choose Save As from the File menu, and in the Save publication as dialog box type **03Work** in the Name box, select the *Projects* folder, and click OK.

Page icon 1 is reverse-highlighted, indicating the first page is selected. To import, create, and modify text and graphics elements on a master page, you must select the master page.

4 Click master-page icon R in the lower-left corner of the publication window.

Adobe PageMaker displays the master page, and the R master-page icon (in the lower-left corner of the publication window) is reverse-highlighted. The page still displays the margin guides you specified in the Document Setup dialog box.

Note: A single-sided publication is marked by a master-page icon R. For double-sided publications, you would see master-page icons L and R (for the left and right master pages).

Creating column guides

With the margins already defined using the Document Setup dialog box, you are ready to specify the column guides. Even though it is possible to vary column guides from page to page, it is suggested that you place column guides on master pages for a consistent look throughout a publication. In addition, specifying column guides on the master page saves you the effort of specifying column guides on individual pages in a publication.

1 Choose Column Guides from the Layout menu, and in the Column Guides dialog box type 2 columns in the Number of columns box, and click OK.

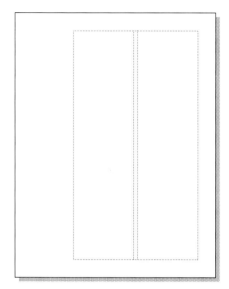

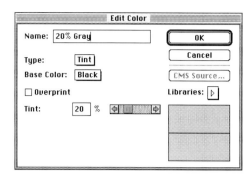

Adobe PageMaker automatically creates columns of equal widths, filling the entire image area between margin guides. Any column guides or ruler guides you create on a master page are automatically displayed on publication pages.

2 Choose Save from the File menu (Command-S).

Adding tints to the Colors palette

In previous lessons you used the Colors palette to apply tints (lightened colors) to text and graphics objects. In this lesson you will use the Define Colors command to add two tints of black to the Colors palette, providing a shortcut to applying the same tint to multiple objects.

1 Choose Define Colors from the Element menu, and in the Define Colors dialog box click the New button.

2 In the Edit Color dialog box type **20% Gray** in the Name box, choose Tint from the Type pop-up menu, choose Black from the Base Color pop-up menu, type **20%** in the Tint box, and click OK.

3 In the Define Colors dialog box click the New button to define another color.

4 In the Edit Color dialog box type **10% Gray** in the Name box, choose Tint from the Type pop-up menu, choose Black from the Base Color pop-up menu, type **10%** in the Tint box, hold down the Option key (to close the chain of dialog boxes), and click OK.

The Colors palette displays the tints 10% Gray and 20% Gray in its list of colors, with a % sign to the left of each tint name.

5 Choose Save from the File menu.

Using the Control palette to resize an object proportionally

After drawing a circle, you will use the Control palette to resize and position it. This circle will serve to frame the page numbers.

1 Magnify the view of the upper-left corner of the page.

2 With the ellipse tool selected in the toolbox, hold down the Shift key (to constrain the ellipse to a circle), and drag to draw a circle of any diameter in the upper-left corner of the page.

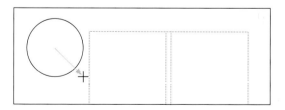

TIP: TO TURN PROPOR-
TIONAL SCALING ON
OR OFF, ACTIVATE THE
CONTROL PALETTE, AND
PRESS THE SPACEBAR.

3 In the Control palette click the Proportional-scaling button (to constrain an object to its original proportions) to select it, type **.85** inch in the Width or the Height box, and press the Return key.

By default, the Proportional-scaling button is deselected, allowing you to scale an object's height and width independently. When activated, you can enter a single value, and the related value changes proportionally.

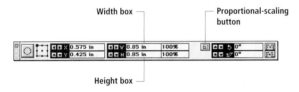

You are ready to position the circle using the Control palette.

4 With the circle still selected, in the Control palette make sure the center reference point of the Proxy icon is selected, type **1** inch in the X box and **.75** inch in the Y box, and press the Return key to align the center of the circle with the specified coordinate position.

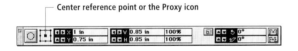

5 In the Colors palette click the Both button, and click 20% Gray to apply the 20% tint of black to the line and fill of the circle.

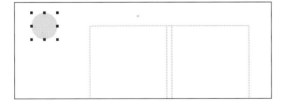

6 Choose Save from the File menu.

Specifying automatic page numbering

To automatically number all pages in this publication, you will place a page-number marker on the master page.

Note: With Adobe PageMaker, it is possible to number the pages of a multiple-publication document consecutively from the first publication through the last, restart the page numbering in each publication, or combine the two methods. You can also tell Adobe PageMaker to begin each successive publication on the next odd or even page number.

1 With the text tool selected, drag to define a text block in the gray circle that is wider than the gray circle (exact height is not important).

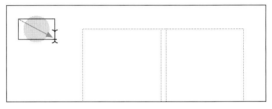

2 In the Control palette choose Minion Semibold from the Font pop-up menu, type **50** points in the Size box, and click the Apply button.

3 Hold down the Command and Option keys, and press P.

The left-aligned page-number marker RM (right master) is displayed in the gray circle, indicating where page numbers will appear.

Note: If your publication has facing pages, you would add the page-number marker on both the right and left master pages.

4 With the pointer tool selected, drag to visually center the letter R in the circle.

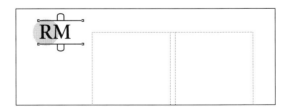

TIP: TO DELETE AN
EXISTING RULER
GUIDE, DRAG
IT OFF THE PAGE.

5 With the text tool selected, double-click the page-number marker to select it.

6 In the Colors palette click Paper to apply the color paper to the page number.

7 Choose Save from the File menu.

Establishing a publication default line style and weight

Before drawing lines (to be printed) over ruler guides and column guides, you will establish a publication default line style and weight.

1 Click the pointer tool in the toolbox to deselect all objects.

2 Choose Line from the Element menu and .5-point line from the submenu to establish a publication default.

3 Choose Guides and Rulers from the Layout menu and Guides in Back from the submenu.

4 From the horizontal ruler, drag to create a horizontal ruler guide at 2.125 inches.

5 From the vertical ruler, drag to create a vertical ruler guide at 1 inch.

The first line segment you will draw is a vertical line.

6 With the constrained-line tool selected in the toolbox, position the crosshair on the intersection of the bottom edge of the gray circle and the 1-inch vertical ruler guide, and drag down to the 2.125-inch horizontal ruler guide to draw a line.

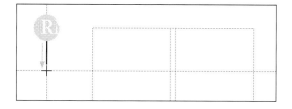

Rather than creating a new vertical ruler guide, you will reposition an existing guide that is no longer needed.

7 With the pointer tool selected, position the cursor over the existing 1-inch vertical ruler guide, hold down the mouse button until the cursor is displayed as a double arrow, drag it until it is aligned with the 2.25-inch mark on the horizontal ruler (using the Control palette if necessary), and release the mouse button to reposition the guide.

The second line segment you will draw is a horizontal line.

8 With the constrained-line tool selected, position the crosshair at the ending point of the line you just drew, and drag right to the intersection of the 2.125-inch horizontal ruler guide and the 2.25-inch vertical ruler guide to draw a second line.

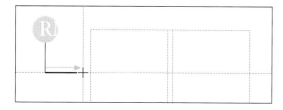

9 Choose View from the Layout menu and Fit in Window from the submenu (Command-0) to view the entire master page.

10 From the horizontal ruler, drag to create a horizontal ruler guide aligned with the bottom margin guide at 10.25 inches.

The 10.25-inch horizontal ruler guide extends beyond the bounds of the bottom margin guide, facilitating precise alignments across the entire page.

The final line segment you will draw is a vertical line.

11 With the constrained-line tool still selected, position the crosshair at the right ending point of the second line you just drew, and drag down to the 10.25-inch horizontal ruler guide to draw a third line.

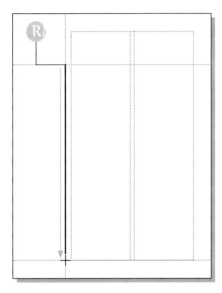

12 Choose Save from the File menu.

Creating the rotated display text

You will create, rotate, and align the display text that is positioned in the left margin of the master page.

1 With the text tool selected, drag to define a text block that spans the width of the image area (between the left and right margin guides).

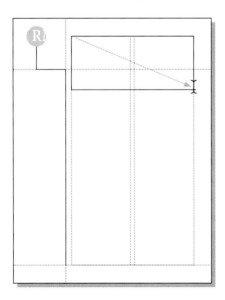

Before typing the text, you will use the Control palette to format the text.

2 In the Control palette choose Minion Display from the Font pop-up menu, type **130** points in the Size box, and click the Apply button.

3 Type **Project** in uppercase and lowercase letters.

4 With the text tool selected, double-click the text to select it; and in the Colors palette click 10% Gray to apply the 10% tint of black to the text.

5 With the pointer tool selected, click the text to select it, and in the Control palette make sure the center point of the Proxy icon is selected, type **90°** in the Rotating box, and click the Apply button.

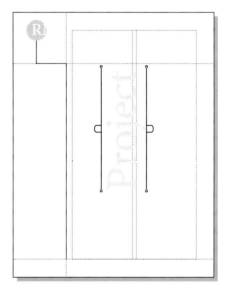

The text is rotated on the center point of the text block.

6 From the horizontal ruler, drag to create a horizontal ruler guide at 9.125 inches.

7 From the vertical ruler, drag to create a vertical ruler guide at approximately 1.56 inches.

8 Choose Guides and Rulers from the Layout menu and Snap to Guides from the submenu to deselect it, making sure it is unchecked.

9 With the pointer tool selected, click the text Project to select it as a text block, and drag it until its baseline is aligned with the 1.56-inch vertical ruler guide, with the bottom edge of the letter P aligned with the 9.125-inch horizontal ruler guide.

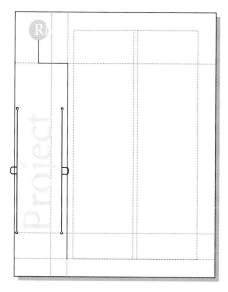

10 Choose Save from the File menu.

Replacing selected text

After copying and pasting the word Project, you will select the pasted text and type more text, replacing the text.

1 With the pointer tool selected, click the text Project to select it as a text block, and choose Copy from the Edit menu (Command-C), and then choose Paste from the Edit menu (Command-V).

The pasted text block is rotated like the copied text block, and the text is formatted like the copied text.

2 With the text tool selected, double-click the pasted text to select it, and type **Plan** in uppercase and lowercase letters to replace the pasted text.

3 Double-click the text Plan to select it, and in the Colors palette click 20% Gray.

This design calls for the text Plan to use a smaller font size.

4 With the text still selected, in the Control palette type **100** points in the Size box, and click the Apply button.

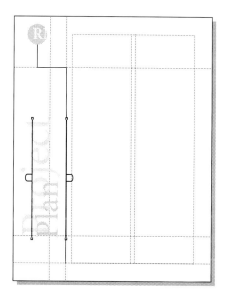

5 With the pointer tool selected, drag the existing 2.25-inch vertical ruler guide to be positioned at approximately 2.15 inches.

6 With the pointer tool still selected, click the text Plan to select it as a text block, and drag it until its baseline is aligned with the 2.15-inch vertical ruler guide, with the stem of the letter P in the text Plan aligned with the stem of the letter t in the text Project as shown below.

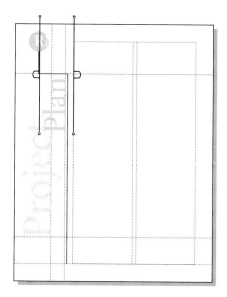

The text Plan overlaps the text Project, and the master page is complete.

7 Choose Select All from the Edit menu (Command-A), and choose Lock Position from the Arrange menu to prevent accidentally modifying the master-page elements.

8 Choose Guides and Rulers from the Layout menu and Clear Ruler Guides from the submenu to delete the ruler guides used to assemble the master page.

9 Choose Save from the File menu.

Displaying and hiding master-page elements

You can display master-page elements on a page-by-page basis, making it possible to create a publication that makes use of master-page elements on certain pages.

1 Click page icon 1 in the lower-left corner of the publication window to view the first page.

Since master-page elements are automatically displayed on each page of the publication, the first page of the publication is displayed along with all master-page elements. By definition, the master page is positioned below the stack, and cannot be moved.

2 Choose Select All from the Edit menu, and notice how none of the master-page elements are selected.

Since the first page is displayed, it is not possible to select text and graphics elements on the master page.

You can easily hide master-page elements on a particular page in your publication, provided it is the current page.

3 With the first page still selected, choose Display Master Items from the Layout menu to deselect it, making sure it is unchecked.

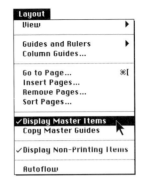

The text and graphics elements that you created are not displayed, and the nonprinting guides (margin, column, and ruler) are not affected. If you were to print this page, none of the master-page elements would be printed.

4 Choose Display Master Items from the Layout menu to select it, making sure it is checked.

The first page of the publication is displayed, along with all master-page elements.

Note: An interim file was saved at this point. To open it, double-click the 03Int1 *file in the* Extras *folder.*

ASSEMBLING THE FIRST PAGE

To assemble the first of three pages of the proposal, you will begin by creating and modifying text. Once the text is formatted, you will create new styles and edit existing styles that you will use throughout the rest of this publication.

Creating the title text

After establishing the character and paragraph specifications for the title text (Bella Coola) that spans the top of the first page of the proposal, you will create the text and apply a 75% tint of black using the Colors palette.

1 With the text tool selected, drag to define a text block that spans the width of the two columns (exact height is not important).

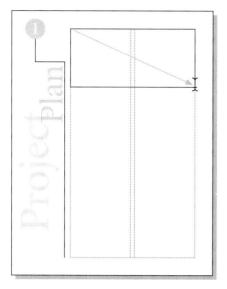

2 In the Control palette choose Birch from the Font pop-up menu, type **100** points in the Size box, and click the All caps button.

Note: By default, Adobe PageMaker automatically sets the leading to 120% of the font size (as indicated in the Control palette).

All caps button

3 With the insertion point still established, choose Paragraph from the Type menu (Command-M).

Paragraph Specifications

Indents:			Paragraph space:			OK
Left	0	inches	Before	0	inches	Cancel
First	0	inches	After	0	inches	Rules...
Right	0	inches				Spacing...

Alignment: Left   Dictionary: US English

Options:
☐ Keep lines together   ☐ Keep with next 0 lines
☐ Column break before   ☐ Widow control   0 lines
☐ Page break before   ☐ Orphan control 0 lines
☐ Include in table of contents

The Paragraph Specifications dialog box prompts you to select the desired paragraph specifications to be applied to the text you will create.

4 In the Paragraph Specifications dialog box click the Spacing button.

The Spacing Attributes dialog box makes it possible to control the amount of space inserted between letters and words, the leading method, and the percentage of autoleading. In this example you will use the Spacing Attributes dialog box to override the proportional (default) leading method with the baseline leading method.

Note: The proportional leading method aligns the baseline of the text one-third of the slug height above the bottom of the slug.

5 In the Spacing Attributes dialog box click the Baseline radio button to select a leading method, hold down the Option key (to close the chain of dialog boxes), and click OK.

Paragraph Spacing Attributes

Word space:		Letter space:		
Minimum	75 %	Minimum	-5 %	OK
Desired	100 %	Desired	0 %	Cancel
Maximum	150 %	Maximum	25 %	Reset

Pair kerning: ☒ Auto above 4 points

Leading method: Autoleading:
○ Proportional   120 % of point size
○ Top of caps
◉ Baseline

The baseline leading method aligns the baseline of the text with the bottom of the leading slug.

6 Type **bella coola** in lowercase letters.

Because you had selected the All caps button in the Control palette, the text is displayed in uppercase letters.

7 With the text tool still selected, drag to select the letter B in the text BELLA, and in the Control palette type **120** points in the Size box, and click the Apply button.

Note: If different leading amounts occur within a single line, Adobe PageMaker uses the largest leading amount for the entire line. Since leading is a character attribute, you can apply more than one leading amount within the same paragraph.

8 Drag to select the letter C in the text COOLA, and in the Control palette type **120** points in the Size box, and click the Apply button.

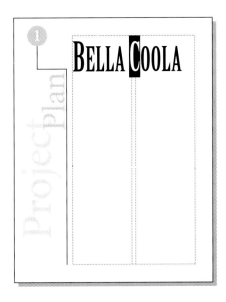

9 With the text tool still selected, triple-click the title text to select it.

10 In the Control palette click the Paragraph-view button, and in the paragraph view of the Control palette click the Force-justify button to force the title text to spread across the width of the text block (that spans the two columns).

— Force-justify button

11 With the text still selected, in the Colors palette make sure Black is selected, and choose 75% from the Tint pop-up menu to apply a 75% tint of black.

12 With the pointer tool selected, click the title text to select it as a text block, hold down the Shift key (to constrain the movement to 45°), and drag the text block to align the top edge of the smaller letters with the top margin guide.

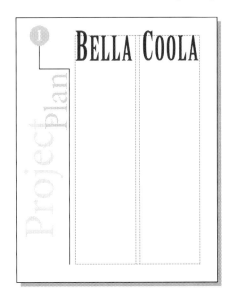

The 120-point letters overlap the top margin.

13 Choose Save from the File menu.

Placing text using the Autoflow command

Use the Autoflow command when you have a lot of text to place. Flowing text automatically means Adobe PageMaker will insert enough pages until all text is placed, eliminating the need for you to insert individual pages.

Time out for a movie

If your system is capable of running Adobe Teach movies, play the movie named *Autoflow* to see a preview of the section on autoflowing text. For information on how to play Adobe Teach movies, see the section What You Need To Know at the beginning of this book.

TIP: TO DELETE A STORY THAT IS COMPRISED OF MULTIPLE TEXT BLOCKS, CLICK THE TEXT WITH THE TEXT TOOL, CHOOSE SELECT ALL FROM THE EDIT MENU, AND PRESS THE DELETE KEY.

1 Choose Place from the File menu (Command-D), and in the Place Document dialog box double-click the *03TextA* file in the *03Lesson* folder.

2 Choose Autoflow from the Layout menu to select it, making sure it is checked.

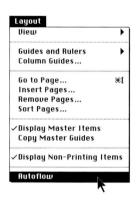

The cursor is displayed as an automatic text-flow icon.

Note: Whenever you have a loaded text icon, you can switch temporarily between manual and automatic text flow by pressing the Command key.

3 Making sure the automatic text-flow icon does not overlap the margin guides or column guides, click in the left column below the title text.

The last lines of text in the story are displayed on page 3 of your publication, indicating Adobe PageMaker has automatically inserted two pages.

4 With the pointer tool selected, click the text in the left column to select it as a text block.

The plus sign in the top windowshade handle indicates that text from the same story is contained in another text block, and the empty bottom windowshade handle indicates the end of the story.

5 Click page icon 2 to view the second page of the publication.

6 With the pointer tool selected, click the text in either column to select it as a text block.

The grayed-out text fills both columns, with the top and bottom windowshade handles of the selected text block displaying plus signs. As was just mentioned, a plus sign in the windowshade handle indicates that text from the same story is contained in another text block.

Plus sign

TIP: TO PAGE FORWARD IN A PUBLICATION, HOLD DOWN THE COMMAND KEY, AND PRESS THE TAB KEY TO VIEW THE PREVIOUS PAGE, HOLD DOWN THE COMMAND AND TAB KEYS, AND PRESS THE SHIFT KEY.

In previous lessons you placed and created stories that were contained in a single text block. Since the story in this lesson is contained in five text blocks, you would say the text in this publication is threaded (through multiple text blocks).

7 Click page icon 1 to view the first page of the publication.

8 With the pointer tool selected, click the text in the left column to select it as a text block.

The first line of text in the left column is positioned where you clicked to place the text, with the empty top windowshade handle indicating the beginning of a story.

Note: If no object had been positioned in the top portion of the right column (or if the object had overlapped the right margin guide), the entire right column would have been filled with text, overlapping the text Bella Coola.

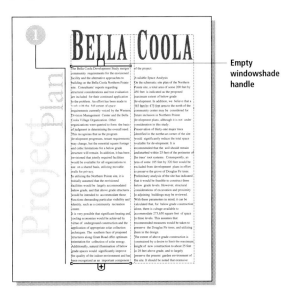

Empty windowshade handle

9 Choose Save from the File menu.

Adjusting the tracking

After formatting the text, you will use the Expert Tracking command to adjust algorithmically the spacing between letters and words (tracking) in the proposal text. This command is useful for

darkening or lightening a page, where type with tight tracking darkens a page, and type with loose tracking lightens a page. You can also use Expert Tracking to adjust the spacing of selected lines of very large or very small type (headlines and captions), or to make text fit in a defined space on a page.

1 With the text tool selected, click the proposal text to establish an insertion point, and choose Select All from the Edit menu to select the entire threaded story.

Note: Once the entire story is formatted, you can apply specific styles to specific paragraphs (such as headlines, subheads, etc.) to override the original formatting, saving you the effort of formatting all paragraphs individually.

2 In the Control palette type .25 inch in the First-line indent box, and click the Justify button.

First-line indent box

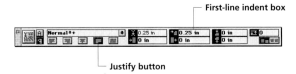

Justify button

The first line of each paragraph is indented, with the left and right edges of the text aligned with the edges of the text block.

3 With the text still selected, in the Control palette click the Character-view button, and in the character view of the Control palette choose Myriad MM 215 Light 600 Normal from the Font pop-up menu, type **9** points in the Size box and **13** points in the Leading box, and click the Apply button.

Now that the text is formatted, you will use the Expert Tracking command to adjust the spacing between letters and words (tracking) in the proposal text.

4 Magnify the view of the proposal text in either column.

Notice how the spacing between letters and words in the proposal text is fairly tight.

TIP: TO SCROLL THE VIEW, HOLD DOWN THE OPTION KEY, AND DRAG THE PAGE IN ANY DIRECTION.

5 With the text tool selected, click the proposal text in either column to establish an insertion point, and choose Select All from the Edit menu to select the entire story.

6 Choose Expert Tracking from the Type menu to display the submenu.

The submenu displays six tracking options. The default tracking option No Track means no tracking has been applied to the text.

7 Choose Very Loose from the submenu, making sure it is checked.

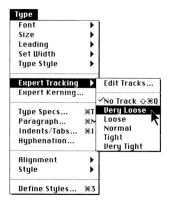

Because Very Loose tracking increases letter spacing for this point size (of this typeface), the loosened tracking makes the page appear lighter.

Note: It is also possible to select a tracking option from the Tracking pop-up menu in the character view of the Control palette.

Now that you have applied type specifications and expert tracking, the text is ready to be aligned with the bottom margin guide.

8 Scroll to view the bottom margin guide.

9 With the pointer tool selected, click the text in the left column to select it as a text block, and drag it until the baseline of the last line of text is aligned with the bottom margin guide.

10 With the pointer tool still selected, click the text in the right column to select it as a text block, and drag it until the baseline of the last line of text is aligned with the bottom margin guide.

11 Choose Save from the File menu.

Varying the number of columns on a page

You can have different numbers of columns on different parts of a single page. In this example, you will create a single column of text below the title text, above the two existing columns of text.

You will begin by reducing the size of the text blocks in the left and right columns to make room for a text block that spans the image area (between the left and right margins).

1 Scroll to view the middle portion of the page.

2 From the horizontal ruler, drag to create a horizontal ruler guide to be aligned with the baseline of the line of text closest to the 4.3-inch mark on the vertical ruler.

This horizontal ruler guide indicates what will be the first line of text in the left and right columns.

3 With the pointer tool selected, click the text in the right column to select it as a text block, and drag the top windowshade handle until it is aligned just above the line of text aligned with the horizontal ruler guide you just created.

4 With the pointer tool still selected, click the text in the left column to select it as a text block, and drag the top windowshade handle until it is just above the line of text in the right column, displaying the first line of text to be aligned with the first line of text in the right column.

Adobe PageMaker automatically flows the text when you resize the text blocks, displaying the first line of text in the threaded story at the top of the first text block.

5 If the baselines of the last line of text in both columns are not aligned with the bottom margin guide, move the text blocks until they are aligned.

With the size of the text blocks reduced, you have space to create a single column of text below the title text.

6 With the text tool selected, drag to select the first three and a half lines in the left column (up to and including the word Bella), and choose Cut from the Edit menu.

7 Position the insertion point at the beginning of the remaining text in the left column (before the word Coola), and press the Delete key to delete the letter space.

8 With the text tool selected, drag to define a text block above the text in the left and right columns, spanning the width of the two columns (exact height is not important), and choose Paste from the Edit menu.

No longer part of the threaded story, the pasted text is a separate story, and will serve as an introductory paragraph. Once formatted into a larger-sized font, this intro text will serve to draw the reader's eye from the larger text into the smaller text of the proposal.

9 Choose Save from the File menu.

Creating and applying a style

Even though you specified the first line of each paragraph in the proposal text to be indented .25 inch, it is possible to override the applied paragraph specifications to remove the indent from any selected paragraph.

1 Make sure the insertion point is still established in the pasted intro text.

2 In the Control palette click the Paragraph-view button, and in the paragraph view of the Control palette type **0** in the First-line indent box, and press the Return key.

The intro paragraph is no longer indented. To make it easier to remove the first-line indent from a few other paragraphs in this publication, you will create a style where the first line of text in a paragraph is aligned to the left edge of the text block. Once created, you will apply this style to selected paragraphs in the proposal text.

3 With the insertion point still established in the pasted intro text, choose Define Styles from the Type menu (Command-3), and in the Define Styles dialog box click the New button.

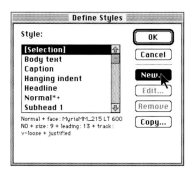

4 In the Edit Styles dialog box type **No indent** in the Name box, hold down the Option key (to close the chain of dialog boxes), and click OK.

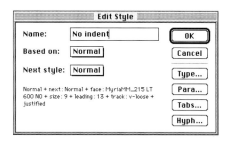

The No indent style has the type and paragraph specifications assigned to the intro text.

5 Choose Styles from the Window menu to display the Styles palette.

Collectively, a publication's styles are called a style sheet, and are listed in the Styles palette. In addition to displaying numerous default styles, the Styles palette displays the style No indent.

Note: You can copy style sheets to other Adobe PageMaker publications and import them from other word-processing applications, so you don't have to re-create styles each time you create a publication.

Now that you have created the style No indent, it is possible to apply it to the first paragraph in the left column below the intro text.

6 With the text tool selected, click the first paragraph in the left column (below the intro text) to establish an insertion point.

Note: When applying a style to a single paragraph, you must establish an insertion point in the target paragraph. When applying a style to multiple, contiguous paragraphs, you must select some text in all target paragraphs.

7 In the Styles palette click No indent to apply the style to the selected paragraph.

Since the intro text is meant to draw the reader's eye into the proposal text, the first paragraph of proposal text looks best without an indentation in the first line of text.

8 Choose Save from the File menu.

Deactivating hyphenation

After formatting the intro text, you will deactivate the hyphenation option.

1 With the text tool selected, triple-click the intro text below the title text to select it.

2 In the Control palette click the Force-justify button to align the left and right edges of the text with the edges of the text block, including the last line of text.

3 In the Control palette click the Character-view button, and in the character view of the Control palette choose Minion Semibold Italic from the Font pop-up menu, type **22** points in the Size box and **39** points in the Leading box, and click the Apply button.

4 With the intro text still selected, in the Colors palette make sure Black is selected, and choose 65% from the Tint pop-up menu to apply a 65% tint of black to the intro text.

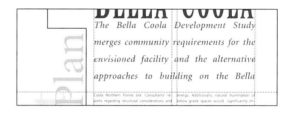

Since the last word on the third line of text is hyphenated, you will deactivate hyphenation to format the intro text to its best advantage.

5 Choose Hyphenation from the Type menu, and in the Hyphenation dialog box click the Off radio button, and click OK.

The formatted text is ready to be aligned.

6 From the horizontal ruler drag to create a horizontal ruler guide at approximately 3.96 inches.

7 With the pointer tool selected, click the intro text to select it as a text block, hold down the Shift key (to constrain the movement to 45°), and drag the text block until the baseline of the last line of text is aligned with the 3.96-inch horizontal ruler guide.

8 Choose Save from the File menu.

Note: An interim file was saved at this point. To open it, double-click the 03Int2 file in the Extras *folder.*

Placing a graphic

After placing and aligning a photograph in the left column, you will reduce the size of the text block in the left column.

After scanning this photograph, it was sized in Adobe Photoshop, and saved in TIFF file format with a resolution of 100 dpi.

1 Scroll to view the bottom of the page.

2 From the horizontal ruler, drag to create a horizontal ruler guide to be aligned with the baseline of the fourth line of text above the bottom margin guide.

To allow for a 3-line caption, you will use this horizontal ruler guide to align the bottom edge of the photograph with the baseline of text in the right column.

Unless you want to place an in-line graphic (a graphic attached to text), it's a good idea to make sure no insertion points are established when using the Place command to import a graphic.

3 Click the pointer tool in the toolbox to make sure no text insertion point is established.

4 Choose Place from the File menu, and in the Place Document dialog box double-click the *03GraphicA* file in the *03Lesson* folder.

5 With the graphics icon displayed, click in the left column to place the photograph.

Depending on where you clicked, the photograph overlaps the text in one or both columns.

6 With the photograph still selected, drag it until its bottom edge is aligned with the horizontal ruler guide, with its right edge aligned with the right edge of the left column.

The photograph extends into the left margin. And now, with the photograph aligned, you are ready to resize the text block in the left column.

7 With the pointer tool selected, click the text above the photograph in the left column to select it as a text block, and drag the bottom windowshade handle to display the last line of text to be approximately one line space above the photograph.

The left column displays 14 lines of proposal text.

8 Choose Save from the File menu.

Editing the default Caption style

Once the caption text is placed below the photograph, you will edit the default Caption style and apply it to the text.

1 Choose Autoflow from the Layout menu to deselect it, making sure it is unchecked.

2 Choose Place from the File menu, and in the Place Document dialog box double-click the *03TextB* file in the *03Lesson* folder.

3 With the loaded text icon displayed, click in the left column below the photograph to place the text.

Since all captions in this publication will be formatted identically, you will save time by editing the existing Caption style to create a custom style. Once created, this style can be applied to each caption in your publication.

4 Choose Define Styles from the Type menu (Command-3).

The Define Styles dialog box displays the default styles that you can apply to text. In addition to creating new styles as you have already done, it is possible to use the Define Styles dialog box to edit an existing style, creating a custom style.

5 In the Define Styles dialog box click Caption in the Style box, and click the Edit button.

6 In the Edit Style dialog box click the Type button.

Even though you can use the character view of the Control palette to format text, the Type Specifications dialog box provides the most complete set of character-formatting options in Adobe PageMaker.

7 In the Type Specifications dialog box choose Minion Semibold Italic from the Font pop-up menu, type **10** points in the Size box and **13** points in the Leading box, hold down the Option key (to close the chain of dialog boxes), and click OK.

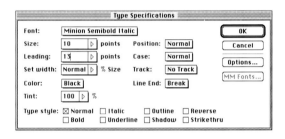

8 With the text tool selected, click the caption text under the photograph to establish an insertion point.

9 In the Styles palette click Caption to apply a style to the selected paragraph.

10 With the pointer tool selected, click the caption text to select it as a text block, drag the bottom windowshade handle until the entire story is displayed, hold down the Shift key (to constrain the movement to 45°), and drag the text block until the baseline of the last line of text is aligned with the bottom margin guide.

11 Choose Save from the File menu.

Editing the default Subhead style

After editing the existing Subhead style to create a custom style for the subheads in this publication, you will apply it to the subhead on the first page.

1 Choose Define Styles from the Type menu, and in the Define Styles dialog box click Subhead 1 in the Style box, and click the Edit button.

2 In the Edit Style dialog box click the Type button, and in the Type Specifications dialog box choose Myriad MM 700 Bold 600 Norm from the Font pop-up menu, type **11** points in the Size box and **13** points in the Leading box, choose Small Caps from the Case pop-up menu, click the Normal check box to select a Type style, hold down the Option key (to close the chain of dialog boxes), and click OK.

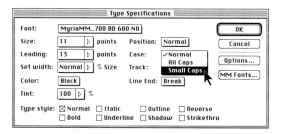

3 With the text tool selected, click the subhead text (Available Space Analysis) in the right column of the first page to establish an insertion point.

4 In the Styles palette click Subhead 1 to apply the style to the subhead text.

5 With the text tool still selected, click the first paragraph below the subhead text you just formatted to establish an insertion point in the paragraph.

6 In the Styles palette click No indent to apply the custom style to the selected paragraph.

The paragraph following the subhead is no longer indented.

7 If necessary, with the pointer tool selected, click the text in the right column to select it as a text block, hold down the Shift key (to constrain the movement to 45°), and drag it until the last line of text is aligned with the bottom margin guide.

The first page is complete.

8 Choose Save from the File menu.

ASSEMBLING THE SECOND PAGE

After applying type specifications to the text on the second page, you will align the text. In addition to formatting and aligning text, you will place two graphics with captions.

Applying styles

After displaying the second page, you will apply the same type specifications to the text on the second page as were applied to the text on the first page of the proposal.

1 Click page icon 2 to view the second page of the publication.

Unless otherwise specified, all master-page elements are displayed within the bounds of the second page.

2 Magnify the view of the text in the lower-half portion of the left column.

3 With the text tool selected, click the subhead text (Light and View Considerations) in the left column to establish an insertion point; and in the Styles palette click Subhead 1.

4 With the text tool still selected, click the first paragraph below the subhead text you just formatted to establish an insertion point in the paragraph.

5 In the Styles palette click No indent to apply the style to the selected paragraph.

6 With the pointer tool selected, click the text in the left column to select it as a text block, hold down the Shift key (to constrain the movement to 45°), and drag the text block until the baseline of the last line of text is aligned with the bottom margin guide, with the first line of text a little below the top margin guide.

7 If necessary, drag a windowshade handle to resize the text block so that it fits between the top and bottom margin guides, again, with the baseline of the last line of text aligned with the bottom margin guide.

You will repeat this procedure to align the text in the right column.

8 With the pointer tool selected, click the text in the right column to select it as a text block, and drag a windowshade handle to resize the text block so that it fits between the top and bottom margin guides, with the baseline of the last line of text aligned with the bottom margin guide.

Both columns of text are aligned with the bottom margin guide.

9 Choose Save from the File menu.

Quick dragging a graphic object

After placing a drawing, you will use the quick-drag technique to move the drawing to be aligned in the lower portion of the left column.

After scanning this drawing, it was sized in Adobe Photoshop, and then saved in TIFF file format with a resolution of 100 dpi.

1 From the horizontal ruler, drag to create a horizontal ruler guide to be aligned with the baseline of the third line of text above the bottom margin guide.

To allow for a 2-line caption, you will use this horizontal ruler guide to align the bottom edge of the drawing with the baseline of text in the right column.

2 Choose View from the Layout menu and Fit in Window from the submenu.

3 Choose Place from the File menu, and in the Place Document dialog box double-click the *03GraphicB* file in the *03Lesson* folder.

4 With the graphics icon displayed, click in the left column to place the drawing.

You will use the quick-drag method to align the drawing on the page.

5 With the drawing still selected, position the cursor in the center of the drawing, and just after you press the mouse button, quickly drag the drawing to display its bounding box, still holding the mouse button down.

6 With the bounding box still displayed, drag the drawing until its bottom edge is aligned with the horizontal ruler guide you just created, with its left and right edges aligned with the left column guides.

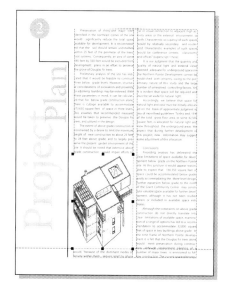

With the drawing aligned, you are ready to resize the text block in the left column.

7 With the pointer tool selected, click the text in the left column to select it as a text block, and drag the bottom windowshade handle to display the last line of text to be one line space above the drawing.

Now that the drawing and text are aligned, you are ready to place the caption text.

8 Choose Place from the File menu, and in the Place Document dialog box double-click the *03TextC* file in the *03Lesson* folder.

9 With the loaded text icon displayed, click in the left column below the drawing to place the text.

10 With the text tool selected, click the caption text to establish an insertion point, and in the Styles palette click Caption to apply a style to the text.

11 Magnify the view of the caption text.

12 With the pointer tool selected, click the caption text to select it as a text block, drag the bottom windowshade handle until the entire story is displayed, hold down the Shift key (to constrain the movement to 45°), and drag the text block until the baseline of the last line of text is aligned with the bottom margin guide.

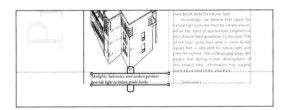

13 Choose Save from the File menu.

Using the Control palette to position a graphic

After placing a second illustration on the second page, you will enter precise values in the Control palette to move it.

The illustration you are about to place and position was created in Adobe Dimensions®, sized in Adobe Photoshop, and saved in TIFF file format with a resolution of 100 dpi.

Note: Adobe Dimensions is a design tool that lets you create and edit 2D Bézier paths and text directly within the program and then extrude, revolve, bevel, and manipulate them for a 3D look.

1 Scroll to view the upper-right portion of the page.

2 Choose Place from the File menu, and in the Place Document dialog box double-click the *03GraphicC* file in the *03Lesson* folder.

3 With the graphics icon displayed, click in the right column to place the illustration.

4 With the illustration still selected, in the Control palette make sure the upper-left reference point in the Proxy icon is selected, type **4.316** inches in the X box and **.417** inches in the Y box, and press the Return key.

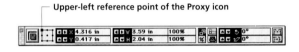

Upper-left reference point of the Proxy icon

The upper-left corner of the illustration is aligned with the specified coordinate position (4.316, .417).

In addition to overlapping the text in the right column, the illustration overlaps text in the left column.

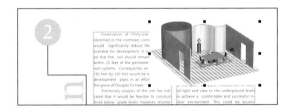

5 Choose Save from the File menu.

Creating a custom text wrap

Since this nonrectangular illustration extends within the bounds of the left column, you will create a custom text wrap that will allow the text to flow around the edges of the illustration.

1 With the pointer tool selected, click the illustration to select it, and choose Text Wrap from the Element menu.

The Text Wrap dialog box prompts you to specify how you want the text to flow around the graphics boundary of the selected object.

2 In the Text Wrap dialog box click the graphics boundary icon (middle icon) to select a Wrap option, make sure the Wrap-all-sides icon (right icon) is selected for the Text flow option, type **0** inch in the Bottom box to specify the Standoff in inches, and click OK.

A rectangular graphics boundary (dotted line) frames the illustration, with the text flowing around the edges of the graphics boundary within both columns. You will customize the shape of this graphics boundary to allow the text to flow around the illustration with greater precision.

3 Position the cursor at the intersection of the bottom edge of the graphics boundary (dotted line) and the left edge of the right column, and click (quickly).

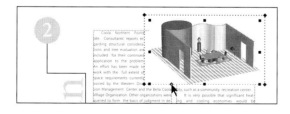

A handle is displayed on the graphics boundary.

Note: Since it is possible to drag a graphics boundary to position it, clicking too slowly will not establish a handle.

4 Position the cursor on the lower-left corner handle of the graphics boundary, hold down the Shift key (to constrain the movement to 45°), and drag the corner graphics handle up until it is aligned with the baseline of the fourth line of text in the left column.

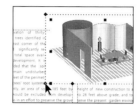 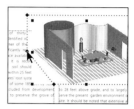

The custom text wrap allows the text to flow along the bounds of the graphics boundary. Since a portion of the graphic overlaps the text, you will adjust the stacking order of objects.

5 Choose Send to Back from the Arrange menu to stack the illustration behind the text and graphics elements.

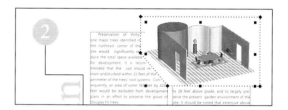

6 Choose Save from the File menu.

Placing, formatting, and aligning a caption

You will place, format, and align a caption to be displayed below the illustration at the top of the right column. Before placing the caption text, you will reduce the size of the text block in the right column to make some space for the 3-line caption.

1 From the horizontal ruler, drag to create a horizontal ruler guide that is aligned with the baseline of text nearest to the 3.4-inch mark on the vertical ruler.

This horizontal ruler guide indicates where the first line of proposal text in the right column will be positioned.

2 With the pointer tool selected, click the proposal text in the right column to select it as a text block, and drag the top windowshade handle until it is just above the line of text aligned with the horizontal ruler guide you just created.

You are ready to place the caption text.

3 Choose Place from the File menu, and in the Place Document dialog box double-click the *03TextD* file in the *03Lesson* folder.

4 With the loaded text icon displayed, click in the right column (below the illustration) to place the text.

Before aligning the caption text, you will apply the Caption style.

5 With the text tool selected, click the caption text to establish an insertion point, and in the Styles palette click Caption to apply a style to the text.

6 From the horizontal ruler, drag to create a horizontal ruler guide aligned with the baseline of the first line of text in the second paragraph in the left column.

You will use this horizontal ruler guide to align the caption text with the text in the left column.

7 With the pointer tool selected, click the caption to select it as a text block, and drag the text block until the baseline of the last line of text is aligned with the horizontal ruler guide you just created.

The second page of this publication is completely assembled.

8 Choose View from the Layout menu and Fit in Window from the submenu.

9 Choose Save from the File menu.

ASSEMBLING THE THIRD PAGE

After formatting and aligning the text on the third page, you will draw a box that will serve to frame an illustration. This boxed illustration and its corresponding caption will span the width of both columns.

Applying styles

You will apply the same formatting specifications applied to the text on the first and second pages of this publication to the text on the third page.

1 Click page icon 3 to view the third page of the publication.

As before, all master-page elements are displayed within the bounds of the third page.

2 If there is no text in the left column on page 3, click page icon 2 to view the second page, click the text in the right column with the pointer tool to select it as a text block, click the red down arrow to load the remaining text, click page icon 3 to view the third page, and with the loaded text icon displayed, click the left column to place the text.

3 Magnify the view of the text in the lower-half portion of the left column.

4 With the pointer tool selected, click the text in the left column to select it as a text block.

The red down arrow in the bottom windowshade handle indicates there is more text to be placed. Before manually flowing the remaining text into the right column, you will format and align the text in the left column.

5 Drag the bottom windowshade handle until it is just below the bottom margin guide to fill the left column with text.

6 With the text tool selected, click the subhead text (Conclusions) to establish an insertion point; and in the Styles palette click Subhead 1.

7 With the text tool still selected, click the first paragraph below the subhead text you just formatted to establish an insertion point in the paragraph; and in the Styles palette click No indent.

With the type and paragraph specifications applied to the text, you are ready to align the text.

8 With the pointer tool selected, click the text in the left column to select it as a text block, hold down the Shift key (to constrain the movement to 45°), and drag the text block until the baseline of the last line of text is aligned with the bottom margin guide, with the first line of text a little below the top margin guide.

9 Choose Save from the File menu.

Manually flowing text into a column

Since the illustration and caption extend across the bottom portion of both columns, you will resize the text block in the left column, and manually flow the remaining text into the right column.

Before reducing the size of the text block in the left column, you will create a horizontal ruler guide to be aligned with text in the left column. You will eventually use this horizontal ruler guide to align the bottom edge of the box that contains an illustration, allowing enough space for a single-line caption.

1 From the horizontal ruler, drag to create a horizontal ruler guide aligned with the baseline of the second line of text above the bottom margin guide.

After drawing the box that will frame the illustration, you will use this horizontal ruler guide to align the box.

2 From the horizontal ruler guide, drag to create a horizontal ruler guide that is aligned with the baseline of text nearest to the 5.9-inch mark on the vertical ruler.

3 With the pointer tool selected, click the text in the left column to select it as a text block, and drag the bottom windowshade handle just below the line of text aligned with the horizontal ruler guide you just created.

As before, the red down arrow in the bottom windowshade handle indicates all text is not displayed.

4 Click the red down arrow in the bottom windowshade handle to load the remaining text in the story.

5 With the loaded text icon displayed, click in the right column to place the text.

The empty bottom windowshade handle of the text block in the right column indicates the end of the story.

6 With the text in the right column still selected as a text block, drag the text block until the last line of text in the right column is aligned with the last line of text in the left column, using the existing horizontal ruler guide.

7 Choose Save from the File menu.

Drawing a box

After creating a box that will frame the final illustration, you will align it with an existing horizontal ruler guide.

1 With the rectangle tool selected in the toolbox, drag to draw a box below the proposal text, spanning the width of the two columns (exact height is not important).

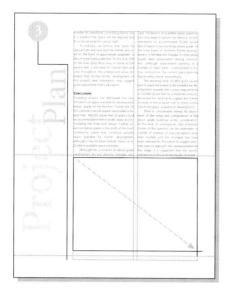

2 In the Control palette type **3.87** inches in the Height box, and press the Return key to establish the height for the box.

3 With the box still selected, choose Line from the Element menu and Hairline from the submenu to assign a line style and weight to the line of the box.

4 With the pointer tool selected, position the cursor on the edge of the box, hold down the Shift key (to constrain the movement to 45°), and drag the box until its bottom edge is aligned with the horizontal ruler guide you created (to be aligned with the second line of text above the bottom margin guide), with the left and right edges of the box still aligned with the margin guides.

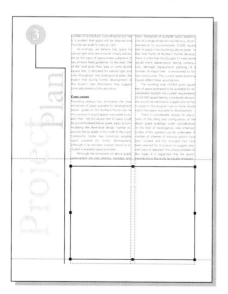

Since the bottom of the box is aligned with what was the baseline of the second line of text above the bottom margin guide, you have provided enough space for the single-line caption.

5 Choose Save from the File menu.

Placing a graphic and caption

After placing the final illustration, you will place, format, and align its corresponding caption.

This illustration was sized in Adobe Photoshop, and saved in TIFF file format with a resolution of 100 dpi.

1 Choose Place from the File menu, and in the Place Document dialog box double-click the *03GraphicD* file in the *03Lesson* folder.

2 With the graphics icon displayed, click within the hairline box to place the illustration.

3 With the illustration still selected, drag it until it is visually centered in the hairline box.

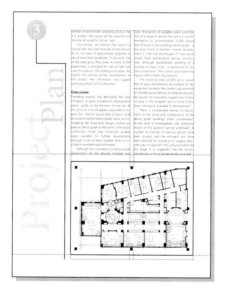

4 Choose Place from the File menu, and in the Place Document dialog box double-click the *03TextE* file in the *03Lesson* folder.

To allow the caption text to span the image area, you will drag to define a text block that spans both columns.

5 With the loaded text icon displayed, drag to define a text block under the boxed illustration that spans both columns to place the caption (exact height is not important).

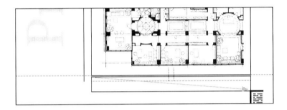

6 With the text tool selected, click the caption text to establish an insertion point, and in the Styles palette click Caption.

7 With the pointer tool selected, click the caption text to select it as a text block, drag the bottom windowshade handle until the entire story is displayed, hold down the Shift key (to constrain the movement to 45°), and drag the text block until the baseline of the text is aligned with the bottom margin guide.

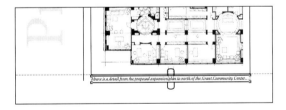

You have completed assembling the entire proposal.

8 Choose View from the Layout menu and Fit in Window from the submenu.

9 Choose Guides and Rulers from the Layout menu and Show Guides from the submenu to hide the column, ruler, and margin guides used to assemble this proposal.

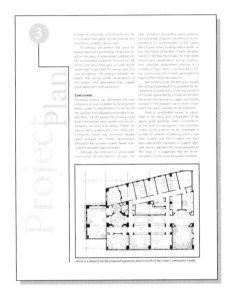

10 Choose Save from the File menu to save the *03Work* publication.

PRODUCING THE PROPOSAL

As was mentioned at the beginning of this lesson, this publication can be printed successfully on any 300 dpi or 600 dpi desktop laser printing device, and then photocopied for on-demand distribution.

1 Choose Print from the File menu (Command-P) to open the Print: Document printing boxes for the type of printer you selected.

2 If you have a PostScript printer, be sure to select a PostScript Printer Description (PPD) from the PPD pop-up menu in the Print: Document dialog box that matches your printer type.

3 In the Print: Document dialog box click the Color button, and in the Print: Color dialog box make sure the Grayscale radio button is selected.

4 In the Print: Color dialog box click the Options button, and in the Print: Options dialog box choose Optimized from the Send Image data pop-up menu.

5 Click the Print button to print the proposal.

6 Close all open publications, and choose Quit from the File menu (Command-Q) to exit the Adobe PageMaker application.

1998 WINTER LECTURE SERIES

THE JAPANESE

GARDEN

As part of its 1998 Winter Lecture Series, we are pleased to invite you and your guests to an evening featuring internationally-known landscape architect and author Jonathon Takei. This is a special opportunity for those interested in examining the challenge of conceiving, planning, constructing, and maintaining the garden that adapts the spirit of the Japanese garden to your needs and our local setting. You will be presented with information for analyzing your site and needs, as well as selecting and maintaining plants, including bonsai. Mr. Takei will also offer his own unique insights into the Japanese concept of the garden's relation to nature, form, space, and time. Seating is limited, so reserve your place early. The lecture begins at 7:30 PM on Thursday, February 19th. For information, call 1-800-555-1412.

THURSDAY

FEBRUARY

NINETEENTH

AT 7:30 PM.

• JAPAN •

No matter how elegant black and white may be, people will always love color. Perhaps you are eager to use color, but your budget will not allow for the cost of film separa-

JAPANESE GARDEN POSTER

tions and press setup normally expected when printing on a press. So why not produce color publications on standard-sized paper using a color copier at your local copy shop? Your publications will reflect many benefits of a four-color printing job, without the expense and effort. ■ The color photographs featured in this poster were scanned on a flatbed scanner, processed and sized in Adobe Photoshop, and saved in TIFF file format at a resolution of 100 dpi. The Japanese characters, representing the Japanese word for garden, were processed in Adobe Illustrator®, saved in EPS file format, imported into Adobe Photoshop, and converted to TIFF file format.

For this lesson you will import, format, and align the text and graphics elements for an 11-inch-by-17-inch color poster, creating the objects that are not available in text or image files. Again, with a limited budget in mind, the publication require-

JAPANESE GARDEN POSTER

ments for this poster call for it to be printed on a 300 dpi color copying device with a PostScript RIP (raster image processor) attached, using tabloid-sized paper.

This lesson covers:

- Defining and applying process colors
- Removing colors from the Colors palette
- Manually cropping a graphic
- Using the Control palette to crop graphics
- Dragging to define a text block
- Using the Text Wrap command
- Establishing a publication default font
- Printing to a color printer.

BEFORE YOU BEGIN

All files and fonts needed for this particular lesson are found on the Adobe PageMaker *Classroom in a Book* CD-ROM disc in the folders *04Lesson* and *Fonts*, respectively.

It should take you approximately 60 minutes to complete this lesson.

Opening an existing document

Let's take a look at the final version of the poster you will create in this lesson.

1 Before launching the Adobe PageMaker program, throw away the *Adobe PageMaker 6.0 Prefs* file to ensure all settings are returned to their default values.

2 Make sure the fonts Myriad MM 215 Light 600 Normal and Trajan Regular are installed.

The inscription on the base of the Trajan column in Rome is an example of classic Roman letterforms, which reached their peak of refinement in the first century A.D. It is believed that the letters were first written with a brush, then carved into stone. These forms provided the basis for Trajan, an Adobe Originals typeface designed by Carol Twombly in 1989. Trajan is an elegant typeface well-suited for display work in books, magazines, posters, and billboards.

3 Double-click the *Adobe® PageMaker® 6.0* icon to launch the Adobe PageMaker program.

4 Choose Open from the File menu (Command-O), and in the Open Publication dialog box double-click the *04Final* file in the *04Lesson* folder.

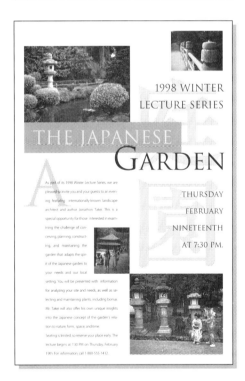

The full view of the page displays a variety of text and graphics elements.

5 Choose Guides and Rulers from the Layout menu and Show Guides from the submenu (Command-J) to display the guides that were used to align the text and graphics elements.

Talk with the operator at your local copy shop

Before assembling a publication to be printed at a copy shop, be sure to find out the maximum imageable area for your specific paper size on the target printing device. Depending on the printing device, the non-imageable area around the edges of the page can equal roughly ¼ inch to ½ inch.

Also, find out whether the operator expects you to deliver an Adobe PageMaker file or a PostScript file made from your publication. For more information about preparing PostScript files, refer to the *Adobe PageMaker 6.0 User Guide.*

Even though you cannot expect precise color matching when printing on a color copier, it's a good idea to run the job once to check for noticeably oversaturated or undersaturated colors. If this is the case, the operator may be able to recalibrate the printing device.

Since this poster was designed to be printed on a 300 dpi CMYK copier with a PostScript RIP attached, all image files were saved in CMYK TIFF file format at a resolution of 100 dpi..

ASSEMBLING THE POSTER

Once most of the graphics elements are placed, positioned, resized, and cropped, you will place, format, and align the text elements. As a finishing touch, you will place the Japanese characters, and adjust the stacking order to move them to the bottom of the stack.

Opening a custom template

You will use a custom template that was created specifically for this lesson. After establishing the dimensions, margins, and ruler guides, this publication was saved as a template, so that when you open it, Adobe PageMaker opens an untitled copy of the template.

1 Choose Open from the File menu, and in the Open Publication dialog box double-click the *04Template* file in the *04Lesson* folder.

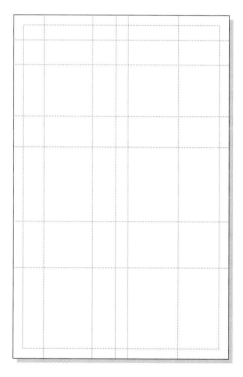

The untitled template displays the established margin guides and ruler guides, with the rulers reflecting the selected unit of measure for this publication, inches. For your protection, the ruler guides have been locked.

2 If you do not have a *Projects* folder, create one now.

3 Choose Save As from the File menu, and in the Save publication as dialog box type **04Work** in the Name box, click the *Projects* folder, and click OK.

Defining process colors

In previous lessons you incorporated spot colors and tints of spot colors into your publications. You may recall that you used spot colors in an effort to limit the number of required film separations (for commercial printing), where each spot color requires an individual film separation.

Unlike spot colors, all process colors require no more than the four film separations: cyan, magenta, yellow, and black (CMYK). Since this is a full-color poster, incorporating process colors into the design will not cause the number of film separations to exceed four.

Note: If you are unfamiliar with the difference between spot and process colors, refer to the Adobe Print Publishing Guide.

1 Choose Define Colors from the Element menu, and in the Define Colors dialog box click the New button.

2 In the Edit Color dialog box type **Putty** in the Name box, choose Process from the Type pop-up menu and CMYK from the Model pop-up menu, and enter the following CMYK values:

Cyan 15%
Magenta 17%
Yellow 23%
Black 12%

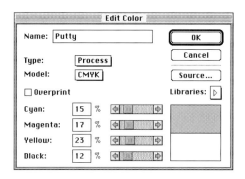

Note: These CMYK values are copied from a swatch book.

3 Click OK to close the Edit Color dialog box, and in the Define Colors dialog box click the New button to define another color.

4 In the Edit color dialog box type **Lemonade** in the Name box, choose Process from the Type pop-up menu and CMYK from the Model pop-up menu, and enter the following CMYK values:

Cyan 0%
Magenta 0%
Yellow 10%
Black 5%

5 Click OK to close the Edit Color dialog box, and in the Define Colors dialog box click the New button.

6 In the Edit Color dialog box type **Lavender** in the Name box, choose Process from the Type pop-up menu and CMYK from the Model pop-up menu, and enter the following CMYK values:

Cyan 5%
Magenta 7%
Yellow 0%
Black 12%

7 Click OK to close the Edit Color dialog box.

The Define Colors dialog box displays the list of colors that the Colors palette will contain. Since you will not use the colors Red, Green, and Blue in this publication, take a moment to remove them.

8 In the Define Colors dialog box click Blue to select it, and click the Remove button.

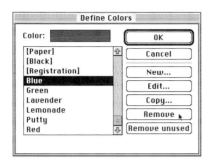

9 Repeat this step two more times, selecting and removing the Green and Red colors, and click OK to close the Define Colors dialog box.

In addition to the bracketed colors, the Colors palette displays Lavender, Lemonade, and Putty.

Note: The bracketed colors [None], [Paper], [Black], and [Registration] cannot be removed from the Colors palette. For more information on these colors, refer to the Adobe PageMaker 6.0 User Guide.

10 Choose Save from the File menu (Command-S).

Applying a process color to a box

After drawing a large box, you will apply the putty color you just specified.

1 With the rectangle tool selected in the toolbox, position the cursor on the intersection of the 5-inch horizontal ruler guide and the left margin guide, and drag down and right to the intersection of the 6.5-inch horizontal ruler guide and the 8.4 vertical ruler guide to draw a box.

2 With the box still selected, in the Colors palette click the Both button to select it, and click Putty to apply the color putty to the line and fill of the box.

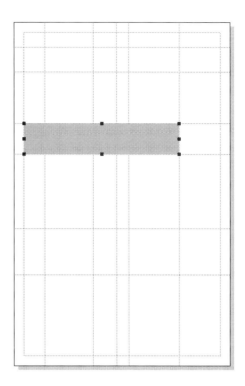

3 Choose Save from the File menu.

Manually cropping a graphic

After placing a photograph in the upper-left corner of your publication, you will use the cropping tool to specify what portions of the photograph will be printed, adjusting the frame (bounding box) surrounding the photograph, and moving the photograph within the frame.

Note: To save printing time, crop graphics before you import them into Adobe PageMaker. Graphics that are cropped in Adobe PageMaker take longer to print than graphics that are cropped before being imported.

1 Choose Place from the File menu (Command-D), and in the Place Document dialog box double-click the *04GraphicA* file in the *04Lesson* folder.

Since this file is 256K or larger, an alert message prompts you to indicate whether or not you want a complete copy of the graphic stored in the publication.

2 Click the No button to prevent duplicating the image data in the *04Work* publication.

Adobe PageMaker will import a low-resolution version of the graphic for display only, establishing a link to the original file.

Note: When you print the publication, the original file must be available and linked; otherwise, Adobe PageMaker prints the low-resolution version of the graphic.

3 With the graphics icon displayed, position the cursor in the upper-left corner of the page, and click to place the photograph.

4 With the photograph still selected, in the Control palette make sure the upper-left reference point in the Proxy icon is selected, type **.32** inch in the X box and **1.1** inch in the Y box, and press the Return key to align the upper-left corner of the graphic with the specified coordinate position.

The photograph slightly overlaps the top edge of the putty-colored box.

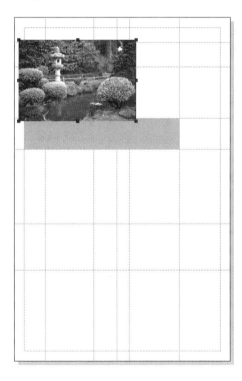

5 With the magnifying glass selected in the toolbox, drag to marquee select the entire photograph.

6 With the cropping tool selected in the toolbox, click the photograph to select it, position the cursor over the lower-left graphics handle of the photograph, making sure the graphics handle shows through the center of the cropping tool, and hold down the mouse button until the cursor is displayed as a double-headed arrow.

7 With the mouse button still held down, drag up and right to the intersection of the top edge of the putty-colored box and the left margin guide, and release the mouse button, cropping the view of the photograph.

8 With the cropping tool still selected, position the cursor over the upper-right graphics handle of the photograph, and drag down and left to the intersection of the 1.235-inch horizontal ruler guide and the 5.8-inch vertical ruler guide, cropping more of the view of the photograph.

Since cropping a graphic does not destroy any image data, you can adjust what portions of the photograph will appear in your publication.

Note: When adjusting the size of a crop, you cannot make the frame larger than the original boundary of the graphic.

9 With the cropping tool selected, position the cursor in the center of the photograph, and hold down the mouse button until the cursor is displayed as a grabber hand.

10 With the mouse button still held down, drag the photograph in any direction within the frame until you see the portions of the photograph you want to appear in your publication.

11 Choose View from the Layout menu and Fit in Window from the submenu.

12 Choose Save from the File menu.

Manually resizing a graphic

After placing and positioning a color TIFF image, you will manually resize it. Normally, you would establish the dimensions and resolution of a graphic before you import it into Adobe PageMaker, as we have done throughout most of this book. For this example, however, you will get satisfactory results resizing the graphic in Adobe PageMaker since you are printing to a lower-resolution device.

1 Choose Place from the File menu, and in the Place Document dialog box double-click the *04GraphicB* file in the *04Lesson* folder.

2 When prompted, click the No button to prevent duplicating the image data in the *04Work* publication.

3 With the graphics icon displayed, click near the center of your page to place the photograph.

4 With the pointer tool selected, drag the photograph until its bottom edge is aligned with the 12.5-inch horizontal ruler guide, with its left edge aligned with the 4-inch vertical ruler guide.

5 With the photograph still selected, position the cursor on the upper-right graphics handle, and hold down the mouse button until the cursor is displayed as a double-arrow.

TIP: TO SELECT A
REFERENCE POINT IN
THE PROXY ICON (IN THE
CONTROL PALETTE) AS
A TWO-WAY ARROW,
DOUBLE-CLICK AN UN-
SELECTED REFERENCE
POINT OR SINGLE-
CLICK A SELECTED
REFERENCE POINT.

6 With the mouse button still held down, hold down the Shift key (to constrain the resizing to be proportional), and drag the graphics handle down and left until it is aligned with the 5.8-inch vertical ruler guide, and release the mouse button.

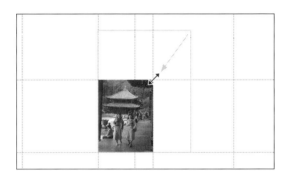

The Control palette indicates the width and height of the photograph have been reduced proportionally to approximately 60% of the original size.

7 Choose Save from the File menu.

Using the Control palette to resize a graphic

After using the Control palette to resize a photograph proportionally, you will align the photograph in the lower-right portion of the page.

1 Choose Place from the File menu, and in the Place Document dialog box double-click the *04GraphicC* file in the *04Lesson* folder.

2 When prompted, click the No button to prevent duplicating the image data in the *04Work* publication.

3 With the graphics icon displayed, click the lower portion of the page to place the photograph.

4 In the Control palette make sure a corner reference point or the center reference point is selected in the Proxy icon, make sure the Proportional-scaling button is selected, type **70%** in either of the Percent-scaling boxes, and press the Return key.

Proxy icon   Proportional-scaling button

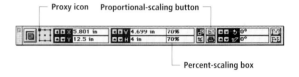

Percent-scaling box

The width and height of the photograph are proportionally reduced to 70% of their original size.

5 Drag to align the bottom edge of the photograph with the bottom margin guide, with its right edge aligned with the right margin guide.

6 Choose Save from the File menu.

Using the Control palette to crop a graphic

Using the Control palette, you will crop the resized lantern photograph so that its upper-left corner is precisely aligned with the lower-right corner of the pagoda photograph.

TIP: TO VIEW THE PAGE IN DISPLAY SIZE FIT IN WINDOW, HOLD DOWN THE OPTION KEY, AND DOUBLE-CLICK THE MAGNIFYING GLASS IN THE TOOLBOX.

1 With the pointer tool selected, click the Pagoda photograph to select it, in the Control palette make sure the lower-right reference point in the Proxy icon is selected, and notice how the X and Y values indicate its coordinate position.

The X and Y values should equal approximately 5.813 and 12.5, respectively.

2 With the pointer tool still selected, click the lantern photograph to select it.

3 In the Control palette click the upper-left reference point in the Proxy icon until it is displayed as a two-way arrow (to crop a graphic using the reference point), click the Cropping button to select it, type **5.813** inches in the X box and **12.5** inches in the Y box, and press the Return key.

Note: If your coordinate position is slightly different, type the exact coordinate values to get a precise alignment.

As before, cropping the photograph has not destroyed any image data.

4 With the cropping tool selected, position the cursor in the center of the photograph, and drag the photograph in any direction within the frame until you see the portions of the photograph you want to appear in your publication.

5 Choose Save from the File menu.

Using the Control palette to move a graphic

Using the Control palette, you will position the final photograph in the upper-right corner of your page.

1 Choose View from the Layout menu and Fit in Window from the submenu (Command-0).

2 Choose Place from the File menu, and in the Place Document dialog box double-click the *04GraphicD* file in the *04Lesson* folder.

3 When prompted, click the No button to prevent duplicating the image data in the *04Work* publication.

4 With the graphics icon displayed, click the upper-right portion of the page to place the photograph.

5 In the Control palette make sure the upper-right point of the Proxy icon is selected as a black box, and type **10.5** inches in the X box and **.5** inches in the Y box, and press the Return key.

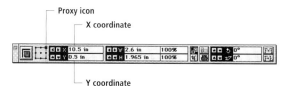

The top edge of the photograph is aligned with the top margin guide, with its right edge aligned with the right margin guide.

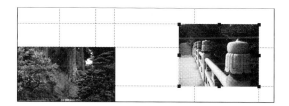

6 Choose Save from the File menu.

Placing text by dragging to define a text block

Up to this point, you have placed text by clicking in a column (where the width of your text block equals the width of the column) or by clicking the pasteboard (where the width of the text block equals the width of the image area between the left and right margins). In this lesson, you will drag to define the bounds of a text block that the text will flow into.

To begin, you will delete an existing vertical ruler guide that is no longer needed.

1 Choose Guides and Rulers from the Layout menu and Lock Guides from the submenu to deselect it, making it possible to delete or modify the existing ruler guides.

2 With the pointer tool selected, position the cursor over the 4-inch vertical ruler guide, and hold down the mouse button until the cursor is displayed as a double-headed arrow.

3 Drag the vertical ruler guide left or right off the page, and release the mouse button to delete the ruler guide.

Now it's a little easier to drag to define the text block within an area bounded by the 1.55-inch and 5.2-inch vertical ruler guides, below the putty-colored box.

4 Choose Guides and Rulers from the Layout menu and Lock Guides from the submenu to make it impossible to delete or modify the remaining ruler guides.

5 Choose Place from the File menu, and in the Place Document dialog box double-click the *04TextA* file in the *04Lesson* folder.

6 With the loaded text icon displayed, position the cursor at the intersection of the 1.55-inch horizontal ruler guide and the bottom edge of the putty-colored box, hold down the mouse button, drag to the intersection of the 5.2-inch vertical ruler guide and the bottom margin guide, and release the mouse button to place the text within the bounds of the text block you have defined.

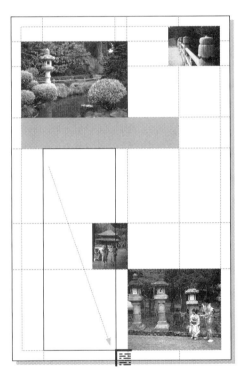

Even though you defined the text block to extend to the bottom margin guide, the bottom edge of the text block does not extend beyond the last line of text.

You are ready to apply type and paragraph specifications to the text.

7 With the text tool selected, click the placed text to establish an insertion point, and choose Select All from the Edit menu (Command-A) to select the entire story.

8 In the Control palette choose Myriad MM 215 Light 600 Normal from the Font pop-up menu, type **14** points in the Size box and **32** points in the Leading box, and click the Apply button.

9 In the Control palette click the Paragraph-view button, and in the paragraph view of the Control palette click the Justify button to align the text with the left and right edges of the text block.

The formatted text overlaps the pagoda photograph.

10 Choose Save from the File menu.

Wrapping text around a graphic

Since the main body of text overlaps the pagoda photograph, use the Text Wrap command to specify how you want text to wrap around the photograph.

1 Magnify the view of the pagoda photograph (in the middle of your publication).

2 With the pointer tool selected, click the right portion of the pagoda photograph (not overlapped by the text) in the middle of the page to select it.

3 Choose Text Wrap from the Element menu, and in the Text Wrap dialog box click the rectangular boundary icon (middle icon) to select a Wrap option, and type **.36** inch in the Left box, **0** inch in the Right box, **0** inch in the Top box, and **0** inch in the Bottom box to set the Standoff in inches, and click OK.

Now that the formatted text wraps around the photograph, you will align the text with the bottom margin guide.

4 Scroll to view the bottom margin guide.

5 With the pointer tool selected, click the main body of text to select it as a text block, hold down the Shift key (to constrain the movement to 45°), and drag the text block until the baseline of the last line of text is aligned with the bottom margin guide.

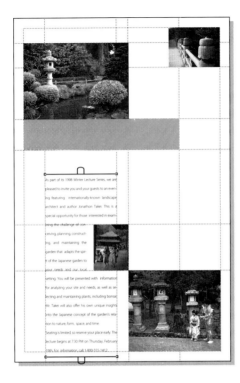

6 Choose Save from the File menu.

Establishing a publication default font

You will create the remaining display text. Since all display text in this publication uses the same font Trajan, you will override the application default font Times, establishing the publication default font to be Trajan.

To override a text formatting default for this publication, you must make sure that no text is selected and no insertion point exists in your publication.

1 Click the pointer tool in the toolbox to make sure no text insertion point exists and no text is selected.

2 Choose Fonts from the Type menu and Trajan Regular from the submenu.

3 With the text tool selected, in the Control palette click the Character-view button to inspect the character view of the Control palette.

The Control palette displays the new publication default font Trajan.

Creating the lavender-colored display text

You will create a lavender-colored A that is positioned at the beginning of the column of text.

1 Scroll to view the top lines of the column of text.

2 With the text tool selected, click below the putty-colored box to establish an insertion point, and type **a**.

The capital A reflects the selected default font Trajan Regular, an all-caps font. Since the insertion point was established in the image area (between the left and right margins), the text block spans the width of the image area.

After formatting the letter A, you will reduce the size of the text block.

3 With the text tool still selected, double-click the text A to select it; in the Control palette type 220 points in the Size box, and click the Apply button.

4 With the text still selected, in the Colors palette click Lavender to apply a color to the text.

5 With the pointer tool selected, click the lavender A to select it as a text block, and drag a right corner handle until it is roughly aligned with the right edge of the text, better organizing your work space.

6 With the lavender A still selected as a text block, drag the text block until the letter is centered over the first word of the formatted text below the putty-colored box.

7 Choose Send to Back from the Arrange menu (Command-B) to display the lavender A behind the formatted text.

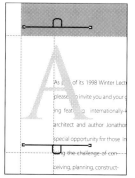 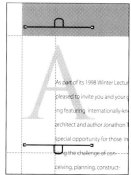

8 Choose Save from the File menu.

Creating the lemonade-colored display text

After dragging to define a text block that spans the width of the putty-colored box, you will apply the paragraph specification that centers the text within the text block, causing the text to be centered in the putty-colored box.

1 Adjust the view of the page so that you can see the entire putty-colored box.

2 With the text tool selected, drag in the putty-colored box to define a text block that spans the width of the putty-colored box (exact height is not important), and type **the japanese** in lowercase letters.

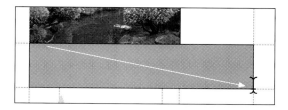

3 With the text tool still selected, triple-click the text to select it, and in the Control palette type **65** points in the Size box, and click the Apply button.

4 In the Control palette click the Paragraph-view button, and in the paragraph view of the Control palette, click the Center-align button to center the text within the text block.

Since the text block spans the putty-colored box, the text is centered in the box.

5 With the text still selected, in the Colors palette click Lemonade to apply a color to the text.

6 With the pointer tool selected, click the lemonade-colored text to select it as a text block, and press the up and down arrow keys (or click the up and down nudge buttons in the Control palette) until the text is vertically centered in the putty-colored box.

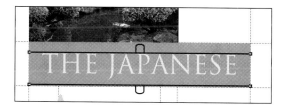

7 Choose Save from the File menu.

Creating the Garden display text

You will create the black display text that overlaps the putty-colored box.

1 With the text tool selected, click the pasteboard to the right of the page to establish an insertion point, and type **garden**.

2 With the text tool still selected, double-click the text garden to select it.

3 In the Control palette click the Character-view button, and in the character view of the Control palette type **80** points in the Size box in the Control palette, and click the Apply button.

4 With the text tool selected, drag to select the letter G in the text GARDEN, and type **110** points in the Size box in the Control palette, and click the Apply button.

5 With the pointer tool selected, click the text GARDEN to select it as a text block, and drag the text block until the top of the 80-point (smaller) capitals is aligned with the bottom edge of the putty-colored box, with the right edge of the text aligned with the right margin guide.

6 With the text GARDEN still selected as a text block, drag a right corner handle until it is roughly aligned with the right edge of the text, reducing the size of the text block.

7 Choose View from the Layout menu and Fit in Window from the submenu.

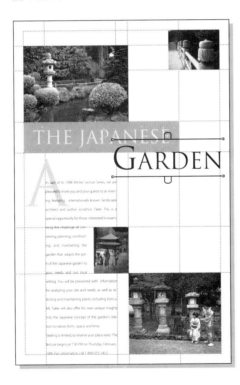

8 Choose Save from the File menu.

Applying a color to line art

After placing and aligning the Japanese characters, you will apply the color lemonade to the characters. Since the bitmapped characters were created in Adobe Illustrator®, and converted to a grayscale TIFF in Adobe Photoshop, it is possible to apply a color to them and view the results. Allowing you to create, manipulate, and refine artwork, Adobe Illustrator includes advanced features for editing, text handling, color support, and more.

1 Choose Place from the File menu, and in the Place Document dialog box double-click the *04GraphicE* file in the *04Lesson* folder.

2 With the loaded text icon displayed, click the page just to the right of the putty-colored box to place the characters.

Depending on where you clicked, the characters overlap several text and graphics elements, since Adobe PageMaker places the object on the top of the stack. As was mentioned before, these characters represent the Japanese expression for garden.

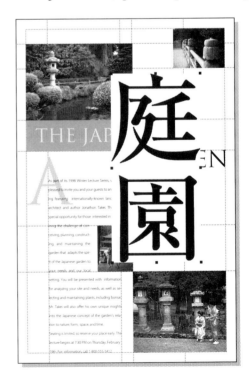

3 With the characters still selected, choose Send to Back from the Arrange menu to place the characters at the bottom of the stack.

4 Drag the characters until they are vertically centered between the two photographs on the right side of the page, with the right edge of the characters aligned with the right margin guide.

5 With the characters still selected, in the Colors palette make sure the Fill button is selected, and click Lemonade to apply the color lemonade to the fill of the characters.

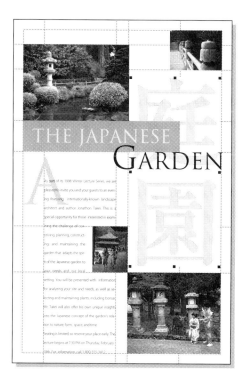

6 Choose Save from the File menu.

Creating the black display text

You will create the black display text that is positioned in the upper-right corner of the page.

1 Magnify the view of the area below the bridge photograph (in the upper-right corner of the page).

2 With the text tool selected, drag to define a text block that spans from the right edge of the photograph above the putty-colored box to the right margin guide (exact height is not important).

3 Type **1998 winter**, press the Return key (to insert a hard-carriage return), and type **lecture series**.

4 With the insertion point still established in the text, choose Select All from the Edit menu.

5 In the Control palette type **35** points in the Size box and **60** points in the Leading box, and click the Apply button.

6 In the Control palette click the Paragraph-view button, and in the paragraph view of the Control palette click the Right-align button to align the text with the right edge of the text block.

7 From the horizontal ruler, drag to create a horizontal ruler guide at 3.5 inches.

Since the guides are set to be displayed behind the text and graphics elements, the lemonade-colored characters partially obscure the view of the ruler guide.

8 Choose Guides and Rulers from the Layout menu and Guides in Front from the submenu to display the guides in front of the text and graphics.

9 With the pointer tool selected, click the text to select it as a text block, and drag a left corner handle until it is roughly aligned with the left edge of the text, and drag the text block until the baseline of the first line of text is aligned with the 3.5-inch horiontal ruler guide, with the right edge of the text aligned with the right margin guide.

10 Choose Save from the File menu.

Creating more black display text

You will create the black display text that is positioned above the lantern photograph in the lower-right corner of the page.

1 Scroll to view the entire second Japanese character above the lantern photograph.

2 With the text tool selected, drag to define a text block over the bottom Japanese character that spans the width of the character (exact height is not important).

3 Type **thursday**, press the Return key, type **february**, press the Return key, type **nineteenth**, press the Return key, and type **at 7:30 p.m.**.

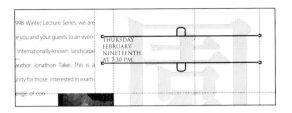

4 With the insertion point still established, choose Select All from the Edit menu.

5 In the Control palette click the Right-align button to align the text with the right edge of the text block.

6 In the Control palette click the Character-view button, and in the character view of the Control palette type **25** points in the Size box and **60** points in the Leading box, and click the Apply button.

7 From the horizontal ruler, drag to create a horizontal ruler guide at approximately 8.7 inches.

8 With the pointer tool selected, click the text (date and time) to select it as a text block, drag a left windowshade handle until it is roughly aligned with the left edge of the text, and drag the text block until the baseline of the first line of text is aligned with the 8.7-inch horizontal ruler guide, with the right edge of the text aligned with the right margin guide.

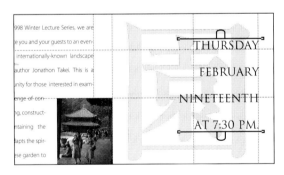

You are finished assembling this poster.

9 Choose View from the Layout menu and Fit in Window from the submenu to view the entire publication.

10 Choose Guides and Rulers from the Layout menu and Show Guides from the submenu to hide the view of the guides.

11 Choose Save from the File menu to save the *04Work* publication.

PRODUCING THIS POSTER

To print this poster at your local copy shop, you will need to deliver the publication, and include all font information and linked image files. When the *04Work* file is open at the copy shop, the operator will execute the following steps.

1 Choose Print from the File menu (Command-P), and in the Print: Document dialog box choose the correct PPD from the PPD pop-up menu (if you are printing to a PostScript device), and click the Paper button

2 In the Print: Paper dialog box choose Tabloid from the Size pop-up menu, make sure the Reduce to fit radio button is selected, and click the Color button.

3 In the Print: Color dialog box make sure the Composite and Color radio buttons are selected.

4 Click the Print button to print the poster.

5 Close all open publications, and choose Quit from the File menu (Command-Q) to exit the Adobe PageMaker application.

BH JOURNAL

British Home Journal • Spring Issue 1998

Special Paint Finishes & Effects Demonstration

The Home Centre is pleased to offer a series of painting demonstrations taught by free-lance painter and designer Mark Waldron Abrahmson.

It's up to you whether you revive an old chair, jazz up a wall, or mask problem surfaces that may include plaster, stripped wood, varnished wood, paper, fabric, tiles, and metal.

Our demonstrations are open to anyone interested in painting finishes and effects, regardless of experience level. The entire series consists of three demonstrations, where each session covers a project from start to finish. You are welcome to attend individual demonstrations.

Class One: Broken Colour

The real essence of the broken colour techniques involves applying a series of multiple colours in broken layers over a coloured background.

Methods discussed here include colour washing, sponging, combing,

Continued on page 2

More Hard Knocks

You can't go wrong using hardwood flooring as a design foundation for luxurious, formal settings, or to provide a light and airy feeling to more informal spaces. In any climate, in any season, wood floors imbue an atmosphere of style and ease, allowing collectors an opportunity to enjoy favorite carpets and textiles.

Parquet: A Natural Mosaic

The word parquet comes from the French word parquetry, which describes the process of creating an inlay of wood in a pattern or mosaic. Masterfully ornate, use parquet flooring whenever you are looking for surface that have decorative strength.

With parquet flooring traditionally utilizing oak and maple, be sure to check whether or not your needs are better met with either pine or fir. These are available as dressed and matched, or tongue and groove, strips of wood, usually prefinished. Ask at your local hardware store for the different grains and strip sizes, most come prefinished.

For laying the floor, you must have a seam or full tile at the center of the room, continuing the pattern in an outward spiral.

The most well known parquet pattern is the checkerboard, although circular wood inlays date back to the sixteenth century when the parquet was designated for royal palaces and theaters. Now your home can exude the grandeur of a palace with ornate, beautiful parquet floors.

This illustration shows an example of a parquet pattern inspired by an antique Islamic carpet design.

Be sure to have a steady grip when disassembling pipe at elbow joints.

Simply redo the loo

PVC or copper pipes in the w/c? If you are hiring a professional to install the plumbing, they should be able to discuss the advantages and disadvantages of each piping system with you.

To install an complete PVC-type plumbing system yourself, you will need to exercise some extra caution when handling PVC materials. For example, the PVC solvent used to fasten pipe joints is engineered to set on contact. The only way to remedy a misaligned joint is to remove it with a saw, discard it, and start again.

Copper piping is similar to working in PVC, yet requires special tools and experience. Far beyond assembling the requisite soldering torch, pipe cutter, flux, and steel wool; soldering copper pipes requires a good deal of expertise. Those with experience always consider the open flame of the soldering torch, since it introduces a fire hazard to any exposed wood. In all cases, you must shield the area with some tin before lighting the soldering torch. In addition, check for any flammable liquids or solvents in your work area, and always work with a fireextinguisher nearby.

part so as
ther dam-
rts can be
g them.
ated by
hen gen-
table top
may en-
s prior
ers. Per-
r to be
in actu-
e wood,
nd be-
y diffi-
screws,
ail, you
th next
h is es-
g a fine
oles
ax. To
ith the
or a add

d ap-
xcess
r glue
uld
three

care-
ob-
hing
e and
ro-
you
stor-

5

You will assemble the elements for a black-and-white newsletter that will be printed on the front and back of a single physical page. In addition to five articles, the newsletter in-

PROMOTIONAL NEWSLETTER

cludes a variety of graphics elements such as borders, display text, photographs, illustrations, and a sidebar box that will serve to frame an article. ■ The graphics elements that you will incorporate into the publication were created using a variety of Adobe image-processing applications. The title graphic for this newsletter was created using Adobe Dimensions. The illustrations were created using Adobe Illustrator. After the photographs and illustrations were scanned on a flatbed scanner, they were imported into Adobe Photoshop to be sized and enhanced, and saved in TIFF file format at a resolution of 100 dpi.

PROMOTIONAL NEWSLETTER

Unlike previous lessons where you imported the text and graphics elements using the Place command, you will drag some of the text and graphics from a library palette that you will assemble yourself. A library palette provides an efficient way to manage collections of frequently used objects in a floating palette. In addition to storing the master-page design for this newsletter publication, the template you will assemble in this lesson will include the library palette, and all styles needed to assemble the newsletter.

This lesson covers:

• Creating a double-sided publication

• Copying styles from one publication to another

• Building a library of text and graphics elements

• Creating a keyline

• Inserting a continued message

• Printing text on a gray background.

BEFORE YOU BEGIN

All files and fonts needed for this lesson are found on the Adobe PageMaker *Classroom in a Book* CD-ROM disc in the folders *05Lesson* and *Fonts*, respectively. The *Extras* folder on the *Classroom in a Book* CD-ROM disc includes the file *05Int1*, an interim file of artwork you may wish to use.

It should take you approximately 2 hours to complete this lesson.

Opening an existing document

Let's take a look at the final version of the newsletter you will assemble in this lesson.

1 Before launching the Adobe PageMaker program, throw away the *Adobe PageMaker 6.0 Prefs* file to return all settings to their default values.

2 Make sure the fonts Adobe Garamond, Adobe Garamond Italic, Adobe Garamond Semibold, Birch, and Myriad MM 700 Bold 600 Normal are installed.

3 Double-click the *Adobe® PageMaker® 6.0* icon to launch the Adobe PageMaker program.

4 Choose Open from the File menu (Command-O), and in the Open Publication dialog box double-click the *05Final* file in the *05Lesson* folder to view the newsletter you will create.

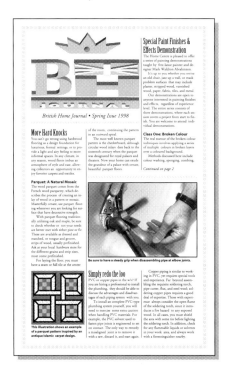

The full view of the double-page spread displays a variety of text and graphics elements. The page icons in the lower-left corner of the publication window indicate this document consists of two pages.

5 Choose Guides and Rulers from the Layout menu and Show Guides from the submenu (Command-J) to display the guides used to assemble this newsletter.

TIP: TO OPEN THE
PREFERENCES DIALOG
BOX, DOUBLE-CLICK
THE POINTER TOOL IN
THE TOOLBOX.

Defining printing requirements

This newsletter (including the TIFF images scanned at a resolution of100 dpi), can be printed successfully on legal-sized paper using a 600 dpi or 800 dpi desktop laser printing device. In this example, a higher-resolution printing device is recommended, because this newsletter includes some text on a gray background. Be forewarned: Faxing a document that has text on a gray background often produces disappointing results.

ASSEMBLING A CUSTOM TEMPLATE

In this lesson you will assemble a custom template for what will be a series of newsletters. With the custom template containing the master page, styles, and a library of text and graphics elements, it will be easy to assemble subsequent newsletters.

Creating a master page

To assemble a master page in a template, you will begin by opening a new publication and saving it as a template.

1 Choose New from the File menu (Command-N), and in the Document Setup dialog box choose Legal from the Page size pop-up menu, click the Facing pages check box to deselect it, type **2** pages in the Number of pages box, type **4p6** in the Inside box, **4p6** in the Outside box, **4p6** in the Top box, and **4p6** in the Bottom box to establish the margin guides, and click OK.

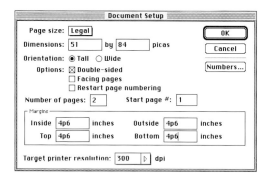

Note: Even though you have not overridden the application default measurement system (inches), it is possible to enter values that are expressed in another unit of measure, since the Adobe PageMaker program will convert the values automatically.

The page icons in the lower-left corner of the publication window indicate the untitled publication consists of two pages. By default, Adobe PageMaker opens page number 1 of a double-sided document as a right page.

2 If you do not have a *Projects* folder, create one now.

3 Choose Save As from the File menu, and in the Save Publication As dialog box type **05Template** in the Name box, click the Template radio button to select it, select the *Projects* folder, and click OK.

Establishing the measurement system and rulers

Because you use the rulers to set up your layout grid, it's a good idea to choose a measurement system before you begin laying out your pages. Since a publication is open, choosing picas as the unit of measure is establishing a publication default, applying the selected measurement system to this publication only.

1 Choose Preferences from the File menu, and in the Preferences dialog box choose Picas from the Measurements in pop-up menu, choose Custom from the Vertical ruler pop-up menu, type **13** points in the Points box (to specify the number of points you want between tick marks on the ruler), and click OK.

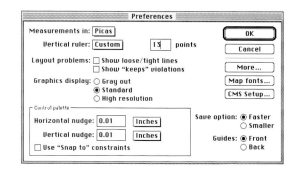

Since you will apply 13-point leading to the body text of the articles, establishing a 13-point vertical ruler will help you align text and graphics.

The *05Template* publication reflects the selected measurement system, picas.

Specifying column guides

With the margins already specified in the Document Setup dialog box, you are ready to specify column guides. In addition to achieving a consistent look throughout a publication, setting the column guides on a master page saves you the effort of specifying columns on every page in a publication.

Notice the L and R master-page icons in the lower-left corner of the publication window. These master-page icons represent the left and right pages of a double-sided publication. In previous lessons you saw how a single-sided publication is marked by an R master-page icon alone.

1 Click the R master-page icon to view the right master page.

Since the Facing pages option was deselected in the Preferences dialog box, Adobe PageMaker highlights the R master-page icon, and displays the right master page as a single page.

Note: When the Facing pages option is activated, the left and right master pages are displayed side-by-side when the L/R master-page icon is selected.

2 Choose Column Guides from the Layout menu, and in the Column Guides dialog box type 3 columns in the Number of columns box, and click OK.

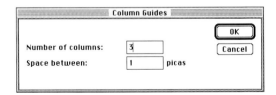

Adobe PageMaker automatically creates three columns of equal widths on the right master page, filling the entire image area between margin guides.

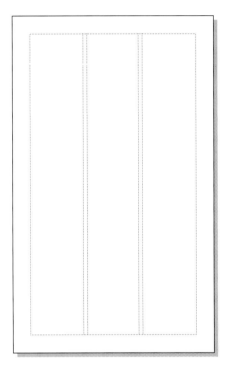

3 Click the L master-page icon to display the left master page.

4 Choose Column Guides from the Layout menu, and in the Column Guides dialog box type 3 columns in the Number of columns box, and click OK to specify column guides on the left master page.

5 Choose Save from the File menu (Command-S).

Creating the border

To cause the border to display on all left pages of the newsletter publication, you will draw a box on the left master page, and use the Control palette to size and position it.

1 With the left master page still displayed, click the rectangle tool in the toolbox to select it, and drag to draw a box of any dimension.

2 In the Control palette make sure the upper-left reference point of the Proxy icon is selected, type **2p7** in the X box, **2p2** in the Y box, **45p10** in the Width box, and **79p7** in the Height box, and press the Return key to resize and position the box.

3 Choose Line from the Element menu and Custom from the submenu, and in the Custom dialog box choose the repeating blocks line (second line style from the bottom) from the Line style pop-up menu, type **8** points in the Line weight box, and click OK.

The border reflects the 8-point repeating blocks line style.

4 Choose Save from the File menu.

Defining a tint

Since you will be applying a 10% tint of black to several objects in the template and the newsletter publication, defining the tint to be added to the Colors palette will streamline your work.

1 Choose Define Colors from the Element menu, and in the Define Colors dialog box click the New button.

2 In the Edit Color dialog box type **10% Gray** in the Name box, choose Tint from the Type pop-up menu, type **10%** in the Tint box, hold down the Option key (to close the chain of dialog boxes), and click OK.

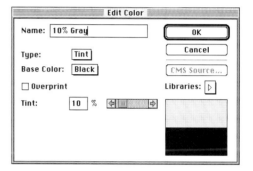

3 With the pointer tool selected, click the border to select it, in the Colors palette click the Line button, and click 10% Gray to apply the color gray to the border.

Now that the border is sized, positioned, and formatted, you are ready to copy and paste it to the right master page.

4 With the border still selected, choose Copy from the Edit menu (Command-C).

5 Click the R master-page icon, and choose Paste from the Edit menu (Command-V) to paste the border to the right master page.

6 With the pasted border selected, in the Control palette make sure the upper-left reference point of the Proxy icon is selected, type **2p7** in the X box and **2p2** in the Y box, and press the Return key to position the border.

The border will be displayed on right and left pages of the newsletter publication.

7 Choose Save from the File menu.

Dragging a graphic from one publication to another

After tiling the open publications in the publication window, you will drag the title graphic from the *05Final* publication to the right master page of your template.

1 With the right master page still displayed, choose Tile from the Window menu to tile the publication window with the open publications.

2 Click the title bar of the *05Final* publication to activate it, and click the R master-page icon to display the right master page.

3 With the pointer tool selected, click the title graphic (BH Journal) in the upper-left corner of the right master page to select it, and drag it to the upper-left corner of the *05Template* document.

4 Click the title bar of the *05Template* document to activate it.

5 From the horizontal ruler, drag to create a horizontal ruler guide at approximately 22p6.

6 With the magnifying glass selected in the tool box, drag to marquee select the upper-left portion of the right master page.

7 With the pointer tool selected, click the copied title graphic to select it, and drag it until its bottom edge is aligned with the 22p6 horizontal ruler guide, with its left and right edges aligned with the left and middle column guides.

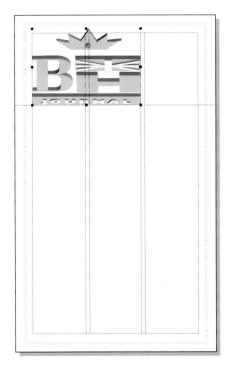

8 Choose Save from the File menu.

Creating, formatting, and aligning the subtitle text

After you create the subtitle text, you will format it and position it below the title graphic that you just positioned in the upper-left corner of the right master page.

1 With the text tool selected, drag to define a text block below the title graphic that spans the width of the left and middle columns (exact height is not important).

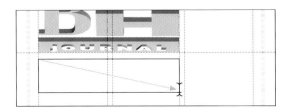

2 Type **British Home Journal** in uppercase and lowercase letters, press the spacebar, hold down the Option key and type **8** (to create a bullet), press the spacebar, and type **Spring Issue 1998**.

3 With the text tool selected, triple-click the subtitle text to select it, and in the Control palette choose Adobe Garamond Italic from the Font pop-up menu, type **17** points in the Size box, and press the Return key.

4 In the Control palette click the Paragraph-view button, and in the paragraph view of the Control palette click the Center-align button to center the text in the text block.

Center-align button

5 With the pointer tool selected, drag the existing 22p6 horizontal ruler guide until it is aligned approximately with the 24p7 mark on the vertical ruler.

6 With the pointer tool still selected, click the subtitle text to select it as a text block, hold down the Shift key (to constrain the movement to 45°), and drag it until the baseline of the text is aligned with the 24p7 horizontal ruler guide.

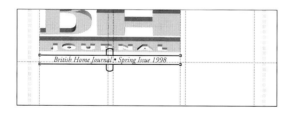

7 Choose Save from the File menu.

Drawing a horizontal divider line

Using the constrained-line tool, you will draw a horizontal line below the subtitle text, spanning the width of the left and middle columns.

1 Drag the existing 24p7 horizontal ruler guide until it is aligned approximately with the 25p11 mark on the vertical ruler.

2 With the constrained-line tool selected in the toolbox, drag to draw a line along the 25p11 horizontal ruler guide, spanning the width of the left and middle columns.

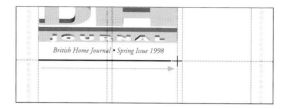

The horizontal ruler guide overlaps the line you just drew.

3 Choose Guides and Rulers from the Layout menu and Guides in Back from the submenu.

4 Choose Line from the Element menu and the 4-point repeating blocks line from the submenu.

5 With the line still selected, in the Colors palette click the Line button to select it, and click 10% Gray to apply the color gray to the line.

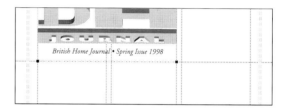

6 Choose Save from the File menu.

The master page is completed, and you are ready to finish assembling the newsletter template.

Building a library of objects

As was mentioned at the beginning of this lesson, Adobe PageMaker provides the ability to arrange collections of text and graphics objects in a library palette, making it possible to store, organize, search for, and retrieve items that you use frequently.

TIP: TO SPECIFY BLACK-AND-WHITE OR COLOR THUMBNAILS IN A LIBRARY PALETTE, CHOOSE PREFERENCES FROM THE FILE MENU, AND SELECT THE DESIRED SETTING.

In this lesson you will create a new library palette, and add four items found in the *05Final* publication to the newly created library palette. Once assembled, you are able to drag individual text and graphics elements from the library palette to the newsletter publication.

1 Click the title bar of the *05Final* publication to activate it.

Note: If you cannot view the title bar, choose 05Final *from the Window menu to activate the* 05Final *publication.*

2 Choose Library from the Window menu, and in the Open Library dialog box double-click the *05Final Library* file in the *05Lesson* folder.

The *05Final Library* palette displays thumbnails that represent text and graphic elements.

Note: If no library exists in a publication, choosing the Library command opens an untitled library palette. You can have only one library palette open at a time.

3 Drag the size box in the *05Final Library* palette to increase the size of the palette, making it possible to see the four thumbnails in the palette.

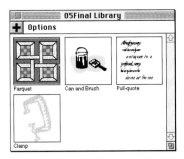

You will create your own library palette, assembling the same collection of text and graphics elements.

4 In the *05Final Library* palette choose New Library from the Options pop-up menu.

Options pop-up menu

5 In the Create New Library dialog box type **05Library** in the Name box, select the *Projects* folder, and click OK.

The *05Final library* palette is closed automatically, since it is not possible to open more than one library at a time.

6 In the *05Library* palette choose Preferences from the Options pop-up menu, and in the Library Preferences dialog box click the Edit items after adding check box to select it, and click OK.

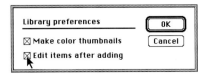

7 With the *05Final* publication activated, click page icon 1 to view the first page.

8 With the pointer tool selected, click the parquet graphic in the lower-left corner of the first page of the *05Final* publication to select it, and click the Add button (the plus sign) in the *05Library* palette.

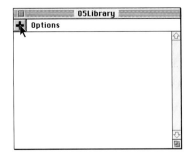

9 In the Item Information dialog box type **Parquet** in the Title box, and click OK.

Note: The Item Information dialog box provides the ability to enter specific keywords that make it possible to search for objects in a library. Use the Description box to attach information (such as resolution, date, author, etc.) to library items to better organize your library.

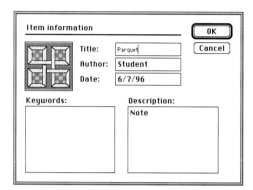

The *05Library* palette displays a thumbnail of the parquet graphic.

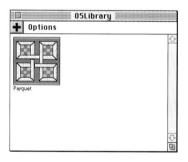

10 Click page icon 2 to view the second page of the *05Final* publication.

11 Magnify the view of the top-half portion of the second page.

12 With the pointer tool selected, click the graphic (paint can/brush) in the upper-right corner of the second page, and click the Add button in the *05Library* palette.

13 In the Item Information dialog box type **Can and brush** in the Title box, and click OK.

In addition to graphics objects, it is possible to place individual text objects in a library palette.

14 With the pointer tool selected, click the pull-quote text (with text wrap) in the middle column of the second page, and click the Add button in the *05Library* palette.

Note: The term pull-quote refers to text that is taken directly from the text of an article, with increased size or weight of the font drawing the reader's interest.

15 In the Item Information dialog box type **Pull-quote** in the Title box, and click OK.

16 With the pointer tool selected, hold down the Command key (to select an object overlapped by another object), click the oversized clamp graphic in the center of the *05Final* publication, and click the Add button in the *05Library* palette.

Note: It may be difficult to view the graphics handles around the clamp graphic that indicate it is selected.

17 In the Item Information dialog box type **Clamp** in the Title box, and click OK.

Even though the thumbnails in the library palette are equally sized, these text and graphics elements (in the *05Library* palette) will retain their original color, dimensions, and previously applied text wrap specifications when placed in your publication.

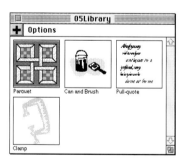

Note: Even though it is uncertain whether or not these objects will be used in subsequent newsletter publications, this exercise is meant to showcase the library palette as a valuable tool for organization.

NEWSLETTER PROMOTIONAL

Lesson 5

TIP: IS THE PARAGRAPH
TAG FOR THIS TEXT. BODY
TEXT IS FRUTIGER
CONDENSED 6 PT, 14 PT
LEADING, 5 PT RIGHT
INDENT, ALL CAPS, RIGHT-
ALIGNED. THE WORD
"TIP:" AND THE COLON
ARE BOLD.

18 Choose Save from the File menu.

Removing and copying Styles

Adobe PageMaker makes it possible to copy styles from an existing Styles palette in a publication to another publication. Before copying styles from the *05Final* publication to your publication, remove the existing styles in the Styles palette of your publication to better organize your Styles palette.

1 Click the title bar of the *05Template* document to activate it.

2 Choose Styles from the Window menu (Command-Y) to open the Styles palette.

3 Choose Define Styles from the Type menu (Command-3), and in the Define Styles dialog box click the first style (below [Selection]), and click the Remove button.

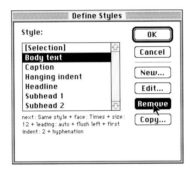

4 With the following style already selected, continue clicking the Remove button until all styles have been removed, and click the Copy button.

5 In the Copy Styles dialog box double-click the *05Final* file in the *05Lesson* folder.

6 In the Define Styles dialog box notice how the copied styles are displayed, and click OK.

The Styles palette displays the copied styles, and the template is now completely assembled.

7 Choose Save from the File menu.

ASSEMBLING THE FIRST PAGE

Using a copy of the template you just created, you will assemble the text and graphics elements for the first page of the newsletter publication. Much like some of the previous lessons, you will position objects to be aligned with objects in adjacent columns.

Opening a copy of the template

After opening an untitled copy of the template you have created, you will name it and save it to the *Projects* folder.

1 Click the close button at the left side of the title bar for *05Template* to close the template you just created.

Closing *05Template* before you reopen it better demonstrates how you would use a custom template.

2 Choose Tile from the Window menu to untile the publication window.

The *05Final* publication is displayed.

3 Choose Open from the File menu, and in the Open Publication dialog box double-click the *05Template* file in the *Projects* folder.

TIP: TO SAVE SPACE ON YOUR DESKTOP, CLOSE THE STYLES PALETTE, AND CHOOSE THE DESIRED STYLE FROM THE STYLE POP-UP MENU IN THE PARAGRAPH VIEW OF THE CONTROL PALETTE.

Adobe PageMaker opens an untitled copy of the template.

4 Drag the size box of the *05Library* palette to reduce the size of the palette.

5 Choose Save As from the File menu, and in the Save publication as dialog box type **05Work** in the Name box, select the *Projects* folder, and click OK.

Placing the first article text

After placing text in the middle column on the front page of your publication, you will apply several of the styles copied from the *05Final* publication.

1 Click page icon 1 to display the first page of the newsletter.

2 Choose Place from the File menu (Command-D), and in the Place Document dialog box double-click the *05TextA* file in the *05Lesson* folder.

3 With the loaded text icon displayed, click in the top portion of the middle column to place the text.

4 With the text tool selected, click the article text to establish an insertion point, choose Select All from the Edit menu (Command-A), and in the Styles palette click 05Article.

5 With the text tool still selected, click the first line of text to establish an insertion point, and in the Styles palette click 05Headline.

6 Click anywhere in the paragraph that follows the headline to establish an insertion point, and in the Styles palette click 05NoIndent.

The style 05NoIndent is identical to the style 05Article, except that the first line of text is not indented.

7 With the magnifying glass selected in the toolbox, drag to marquee select the lower-half portion of the entire page.

8 With the pointer tool selected, click the text in the middle column to select it as a text block, and drag the text block until the baseline of the last line of text is aligned with the bottom margin guide.

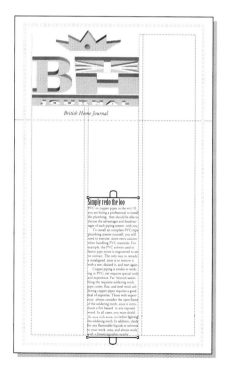

With the text aligned with the bottom margin guide, it is possible to use this text to align other objects in the newsletter.

9 Choose Save from the File menu.

Placing a caption

After placing caption text at the bottom of the left column, you will apply a style to the text, and align it with the bottom margin guide.

1 Choose Place from the File menu, and in the Place Document dialog box double-click the *05TextB* file in the *05Lesson* folder.

2 With the loaded text icon displayed, click in the lower portion of the left column to place the text.

3 With the text tool selected, click the caption text to establish an insertion point, and in the Styles palette click 05Caption.

4 With the pointer tool selected, click the caption to select it as a text block, and drag the text block until the baseline of the last line of text is aligned with the bottom margin guide.

5 Choose Save from the File menu.

Dragging a graphic from the 05Library palette

Before you drag the parquet graphic from the *05Library* palette to the newsletter publication, you will create the horizontal ruler guide to be used for aligning the graphic.

1 From the horizontal ruler, drag to create a horizontal ruler guide aligned with the baseline of the fourth line of text (in the middle column) above the bottom margin guide.

As was just mentioned, the text in the middle column makes it possible to align some of the text and graphics elements.

2 If the *05Library* palette is not displayed, choose Library from the Window menu.

3 With the *05Library* palette displayed, position the cursor on the Parquet thumbnail, hold down the mouse button, and drag the thumbnail until the cursor is displayed as a graphics icon.

4 With the mouse button still held down, drag the Parquet thumbnail from the *05Library* palette to the bottom of the left column, and release the mouse button.

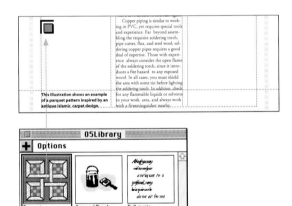

5 Drag the parquet illustration until its bottom edge is aligned with the horizontal ruler guide you just created, with its left and right edges aligned with the left column guides.

The parquet graphic has retained its original size and color as found in the *05Final* publication.

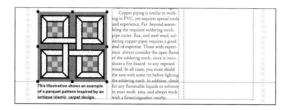

6 Choose Save from the File menu.

Placing and formatting the second article text

After placing and formatting the article text in the left column, you will align it with the text in the middle column.

1 Scroll to the top portion of the left column below the title graphic and subtitle text.

2 Choose Place from the File menu, and in the Place Document dialog box double-click the *05TextC* file in the *05Lesson* folder.

3 With the loaded text icon displayed, click below the title graphic and subtitle text in the left column to place the text.

4 With the text tool selected, click the article text to establish an insertion point, choose Select All from the Edit menu, and in the Styles palette click 05Article.

5 With the text tool still selected, click the first line of the article text to establish an insertion point, and in the Styles palette click 05Headline.

6 Click anywhere in the paragraph that follows the headline text to establish an insertion point, and in the Styles palette click 05NoIndent.

7 Click the tenth line of text (subhead text) that follows a line space to establish an insertion point, and in the Styles palette click 05Subhead.

8 Click anywhere in the paragraph that follows the subhead text to establish an insertion point, and in the Styles palette click 05NoIndent.

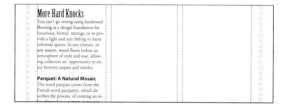

Now that you have applied styles to the text, the text is ready to be positioned.

9 Choose Save from the File menu.

Positioning the second article text

You will use the Text Wrap command to help you resize the text block in the left column.

1 With the pointer tool selected, click the article text in the left column to select it as a text block, hold down the Shift key (to constrain the movement to 45°), and drag the text block until the headline is about two line spaces below the horizontal divider line (gray repeating blocks).

Note: The baseline of the headline text should be aligned approximately with the 28p11 mark on the vertical ruler.

Now that you are ready to resize the text block, notice how difficult it is to see the bottom windowshade handle over the gray parquet illustration. Applying a text wrap to the parquet graphic will force the bottom windowshade handle above the illustration, making it possible for you to view it.

2 With the pointer tool selected, click the parquet illustration to select it.

3 Choose Text Wrap from the Element menu, and in the Text Wrap dialog box click the rectangular boundary icon (middle icon) to select a Wrap option, type **0p** in the Top box and **0p** in the Bottom box to set the Standoff in picas, and click OK.

4 From the horizontal ruler, drag to create a horizontal ruler guide to be aligned with the baseline of the line of text in the middle column that is about one line space above the parquet graphic.

5 With the pointer tool still selected, click the text in the left column to select it.

The text wrap specification has made it possible to view the bottom windowshade handle.

6 Drag the bottom windowshade handle until it is just below the horizontal ruler that you just created.

7 With the text in the left column still selected, hold down the Shift key (to constrain the movement to 45°), and drag the text block until the baseline of the last line of text is aligned with the horizontal ruler guide you just created; again, with the headline about two line spaces below the horizontal divider line as shown in the illustration below.

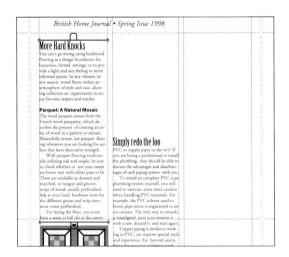

The red down arrow in the bottom windowshade handle indicates the end of the story is not displayed.

8 Click the red down arrow in the bottom windowshade handle to load the remaining text.

9 With the loaded text icon displayed, click in the middle column below the repeating block line to place the text.

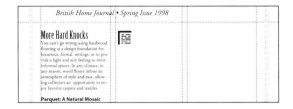

10 From the horizontal ruler, drag to create a horizontal ruler guide that is aligned with the baseline of the first line of text below the headline.

11 With the pointer tool selected, click the selected article text at the top of the middle column to select it as a text block, hold down the Shift key (to constrain the movement to 45°), and drag the text block until the baseline of the third line of text is aligned with the horizontal ruler guide you just created.

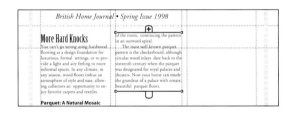

12 Choose Save from the File menu.

Aligning the first article text

Now that the text in the left column can serve to align the remaining text and graphics elements, you will reposition the first article text, manually flowing half of the first article text in the middle column into the right column.

1 With the pointer tool selected, click the text in the lower portion of the middle column to select it as a text block.

2 Drag the bottom windowshade handle up until the last line of text displayed in the text block is the last line of text in the second paragraph, reducing the size of the text block.

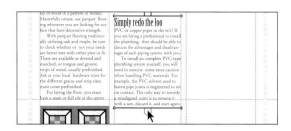

3 With the first article text still selected as a text block, hold down the Shift key (to constrain the movement to 45°), and drag the text block until the baseline of the last line of displayed text is aligned with the bottom margin guide.

The red down arrow in the bottom windowshade handle indicates the end of the story is not displayed.

4 Click the red down arrow to load the remaining text.

5 With the loaded text icon displayed, position the cursor in the right column, roughly aligned with the headline text of the first article in the middle column, and click to place the text.

6 With the text in the right column selected as a text block, drag the bottom windowshade handle until the entire story is displayed, hold down the Shift key (to constrain the movement to 45°), and drag the text block until the baseline of the last line of text is aligned with the bottom margin guide.

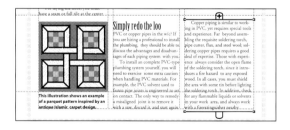

7 Choose Save from the File menu.

Placing the graphic

You will place the photograph that spans the middle and right columns of the first page.

1 Drag the existing horizontal ruler guide (currently aligned with the last line of text in the left column) up two lines, to be aligned with the baseline of the third line of text above the parquet graphic in the left column.

You will align the bottom edge of the photograph to this ruler guide.

2 Scroll to view the empty portion of the middle column (between text blocks).

3 Choose Place from the File menu, and in the Place Document dialog box double-click the *05GraphicA* file in the *05Lesson* folder.

4 With the graphics icon displayed, roughly align the cursor below the article text at the top of the middle column, and click to place the photograph.

5 With the photograph selected, drag it until its bottom edge is aligned with the horizontal ruler guide you just created, with its left and right edges aligned with the middle and right column guides.

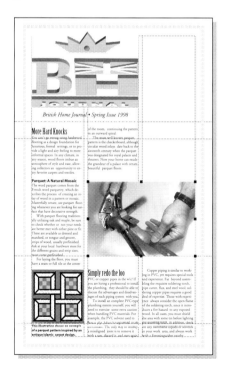

6 Choose Save from the File menu.

Creating a keyline

In a previous lesson you used the rectangle tool to draw boxes that framed graphics with a border. For this lesson you will use the Keyline command to create a border (or keyline) around the photograph. Even though keyline can be used in traditional printing to prepare work for film separations, for this lesson you will create a keyline for purely decorative purposes.

Note: For more information on using the Keyline command, refer to the Adobe Print Publishing Guide.

1 With the pointer tool selected, click the photograph to select it.

2 Choose PageMaker Plug-ins from the Utilities menu and Keyline from the submenu, and in the Keyline dialog box make sure the Bring keyline to front of object button is selected, and click the Attributes button.

3 In the Fill and Line dialog box choose Hairline from the Line pop-up menu, and click OK.

4 In the Keyline dialog box click OK to close it.

The photograph is displayed with the hairline keyline (black border).

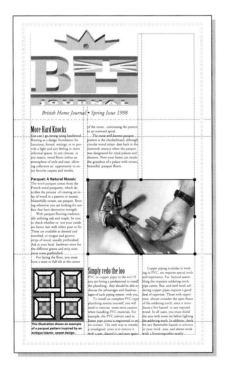

5 Choose Save from the File menu.

Placing a caption

After placing the caption text below the photograph, you will apply a style and align the text.

1 Drag the existing horizontal ruler guide (currently aligned with the bottom edge of the photograph) down one line to be aligned with the baseline of the second line of text above the parquet graphic (in the left column).

Note: To avoid selecting an object when you want to select a horizontal or vertical ruler guide, position the cursor on the ruler guide where it does not overlap text or graphics elements.

2 Choose Place from the File menu, and in the Place Document dialog box double-click the *05TextD* file in the *05Lesson* folder.

3 With the loaded text icon displayed, drag to define a text block below the photograph, spanning the width of the middle and right columns (exact height is not important).

4 With the text tool selected, click the caption text to establish an insertion point, and in the Styles palette click 05Caption.

5 With the pointer tool selected, click the caption text to select it as a text block, hold down the Shift key (to constrain the movement to 45°), and drag the text block until the baseline of text is aligned with the horizontal ruler guide you just created, with the left edge of the text aligned with the left edge of the middle column.

6 Choose Save from the File menu.

Placing the third article text

After placing the third article text in the right column on the first page of your publication, you will apply the styles to the text.

1 Choose Place from the File menu, and in the Place Document dialog box double-click the *05TextE* file in the *05Lesson* folder.

2 With the loaded text icon displayed, click in the top portion of the right column to place the text.

3 With the pointer tool selected, click the third article text in the right column to select it as a text block, hold down the Shift key (to constrain the movement to 45°), and drag the text block to position the first line of text just below the top margin guide.

4 With the third article text still selected as a text block, drag the bottom windowshade handle just above the photograph, reducing the size of the text block.

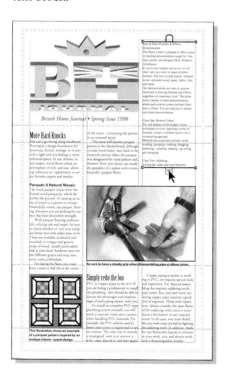

After formatting the text, you will align this text block with text in the middle column.

5 With the text tool selected, click the third article text to establish an insertion point, choose Select All from the Edit menu, and in the Styles palette click 05Article.

6 With the text tool still selected, click the first line of text, and in the Styles palette click 05Headline.

7 Click anywhere in the paragraph that follows the headline to establish an insertion point, and in the Styles palette click 05NoIndent.

8 Click the subhead text that follows a line space to establish an insertion point, and in the Styles palette click 05Subhead.

9 Click anywhere in the paragraph that follows the subhead text to establish an insertion point, and in the Styles palette click 05NoIndent.

You will finish applying styles to the remaining text in this story later.

10 With the pointer tool selected, click the third article text in the right column to select it as a text block, hold down the Shift key (to constrain the movement to 45°), and drag the text block until the baseline of the first line of text that follows the subhead is aligned with the existing ruler guide that is aligned with the baseline of the third line of text in the middle column.

11 With the text in the right column still selected as a text block, drag the bottom windowshade handle until the last line of text is displayed about three line spaces above the photograph as shown in the illustration below.

Once you place the remaining text of the third article on the second page, it will be possible to insert a continued message in the extra space between the text in the right column and the photograph.

12 Choose Save from the File menu.

Drawing a second horizontal divider line

To visually delineate the photograph and its corresponding article in the lower-right portion of the page, you will use the constrained-line tool to draw another horizontal divider line just above the photograph.

1 Choose View from the Layout menu and Fit in Window from the submenu.

2 From the horizontal ruler, drag to create a horizontal ruler guide at approximately 39p10.

3 With the constrained-line tool selected in the toolbox, drag to draw a line along the 39p10 horizontal ruler guide, spanning the width of the left and middle columns.

4 Choose Line from the Element menu and the 4-point repeating blocks line from the submenu to apply a line style and weight.

5 With the line still selected, in the Colors palette click the Line button to select it, and click 10% Gray to apply the color gray to the line.

6 Choose Save from the File menu.

Drawing vertical lines between columns

After establishing the hairline line style as a publication default, you will draw three vertical lines that are centered between the columns in the gutters to visually separate the text.

1 Click the pointer tool to deselect all objects, and choose Line from the Element menu and Hairline from the submenu.

The line style publication default is set to hairline.

2 With the magnifying glass selected in the toolbox, drag to marquee select the entire page above the photograph.

3 From the horizontal ruler, drag to create a horizontal ruler guide that is aligned with the cap height (top edge of the letters) of the headline text in the right column.

4 From the horizontal ruler, drag to create a horizontal ruler guide that is aligned with the baseline of the last line of text (above the photograph) in the middle column.

5 With the constrained-line tool selected in the toolbox, position the cursor at the intersection of the horizontal ruler guide and the approximate center of the right gutter, and drag to the horizontal ruler guide you just created to draw a line.

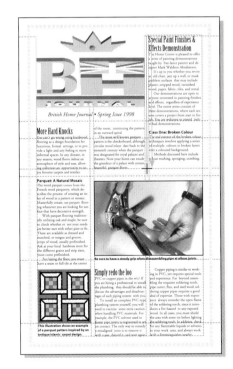

The line reflects the publication default line style (hairline) and the application default color Black.

6 From the horizontal ruler, drag to create a horizontal ruler that is aligned with the top edge of the headline text in the left column.

7 With the constrained-line tool selected, position the cursor at the intersection of the horizontal ruler guide and the approximate center of the left gutter, and drag to the bottom margin guide to draw another line.

8 From the horizontal ruler, drag to create a horizontal ruler that is aligned with the top edge of the headline text in the middle column.

9 With the constrained-line tool selected, position the cursor at the intersection of the horizontal ruler guide and the approximate center of the right gutter, and drag to the bottom margin guide to draw another line.

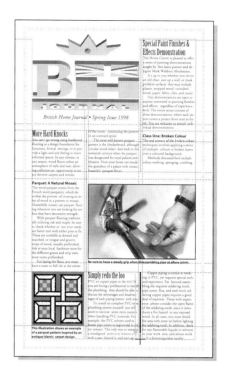

10 If the vertical lines are not centered in the gutters, select a line with the pointer tool, and press the left and right arrow keys (or click the left and right nudge buttons in the Control palette) to adjust the position of the lines.

The first page will be completely assembled, except for the continued message that you can insert after placing the remaining text of the third article on the second page.

11 Choose View from the Layout menu and Fit in Window from the submenu.

12 Choose Save from the File menu.

Note: Interim file 05Int1 *was saved at this point. To open it, double-click the* 05Int1 *file in the Extras folder.*

ASSEMBLING THE SECOND PAGE

In addition to placing, formatting, and aligning text and graphics elements on the second page, you will create a sidebar box that contains text.

Creating the sidebar box

After creating a sidebar box, you will create a smaller box (that will serve to frame the sidebar heading text), and position it at the top of the sidebar box, and then group the boxes together.

1 Click page icon 2 to view the second page.

2 With the rectangle tool selected in the toolbox, drag a box of any dimension in the lower-left corner of the back page.

3 In the Colors palette make sure the Both button is selected, and click 10% Gray to apply the color gray to the line and fill of the box.

4 In the Control palette make sure the center reference point or one of the corner reference points in the Proxy icon is selected, type **13p4** in the Width box and **32p10** in the Height box, and press the Return key to resize the gray box.

5 With the pointer tool selected, click the gray box to select it, and drag it until its bottom edge is aligned with the bottom margin guide, with its left and right edges aligned with the left column guides.

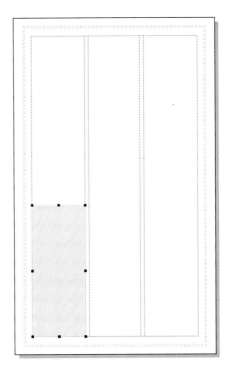

6 With the rectangle tool selected in the toolbox, drag a small box near the top of the gray sidebar box.

7 With the box selected, in the Colors palette make sure the Both button is selected, and click Black to apply the color black to the line and fill of the box.

8 Magnify the view of the top of the sidebar box.

9 With the pointer tool selected, click the black box to select it, and in the Control palette type **13p4** in the Width box and **3p1** in the Height box, and press the Return key to resize the box.

10 Drag the black box until its bottom edge is aligned with the top edge of the gray sidebar box, with its left and right edges aligned with the left column guides.

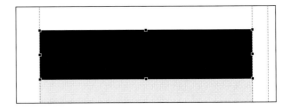

11 With the black box still selected, hold down the Shift key (to select multiple objects), click the gray sidebar box to select it, and choose Group from the Arrange menu (Command-G).

Grouping the two boxes together will ensure they will remain aligned with each other even if they are moved.

12 With the group still selected, choose Lock Position from the Arrange menu (Command-L) to make it impossible to accidentally move the grouped boxes.

13 Choose Save from the File menu.

Overriding a style in a paragraph

After placing and applying styles to the text in the sidebar box, you will override a paragraph specification for one of the styles in a selected paragraph.

1 Choose Place from the File menu, and in the Place Document dialog box double-click the *05TextF* file in the *05Lesson* folder.

2 With the loaded text icon displayed, click in the upper portion of the gray sidebar box to place the text.

3 Magnify the view of the entire sidebar box.

4 With the text tool selected, click the sidebar text to establish an insertion point, choose Select All from the Edit menu, and in the Styles palette click 05Sidebar.

5 With the text tool still selected, click the first line of text in the sidebar text, and in the Styles palette click 05Headline.

Using the Control palette, you will override the style 05Headline.

6 In the Control palette click the Paragraph-view button, and in the paragraph view of the Control palette click the Center-align button.

Notice how the Styles palette and the paragraph view of the Control palette display the style of the selected paragraph (the headline text) as 05Headline+. Since you overrode a paragraph specification for the 05Headline style, Adobe PageMaker displays the modified style as 05Headline+, with the plus sign indicating the style was modified for the selected paragraph.

7 With the text tool selected, triple-click the headline text to select it, and in the Colors palette click Paper to reverse the text out of the sidebar box.

Now that the sidebar text is formatted, you are ready to align it.

8 From the horizontal ruler, drag to create a horizontal ruler guide at 46p.

9 Choose Guides and Rulers from the Layout menu and Guides in Front from the submenu.

Since this particular newsletter design does not dictate the sidebar text be aligned with text in adjacent columns, you will align it with the 46p horizontal ruler guide.

10 With the pointer tool selected, click the text in the sidebar to select it as a text block, hold down the Shift key (to constrain the movement to 45º), and drag the text block until the baseline of the paper-colored headline text is aligned with the 46p horizontal ruler guide.

11 With the sidebar text still selected as a text block, drag the bottom windowshade handle until the entire story is displayed.

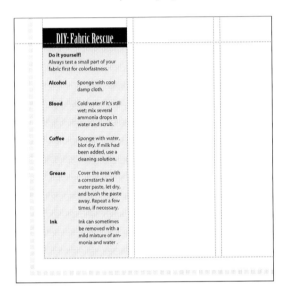

12 Choose Save from the File menu.

Placing the fourth article text

After placing and formatting the fourth article text, you will align it with the bottom margin guide so that you can use it as a ruler, making it possible to align text and graphics elements throughout this page.

1 Choose View from the Layout menu and Fit in Window from the submenu.

2 Choose Autoflow from the Layout menu to select it, making sure it is checked.

3 Choose Place from the File menu, and in the Place Document dialog box double-click the *05TextG* file in the *05Lesson* folder.

4 With the loaded text icon displayed, click in the top portion of the middle column to place the text.

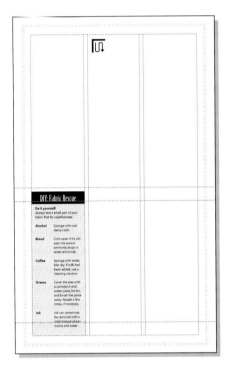

The text flows into the middle and right columns of the second page.

Note: If the placed text had flowed onto the third page, choose Remove Pages from the Layout menu, and in the Remove dialog box type 3 in the Remove page(s) box and 3 in the through box, and click OK to delete the third page.

5 With the text tool selected, click the placed text on the second page to establish an insertion point, choose Select All from the Edit menu, and in the Styles palette click 05Article.

6 Magnify the view of the first lines of text.

7 With the text tool selected, click the first line of the fourth article text in the middle column, and in the Styles palette click 05Headline.

8 Click the paragraph that follows the headline to establish an insertion point, and in the Styles palette click 05NoIndent.

9 Click the first subhead text that follows a line space, and in the Styles palette click 05Subhead.

10 Click anywhere in the next line of text (following the first subhead) to establish an insertion point, and in the Styles palette click 05NoIndent.

11 Repeat the previous two steps for the remaining subhead and corresponding paragraph in this text block, applying the 05Subhead style and the 05NoIndent style, respectively.

Now that the fourth article text is formatted, you will align the text with the bottom margin guide.

12 With the pointer tool selected, click the fourth article text to select it as a text block, hold down the Shift key (to constrain the movement to 45º), and drag the text block until the last line of text is aligned with the bottom margin guide, with the headline text just below the top margin guide.

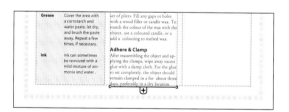

Note: To verify that your text block is properly sized and aligned in the middle column, make sure the baseline of the headline text is aligned with approximately 6p6 on the vertical ruler; again, with the baseline of the last line of text aligned with the bottom margin guide.

You are ready to create the horizontal ruler guides that will help you align the text and graphics elements in adjacent columns.

13 Choose View from the Layout menu and Fit in Window from the submenu, and then magnify the view of the lower-half portion of the page.

14 From the horizontal ruler, drag to create a horizontal ruler guide aligned with the baseline of the fourth line of text above the bottom margin guide.

As before, you will use this horizontal ruler guide to align the bottom edge of a photograph with the text, allowing enough space for a 3-line caption.

15 From the horizontal ruler, drag to create a horizontal ruler guide aligned with the baseline of the line text in the middle column that is about one line space above the sidebar box in the left column.

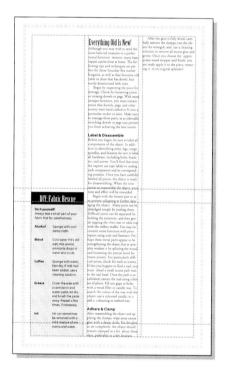

Later, you will use this horizontal ruler guide to align the last line of text of the article in the left column.

16 Choose Save from the File menu.

Placing the second graphic

After placing a second photograph that spans the middle and right columns of the second page, you will reduce the size of the text block in the middle column.

1 Choose Place from the File menu, and in the Place Document dialog box double-click the *05GraphicB* file in the *05Lesson* folder.

2 When prompted, click the No button to prevent duplicating the image data to the *05Work* publication.

3 With the graphics icon displayed, click the lower portion of the page to place the photograph.

The photograph overlaps the text in the middle column (or even the sidebar box).

4 Drag the photograph until its bottom edge is aligned with the horizontal ruler guide that is four line spaces above the bottom margin guide, with its left and right edges aligned with the edges of the middle and right column guides.

5 With the pointer tool selected, click the text in the middle column to select it as a text block, and drag the bottom windowshade handle about two line spaces above the photograph.

Note: The baseline of the last line of text in the middle column should be aligned approximately with the 56p9 mark on the vertical ruler.

7 Choose Save from the File menu.

Creating a keyline

You will use the Keyline command to create a border around another photograph.

1 With the pointer tool selected, click the photograph to select it.

2 Choose PageMaker Plug-ins from the Utilities menu and Keyline from the submenu, and in the Keyline dialog box click the Bring keyline to front of object button, and then click the Attributes button.

3 In the Fill and Line dialog box choose Hairline from the Line pop-up menu, and click OK.

4 In the Keyline dialog box click OK to close it.

The photograph is displayed with the hairline keyline (black border).

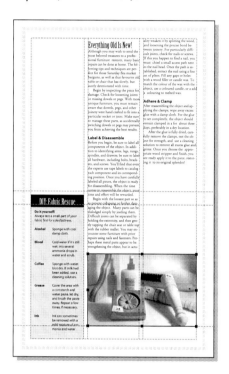

5 Choose Save from the File menu.

Placing a caption

You will place a caption to be positioned below the photograph on the second page.

1 Magnify the view of the page below the photograph.

2 Choose Place from the File menu, and in the Place Document dialog box double-click the *05TextH* file in the *05Lesson* folder.

3 With the loaded text icon displayed, drag to define a text block below the photograph that spans the width of the photograph (exact height is not important) to place the text.

Note: Even though the Autoflow option is activated, the text flows within the bounds of the text block you defined.

4 With the text tool selected, click the caption text to establish an insertion point, and in the Styles palette click 05Caption.

5 With the pointer tool selected, click the caption text to select it as a text block, drag the bottom windowshade handle until the entire story is displayed, hold down the Shift key (to constrain the movement to 45º), and drag the text block until the baseline of the last line of text is aligned with the bottom margin guide.

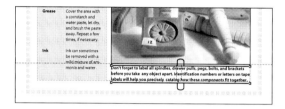

6 Choose Save from the File menu.

Manually flowing the text from the first page

Since the first page included an article that was to be continued on the second page, you will return to the first page to load the remaining text, and manually flow it into the left column on the second page.

1 Click page icon 1 to view the first page.

2 With the pointer tool selected, click the text in the top portion of the right column to select it as a text block, and click the red down arrow in the bottom windowshade handle to load the remaining text.

3 Click page icon 2 to view the second page.

4 Choose View from the Layout menu and Fit in Window from the submenu.

5 With the loaded text icon displayed, click in the top portion of the left column to place the text.

Before aligning the text, you will finish applying styles to the text.

6 Magnify the view of the top portion of the second page.

7 With the text tool selected, click the subhead text that follows a line space to establish an insertion point, and in the Styles palette click 05Subhead.

8 Click the paragraph that follows the subhead to establish an insertion point, and in the Styles palette click 05NoIndent.

9 Repeat the two previous steps to the remaining subhead and corresponding paragraph in this text block, applying the styles 05Subhead and 05NoIndent, respectively.

10 With the pointer tool selected, click the text in the left column to select it as a text block, drag the bottom windowshade handle down to make sure the entire story is displayed, hold down the Shift key (to constrain the movement to 45º), and drag the text block until the baseline of the last line of text is aligned with the existing horizontal ruler guide that is aligned about one line space above the sidebar box.

11 Choose Save from the File menu.

Inserting a continued message

Now that the entire story of the third article text is displayed in the newsletter publication, it is possible to use the Add Con't Line command to add a message at the bottom of the right column on the first page that indicates the article is continued on the next page.

1 Click page icon 1 to view the first page.

2 With the pointer tool selected, click the third article text in the top portion of the right column to select it as a text block, and choose PageMaker Plug-ins from the Utilities menu and Add Con't Line from the submenu, and in the Continuation Notice dialog box click the Bottom of text block radio button to select it, and click OK.

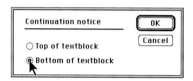

3 With the Command key held down, in the Styles palette click the style Cont On.

4 In the Edit Style dialog box click the Type button, and in the Type Specifications dialog box choose Adobe Garamond Italic from the Font pop-up menu, choose 12 points from the Size pop-up menu, click the Normal button to select a type style, and click OK.

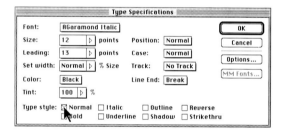

5 In the Edit Style dialog box click the Paragraph button, and in the Paragraph Specifications dialog box choose Left from the Alignment pop-up menu, and click the Rules button.

6 In the Paragraph Rules dialog box make sure the Rule above paragraph button is deselected, make sure the Rule below paragraph button is deselected, hold down the Option key (to close the chain of dialog boxes), and click OK.

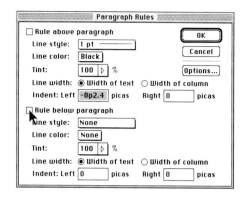

Now that you have applied the type and paragraph specifications to the style Cont On, you are ready to align the text Continued on page 2 with text in the adjacent column.

7 Magnify the top-half portion of the entire page.

8 With the pointer tool selected, click the continued message text to select it as a text block, hold down the Shift key (to constrain the movement to 45°), and drag the text block until the baseline of text is aligned with the existing horizontal ruler guide aligned with the baseline of the last line of text in the middle column.

Even though you have inserted a text block that contains the continued message, the third article text flows independently of it.

9 Choose View from the Layout menu and Fit in Window from the submenu.

10 Choose Save from the File menu.

Dragging objects from the library palette

You will place several text and graphics elements in the middle and right columns.

1 Click page icon 2 to view the second page.

2 From the horizontal ruler, drag to create a horizontal ruler guide that is aligned with the baseline of the line of text in the left column that is nearest to 25p on the vertical ruler.

3 With the *05Library* palette displayed, drag the Pull-quote thumbnail from the *05Library* palette to the middle of the middle column, and release the mouse button.

4 Drag to center the pull quote in the middle column until the baseline of the first line of text in the pull quote is aligned with the horizontal ruler guide you just created.

The text wrap that was already applied to the pull-quote text is retained.

After repositioning the text block in the right column to provide enough space for the Can and Brush graphic, you will drag the Can and Brush thumbnail from the *05Library* palette to the page.

6 With the pointer tool selected, click the text in the right column to select it as a text block, and drag the text block until the last line of text is aligned with the existing horizontal ruler guide that is aligned with the last line of text in the middle column.

7 Drag the Can and Brush thumbnail from the *05Library* palette to the top of the right column, and release the mouse button.

8 Drag to center it at the top of the right column, allowing it to slightly overlap the top margin guide as shown in the illustration below.

After dragging the Clamp thumbnail from the *05Library* palette, you will adjust the stacking order to position the clamp graphic at the bottom of the stack (behind the text).

9 Drag the Clamp thumbnail from the *05Library* palette to position the graphic so that it overlaps the middle and right columns, a few lines above the photograph.

10 With the clamp graphic still selected, choose Send to Back from the Arrange menu (Command-B) to position the graphic at the bottom of the stack.

11 Choose Save from the File menu.

Drawing vertical lines between columns

As with the first page, you will draw vertical lines that are centered between the columns.

1 From the horizontal ruler, drag to create a horizontal ruler that is aligned with the top edge of the headline text in the middle column.

2 With the constrained-line tool selected in the toolbox, position the cursor at the intersection of the horizontal ruler guide and the approximate center of the left gutter, and drag to the bottom margin guide to draw a line.

The line reflects the default publication line style (hairline) that you have already established.

3 With the constrained-line tool selected, position the cursor at the intersection of the horizontal ruler guide and the approximate center of the right gutter, and drag to the horizontal ruler guide aligned with the baselines of the last lines of text in the middle and right columns to draw another line.

4 If the lines are not centered in the gutter, select a line with the pointer tool, and press the left and right arrow keys (or click the left and right nudge buttons in the Control palette) to adjust the position of the line.

You have completed assembling the newsletter publication.

5 Choose View from the Layout menu and Fit in Window from the submenu.

6 Choose Guides and Rulers from the Layout menu and Show Guides from the submenu to hide the guides used to assemble this newsletter.

7 Choose Save from the File menu to save the *05Work* publication.

8 Close all open publications, and choose Quit from the File menu (Command-Q) to exit the Adobe PageMaker application.

PRODUCING THE NEWSLETTER

This publication can be printed successfully on any 600 dpi or 800 dpi desktop laser printing device, and then photocopied for on-demand distribution. Since the newsletter will be printed

on both sides of a single, legal-sized page, you will get the best results if the paper stock is heavy enough to prevent the ink on one side of the publication from showing through to the other side.

1 Choose Print from the File menu (Command-P), and in the Print: Document dialog box choose the correct PPD from the PPD pop-up menu (if you are printing to a PostScript device).

The lower the resolution of your desktop laser printing device, the more likely the gray elements in your publication will show a large dot pattern. To remedy this, adjust the screen frequency as described in the next step.

2 Click the Color button, and in the Print: Color dialog box choose 65 lpi/90 lpi from the Optimized screen pop-up menu to refine the dot pattern in the gray elements, and make sure the Grayscale radio button is selected.

3 In the Print: Color dialog box click the Options button, and in the Print: Options dialog box choose Optimized from the Send Image data pop-up menu.

If your printer allows you to print on both sides of the paper, be sure to specify the duplexing options as follows.

4 Click the Paper button if you are printing on a PostScript device, or click the Options button if you are printing on a non-PostScript device; and in the printing dialog box select the duplex option that indicates how you want your pages oriented when they print.

5 Click the Print button to print the newsletter.

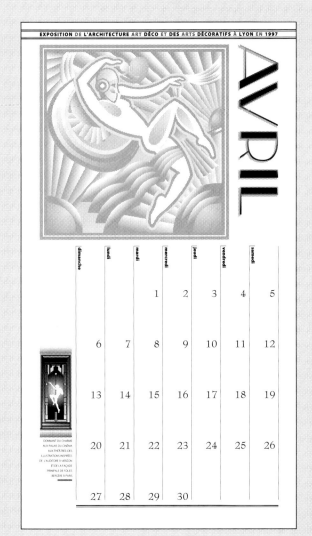

AVRIL

dimanche	lundi	mardi	mercredi	jeudi	vendredi	samedi
		1	2	3	4	5
6	7	8	9	10	11	12
13	14	15	16	17	18	19
20	21	22	23	24	25	26
27	28	29	30			

DONNANT DU CHARME
AUX PALAIS DU CINÉMA
AUX THÉÂTRES, DES
ILLUSTRATIONS INSPIRÉES
DE L'AUDITOIRE À VIERZON
ET DE LA FAÇADE
PRINPALE DE FOLIES
BERGÈRE A PARIS.

MAI

dimanche	lundi	mardi	mercredi	jeudi	vendredi	samedi
				1	2	3
4	5	6	7	8	9	10
11	12	13	14	15	16	17
18	19	20	21	22	23	24
25	26	27	28	29	30	31

CES ILLUSTRATIONS
MONTRENT LES FIGURES
EXUBÉRANTES QUI
ORNAIENT LES FAÇADES
DES MONUMENTS ET
DONNAIENT DU
CHARME À L'ARCHI
TECTURE MODERNE

• F R A N C E •

6

In this lesson, you will assemble the text and graphics for two individual months of a three-color calendar. In addition to the color black, this calendar incorporates a rich gold-

ART DECO CALENDAR

en spot color, PANTONE 128 CVC, and a bordeaux red spot color, PANTONE 202 CVC. ■ The theme of the calendar revolves around the influence of the Art Deco style on architecture and the decorative arts. Directly reflecting the Art Deco theme, the four illustrations featured in this calendar were created in Adobe Illustrator, and saved in Encapsulated PostScript (EPS) file format. Since the illustrations were inspired from figures that once appeared on well-known buildings in French cities, the calendar features text that is in French.

As you have seen in previous lessons, it is possible to import a grayscale TIFF image, apply a color to the image in Adobe PageMaker, and then view the results of the applied color. Unlike TIFF image files, the Adobe PageMaker application does not

ART DECO CALENDAR

display the results of a color applied to imported EPS image files, although EPS images will print with the applied color. In the event that you would want to apply a different color to an EPS image file, it would probably work best to apply the desired color in the original authoring program, view the results, and then re-import it into your Adobe PageMaker publication.

This lesson covers:

• Using the Control palette to move a text block

• Using the Multiple Paste command

• Manually threading and re-threading a story

• Specifying a power paste

• Replacing text and graphics using the Place command

• Inserting a page

• Correcting an uneven rag

• Changing the hyphenation for a word.

BEFORE YOU BEGIN

All files and fonts needed for this lesson are found on the Adobe PageMaker *Classroom in a Book* CD-ROM disc in the folders *06Lesson* and *Fonts*, respectively. In addition, the *Extras* folder on the *Classroom in a Book* CD-ROM disc includes the *06Int1* file, an interim file of artwork that you may wish to use.

It should take you approximately 1 hour to complete this lesson.

Opening an existing publication

Let's take a look at the final version of the two months of a calendar you will assemble in this lesson.

1 Before launching the Adobe PageMaker program, throw away the *Adobe PageMaker 6.0 Prefs* file to ensure all settings are returned to their default values.

2 Make sure the fonts Bernhard Modern Roman, Myriad MM 830 Black 700 Semiextended, Myriad MM 830 Black 600 Normal, and Myriad MM 215 Light 600 Normal are installed.

Lucian Bernhard was one of this century's eminent graphic designers, and Bernhard Modern is his enduring masterpiece of type design. Originally cut in metal in 1937, Bernhard Modern seems to presage the demise of letterpress printing and the eventual rise of digital typography.

3 Double-click the *Adobe® PageMaker® 6.0* icon to launch the Adobe PageMaker program.

4 Choose Open from the File menu (Command-O), and in the Open Publication dialog box double-click the *06Final* file in the *06Lesson* folder.

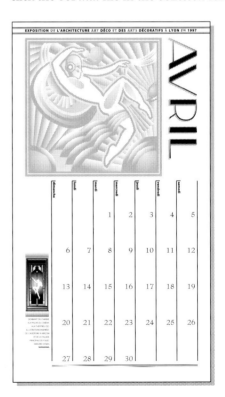

The publication window displays a single page representing the month *Avril* (April in French). The two Art Deco illustrations include the use of two spot colors, and the page icon in the lower-left corner of the display window indicates the publication consists of two pages.

5 Click page icon 2 to view the page representing the month *Mai* (May in French).

6 Click page icon 1 to return to the month Avril.

7 Choose Guides and Rulers from the Layout menu and Show Guides from the submenu (Command-J) to display the guides used to assemble this calendar.

Talk with your printer

Since this calendar is designed to be printed on a commercial printing press, be sure to talk with your printer and your service provider about the requirements of the project and the services you require.

In previous lessons, you imported TIFF images with resolutions that had been established in an authoring system, such as or Adobe Illustrator or Adobe Photoshop. In this lesson, you will be importing EPS images that were created in Adobe Illustrator. While it is possible for an EPS file to contain a bitmapped image (with an established resolution), the EPS images in this project are in vector file format (with no established resolution), and will print according to the selected print resolution of the output device.

With the double lines of the top banner extending to the edges of the page, you or your service provider must extend the lines beyond the edge of the page to construct a bleed. A bleed will ensure that when the printed paper is trimmed, the ink coverage will extend to the very edge of the page. Your printer can indicate the size of the bleed that needs to be constructed. For more information on constructing bleeds, refer to the *Adobe Print Publishing Guide*.

After verifying the size of the bleed and the line screen frequency with your printer, talk with your service provider to determine who will perfom the prepress tasks and how you should deliver this publication to your service provider.

ASSEMBLING THE FIRST MONTH

In addition to placing, formatting, and positioning graphics elements, you will create some of the text and graphics yourself.

Opening a copy of a template

To make it a little easier to align the text and graphics, you will open a copy of an existing template that has the margin and most of the ruler guides already established. To prevent you from accidentally moving or deleting any of these guides, they have been locked.

1 Choose Open from the File menu, and in the Open Publication dialog box double-click the *06Template* file in the *06Lesson* folder.

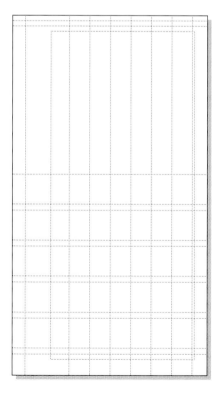

The untitled copy of the template displays the page boundary, margins, and ruler guides that have been established for this publication.

2 If you do not have a *Projects* folder, create one now.

3 Choose Save As from the File menu, and in the Save publication as dialog box type **06Work** in the Name box, select the *Projects* folder, and click OK.

Placing the first graphic

You will begin by placing the large illustration, and positioning it in the top portion of the page. Inspired by the main facade of the Folies-Bergére in Paris, this illustration was created and colored in Adobe Illustrator, and saved as an EPS file.

1 Choose Place from the File menu (Command-D), and in the Place Document dialog box double-click the *06GraphicA* file in the *06Lesson* folder.

2 When prompted, click the No button to prevent duplicating the image data to the *06Work* publication.

3 With the graphics icon displayed, click the page to place the graphic.

4 Notice how the Colors palette displays the spot color PANTONE 129 CVC.

When you import an EPS graphic containing spot colors, Adobe PageMaker automatically lists the spot colors in the Colors palette.

Note: Since Adobe PostScript does not have a standard method of describing process color information, Adobe PageMaker does not list process colors imported in EPS files from other programs.

5 In the Control palette make sure the upper-left reference point in the Proxy icon is selected, type .625 inch in the X box and .75 inch in the Y box, and press the Return key to align the upper-left corner of the illustration with the specified coordinate position.

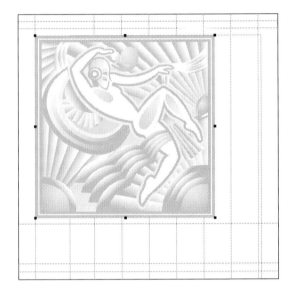

6 Choose Save from the File menu (Command-S).

Placing and positioning the Avril graphic

The characters that spell the word *Avril* were created and colored in Adobe Illustrator, and saved as an EPS file. As was mentioned before, *Avril* is the French word for April.

1 Choose Place from the File menu, and in the Place Document dialog box double-click the *06GraphicB* file in the *06Lesson* folder.

2 With the graphics icon displayed, click the upper-right corner of the page to place the illustration.

The Avril graphic has already been rotated on its side.

TIP: TO SELECT THE
CONSTRAINED-LINE
TOOL, HOLD DOWN
THE SHIFT KEY AND
PRESS THE F6 KEY.

3 In the Control palette make sure the upper-right reference point in the Proxy icon is selected, and type **8.875** inches in the X box and **.75** inch in the Y box, and press the Return key.

Upper-left reference point of the Proxy icon

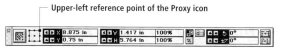

The Avril image is positioned to the right of the large illustration.

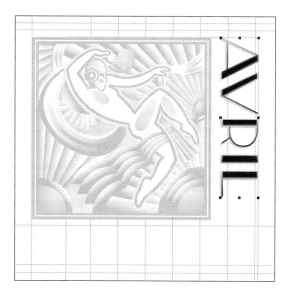

4 Choose Save from the File menu.

Drawing a double-segment line

You will use the constrained-line tool to draw a double-segment line.

1 Magnify the view of the entire page below the large illustration.

You begin by drawing a vertical line.

2 With the constrained-line tool selected in the toolbox, use the X and Y indicators in the Control palette to position the cursor on the coordinate position (1.875, 7.5), hold down the mouse button, and drag down to the 16-inch horizontal ruler guide, and release the mouse button to draw a line.

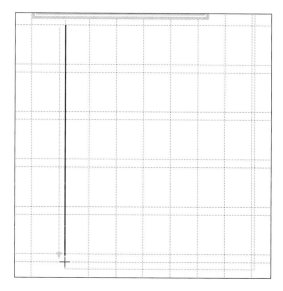

The left margin guide obscures the view of the line you just drew.

3 Choose Guides and Rulers from the Layout menu and Guides in Back from the submenu to display the left margin guide behind the line you just drew.

4 With the line still selected, choose Line from the Element menu and the .5-point line from the submenu to apply a line style and weight to the line.

Now you will draw the horizontal segment of the double-segment line.

5 With the constrained-line tool selected in the toolbox, position the cursor at the top end of the line you just drew, and drag to the right along the 7.5-inch horizontal ruler guide to the 2-inch mark on the horizontal ruler to draw a line.

6 With the line still selected, choose Line from the Element menu and the .5-point line from the submenu.

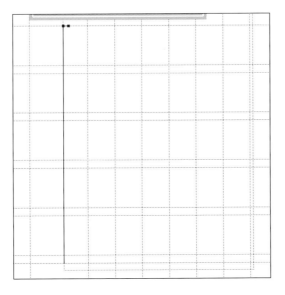

7 Choose Save from the File menu.

Creating the weekdays text

After entering the text Dimanche (Sunday in French), you will specify the font and size for the text, and then rotate and align the text using the Control palette. In most cases you would probably want to drag a text block to align text, but for this exercise using the Control palette to position the text will work as well.

1 With the text tool selected, drag to define a text block approximately one inch wide (exact height is not important), and type **dimanche** in lowercase letters.

2 With the text tool still selected, double-click the text dimanche to select it, and in the Control palette choose Myriad MM 830 Black 600 Normal from the font pop-up menu, type **12** points in the Size box, and click the Apply button.

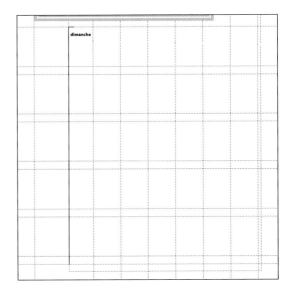

3 In the Control palette click the Paragraph-view button, and in the paragraph view of the Control palette click the Left-align button to align the text with the left edge of the text block.

Left-align button

4 With the pointer tool selected, click the text to select it as a text block; and in the Control palette make sure the center reference point in the Proxy icon is selected, type **-90** degrees in the Rotate box, and press the Return key.

Rotate box

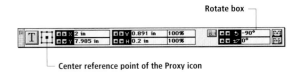

Center reference point of the Proxy icon

5 In the Control palette make sure the upper-right point of the Proxy icon is selected, and type **2.1** inches in the X box and **7.54** inches in the Y box, and press the Return key to move the text block.

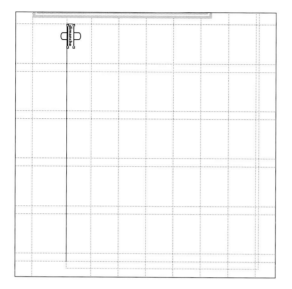

6 Choose Save from the File menu.

Using the Multiple Paste command

To save you the effort of drawing the repeating double-segment lines and positioning the remaining weekdays text, you will use the Multiple Paste command to do the work for you. The Multiple Paste command makes it possible to paste multiple copies of text or graphics elements. Like the Paste command, the Multiple Paste command copies whatever contents were last copied to the Clipboard.

1 Choose View from the Layout menu and Fit in Window from the submenu (Command-0).

2 Click the close box of the Control palette to close it, making it possible to view the lower portion of the page.

Since you cannot reverse multiple-paste actions using the Undo command, it's a good idea to save your work before choosing the Multiple Paste command, making it possible to choose the Revert command from the File menu to revert to the last-saved version of a publication. Since you just saved the *06Work* publication, you are ready to proceed.

3 With the pointer tool selected, drag to marquee select the two-segment line and the text, and choose Copy from the Edit menu (Command-C).

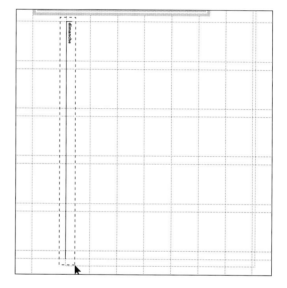

4 Choose Multiple Paste from the Edit menu, and in the Multiple Paste dialog box type **7** copies in the Paste box, **1** inch in the Horizontal offset box, and **0** inch in the Vertical offset box, and click OK.

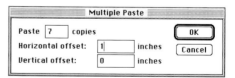

The seven copies are vertically aligned to the right of the original, one inch apart. The positive value entered in the Horizontal offset box in the Multiple Paste dialog box moved each copy one inch to the right, and the zero value in the Vertical offset box caused each copy to retain the original vertical position.

Note: Once you edit the seventh copy, it will serve to visually frame the right edge of the calendar design.

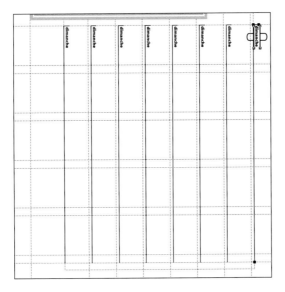

Note: Negative values entered in the Horizontal and Vertical offset boxes move copies to the left and up, respectively.

5 Choose Save from the File menu.

Replacing the copied weekday text

Now that the text and double-segment lines are in place, it's easy to select each copy of the weekday text *dimanche* (Sunday), and replace it with the correct weekday text.

1 Magnify the view of the copied weekday text.

2 With the text tool selected, double-click the first copy of weekday text to the right of the original to select it, and type **lundi** (Monday) in lowercase letters.

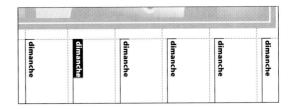

3 With the text tool still selected, double-click the second copy of weekday text, and type **mardi** (Tuesday) in lowercase letters.

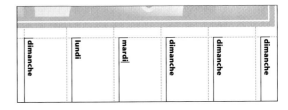

4 Double-click the third copy of text, and type **mercredi** (Wednesday) in lowercase letters.

5 Double-click the fourth copy of text, and type **jeudi** (Thursday) in lowercase letters.

6 Double-click the fifth copy of text, and type **vendredi** (Friday) in lowercase letters.

7 Double-click the sixth copy of text, and type **samedi** (Saturday) in lowercase letters.

You will modify the seventh (rightmost) copy, allowing only the vertical line segment to remain as a design element.

8 With the pointer tool selected, click the seventh (rightmost) copy of weekday text to select it as a text block, hold down the Shift key (to select multiple objects), click the rightmost horizontal line segment, and press the Delete key to delete the selected objects.

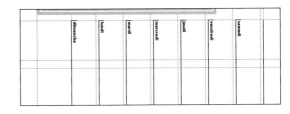

9 Choose Save from the File menu.

Placing and formatting the numbers text

After placing the numbers text, you will format the text and resize the text block.

1 Choose View from the Layout menu and Fit in Window from the submenu.

2 Choose Place from the File menu, and in the Place Document dialog box double-click the *06TextA* file in the *06Lesson* folder.

3 With the loaded text icon displayed, drag to define a .5-inch-wide text block (height not important) on the pasteboard to the left of the page to place the text.

4 With the text tool selected, click the placed text to establish an insertion point, and choose Select All from the Edit menu to select the entire story.

5 Choose Control palette from the Window menu (Command-') to open the Control palette.

6 In the Control palette click the Right-align button to align the numbers text to the right edge of the text block.

7 In the Control palette click the Character-view button, and in the character view of the Control palette choose Bernhard Modern Roman from the Font pop-up menu, type **26** points in the Size box, and click the Apply button.

8 If necessary, click the numbers text with the pointer tool, and adjust the width of the text block to be more closely aligned with the left edge of the text.

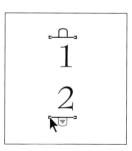

9 Choose Save from the File menu.

Positioning the text block

After dragging the text block onto the page, you will align the text block in the designated calendar grid position.

1 With the pointer tool selected, click the numbers text to select it as a text block, and drag the text block just to the left of the weekdays text.

2 With the zoom tool selected in the toolbox, drag to marquee select the middle section of the page, magnifying the view of the weekdays and the first two weeks of the month.

3 With the pointer tool selected, click the numbers text to select it as a text block, drag the bottom windowshade handle up until only the first line of text (the number 1) of the story is displayed.

4 Choose Guides and Rulers from the Layout menu and Snap to Guides from the submenu (Shift key, Command key-G) to select it, making sure it is checked.

Activating the Snap to Guides option will help you align the individual text blocks in the calendar grid.

5 With the numbers text still selected as a text block, drag the text block to the first grid position below the text *mardi* (Tuesday), aligning the baseline of the first line of text with the 9.203-inch horizontal ruler guide, with the right edge aligned with the 4.766-inch vertical ruler guide.

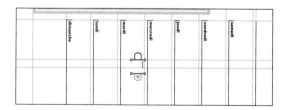

Note: If necessary, press the arrow keys (or click the nudge buttons in the Control palette) to align the text block.

6 Choose Save from the File menu.

Threading text blocks

Using the ruler guides that are provided, you will thread each line of the numbers text by dragging to define the remaining 29 text blocks.

1 With the pointer tool selected, click the numbers text to select it as a text block, and click the red down arrow in the bottom windowshade handle to load the remaining text.

2 With the loaded text icon displayed, position the cursor at the intersection of the Mercredi (Wednesday) vertical line and the top horizontal ruler guide in the grid, and drag to define a text block that extends to the lower-right corner of the grid position as shown in the illustration below.

 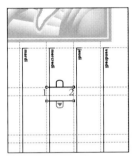

If you succeeded in aligning the right edge of the text block with the 5.766-inch vertical ruler guide, the right edge of the number 2 should also be roughly aligned with the same vertical ruler guide (because the text is formatted to be right-aligned).

Note: As you drag to define a text block to be aligned with ruler guides, the edges of the text block are displayed in red when precisely aligned with the ruler guides.

3 Again, click the red down arrow in the bottom windowshade handle to load the remaining text, and drag to define a text block in the *jeudi* (Thursday) grid position.

4 Repeat the previous step until all thirty numbers are placed in the calendar, using the horizontal and vertical ruler guides that are provided.

dimanche	lundi	mardi	mercredi	jeudi	vendredi	samedi
			1	2	3	4	5
6	7	8	9	10	11	12
13	14	15	16	17	18	19
20	21	22	23	24	25	26
27	28	29	30			

Note: An interim file was saved at this point. To open it, double-click the 06Int1 *file in the* Extras *folder.*

Although this exercise may have seemed repetitious, this lesson will demonstrate the advantage of this approach when creating the next month.

Note: If the text blocks you define for the double-digit numbers are not wide enough for both numbers, Adobe PageMaker will either tighten the tracking (letter spacing) between the numbers or display only one digit of the number.

5 Choose Save from the File menu.

Grouping the numbers text blocks

Now that all text blocks are positioned in the month, take a moment to protect your work by grouping the numbers text blocks together.

1 Choose View from the Layout menu and Fit in Window from the submenu, and make sure the Control palette does not obscure the view of the numbers text.

2 With the pointer tool selected, drag to mar-quee select all numbers text blocks.

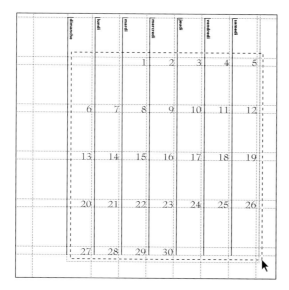

3 Choose Group from the Arrange menu (Command-G) to group selected text blocks into a single entity.

To better organize your work space, grouping the text blocks will maintain the relative alignment of the text blocks, even if you accidentally move the group.

4 Choose Save from the File menu.

Drawing a line

You will draw a single horizontal line that anchors the bottom edge of the calendar design, aligning it with the bottom margin guide.

1 Magnify the view of the bottom portion of the entire page.

2 With the constrained-line tool selected in the toolbox, position the cursor on the left margin guide (aligned with the leftmost vertical hairline) and the bottom margin guide, and drag to draw a line that extends to the right margin guide.

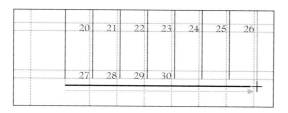

3 Choose Line from the Element menu and the 5-point double line (heavy over light) from the submenu to apply a line style and weight.

4 Choose Save from the File menu.

Placing a graphic and a caption

You will place an illustration and caption in the lower-left corner of the calendar. Inspired by the figure that appeared on the entrance doors to the auditorium at Vierzon, this illustration was created in Adobe Illustrator, and saved as an EPS file.

1 Choose Place from the File menu, and in the Place Document dialog box double-click the *06GraphicC* file in the *06Lesson* folder.

2 With the graphics icon displayed, click the lower-left corner of the page to place the illustration.

3 In the Control palette make sure the upper-right reference point in the Proxy icon is selected, type **1.754** inches in the X box and **10.87** inches in the Y box, and press the Return key.

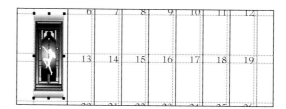

4 Choose Place from the File menu, and in the Place Document dialog box double-click the *06TextB* file in the *06Lesson* folder.

5 With the loaded text icon displayed, click below the small illustration to place the text.

Note: In English the caption reads: Illustrations inspired by the auditorium at Vierzon and the main facade of the Folies-Bergére in Paris glamorized cinemas and theatres.

6 With the caption text selected as a text block, in the Control palette type **1.142** in the Width box, and press the Return key to resize the text block.

7 Magnify the view of the small illustration and the caption text.

8 With the pointer tool selected, click the caption text to select it as a text block, and drag the bottom windowshade handle to display the entire story.

9 In the Control palette make sure the upper-left reference point in the Proxy icon is selected, type .61 inch in the X box and 14 inches in the Y box, and press the Return key to move the text block.

10 With the text tool selected, triple-click the caption text to select it.

11 In the Control palette choose Myriad MM 215 Light 600 Normal from the font pop-up menu, type 7.5 points in the Size box and 12 points in the Leading box, and click the All caps button.

12 In the Control palette click the Paragraph-view button, and in the paragraph view of the Control palette click the Right-align button to align the text with the right edge of the text block.

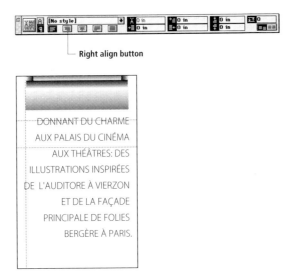

Right align button

13 Choose Save from the File menu.

Using the Control palette to draw a line

To enhance the design, you will use the Control palette to draw a line below the caption, applying a 60% tint of black to the line.

1 With the constrained-line tool selected in the toolbox, position the cursor below the caption text, and hold down the mouse button until the cursor is displayed as a crosshair.

2 With the mouse button still held down, use the Width indicator in the Control palette to draw a line that is approximately .5 inch wide, and release the mouse button.

Note: If you drag too quickly, the Control palette will not display the dimensions.

3 With the line still selected, in the Control palette make sure the right reference point in the Proxy icon is selected, type 1.746 inches in the X box and 15.398 inches in the Y box, and press the Return key to move the line.

4 Choose Line from the Element menu and the 4-point line from the submenu.

5 In the Colors palette click the Line button, make sure Black is selected, and choose 60% from the Tint pop-up menu to apply the color gray to the line.

6 Choose Save from the File menu.

Power pasting the banner lines

After drawing a horizontal line that will frame the banner text (not yet placed) above the large illustration, you will power paste a copy of the double line. When an object is power pasted, the pasted object is aligned with the copied object, providing a positioning shortcut for some situations.

1 Choose View from the Layout menu and Fit in Window from the submenu, and then magnify the view of the entire page above the large illustration.

2 With the constrained-line tool selected in the toolbox, position the cursor on the left edge of the page, aligned with the .25-inch (top) horizontal ruler guide, and drag to draw a line that extends to the right edge of the page.

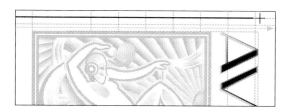

3 Choose Line from the Element menu and the 5-point double line (heavy over light) from the submenu.

4 With the line still selected, choose Copy from the Edit menu, hold down the Option key (to specify the pasted object be aligned with the copied object), and choose Paste from the Edit menu.

The pasted line is precisely aligned with the original line.

Before positioning the pasted line, you will apply a complementary line style (light over heavy) to it.

5 With the pasted line still selected, choose Line from the Element menu and the 5-point double line (light over heavy) from the submenu.

6 Hold down the Shift key (to constrain the movement to 45°), and drag the pasted line until it is aligned with the .547-inch horizontal ruler guide.

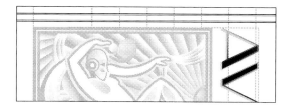

7 Choose Save from the File menu.

Placing the banner text

After placing the banner text, you will format and align it between the double lines.

1 Choose Place from the File menu, and in the Place Document dialog box double-click the *06TextC* file in the *06Lesson* folder.

2 With the loaded text icon displayed, drag to define a text block that extends from the .625-inch vertical ruler guide to the right margin guide, above the double lines (exact height is not important) to place the text.

Note: In English the banner reads: 1997 Lyon Exposition of Art Deco Architecture and Decorative Arts.

3 With the text tool selected, triple-click the banner text to select it, and in the Control palette choose Myriad MM 830 Black 700 Semiextended from the font pop-up menu, type **12.5** points in the Size box and **.05** em space in the Kerning box, and click the All caps button.

4 In the Control palette click the Paragraph-view button, and in the paragraph view of the Control palette click the Force-justify button to force the text to be aligned with the left and right edges of the text block.

5 With the text still selected, in the Colors palette make sure Black is selected, and choose 60% from the Tint pop-up menu.

6 With the pointer tool selected, click the banner text to select it as a text block, and press the up and down arrow keys (or click the nudge buttons in the Control palette) until the text is vertically centered between the pair of double-lines.

7 As a finishing touch, select the text tool, drag to select the word EXPOSITION, and in the Colors palette make sure Black is selected, and choose 100% from the Tint pop-up menu.

8 Continue repeating this step for the remaining alternating words L'ARCHITECTURE, DÉCO, DES, DÉCORATIFS, LYON, and 1997, applying the color black to each one.

This month is complete, and you are ready to create the next month.

9 Choose View from the Layout menu and Fit in Window from the submenu to view the entire page.

10 Choose Save from the File menu.

ASSEMBLING THE SECOND MONTH

The following steps are designed to save you as much effort as possible in assembling the month *Mai* (May in French), allowing you to modify the month and days using most of the text and graphics elements already in place for the assembled month.

Inserting a page

After inserting a page in the publication, you will power paste the text and graphics elements from the first page to the second page.

1 With the pointer tool selected, choose Select All from the Edit menu to select all text and graphics elements on the page.

2 Choose Copy from the Edit menu to copy the selection to the Clipboard.

3 Choose Insert Pages from the Layout menu, and in the Insert Pages dialog box make sure 1 page is displayed in the Insert page(s) box, and click the Insert button.

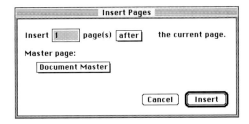

The publication window displays the inserted page.

4 Hold down the Option key (to specify the pasted object be aligned with the copied object), and choose Paste from the Edit menu to paste the contents of the Clipboard to the inserted page.

The pasted text and graphics elements are aligned on the second page.

5 Choose Save from the File menu.

Replacing the large illustration graphic

The following steps demonstrate how to use the Place command to replace the large illustration with another image. Like the first illustration, this image was created in Adobe Illustrator, and saved as an EPS file.

1 With the pointer tool selected, click the large illustration to select it.

2 Choose Place from the File menu, and in the Place Document dialog box *single*-click the *06GraphicD* file in the *06Lesson* folder to select it, click the Replacing entire graphic radio button to select it, and click OK.

3 If prompted, click the No button to prevent duplicating the image data to the *06Work* publication.

4 Choose Save from the File menu.

Replacing the Avril graphic

The following steps demonstrate how to use the Place command to replace the Avril graphic with the Mai graphic. Like the Avril graphic, the Mai image was created in Adobe Illustrator, and saved as an EPS file.

1 With the pointer tool still selected, click the Avril graphic in the upper-right portion of the page to select it.

2 Choose Place from the File menu, and in the Place Document dialog box *single*-click the *06GraphicE* file in the *06Lesson* folder to select it, click the Replacing entire graphic radio button to select it, and click OK.

The page is displayed with the Mai graphic in place of the Avril graphic. Since the Avril graphic is taller than the Mai graphic, the Mai graphic has been stretched to fill the boundaries of the Avril graphic.

3 With the Mai graphic selected, in the Control palette make sure the upper-right reference point in the Proxy icon is selected (to maintain the alignment of the upper-right corner of the graphic), type **100%** in the Height and Width Percent scaling boxes, and click the Return key to resize the graphic to its original size.

Width percent scaling box ⌐

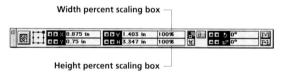

Height percent scaling box ⌐

4 Choose Save from the File menu.

Replacing the small illustration graphic

You are ready to use the Place command to re-place the small illustration with another image.

1 Magnify the view of the lower-left portion of the page, including the small illustration and the caption below it.

2 With the pointer tool selected, click the small illustration in the lower-left portion of the page to select it.

3 Choose Place from the File menu, and in the Place Document dialog box *single*-click the *06GraphicF* file in the *06Lesson* folder to select it, click the Replacing entire graphic radio button to select it, and click OK.

4 Choose Save from the File menu.

Correcting an uneven rag

After replacing the caption text with another caption, you will insert a soft-carriage return and a hyphen to improve the appearance of an uneven rag along the left edge of the caption text.

Note: The term rag refers the uneven edge of unjustified text, as opposed to the even (or flush) edge of justified text.

1 With the pointer tool selected, click the caption text below the small illustration to select it as a text block.

2 Choose Place from the File menu, and in the Place Document dialog box *single*-click the *06TextD* file in the *06Lesson* folder to select it, click the Replacing entire story radio button to select it, and click OK.

Note: In English the caption reads: These illustrations show the exuberant figures that served to glamorize modern architecture, appearing on the facades of many buildings.

You are ready to format the new caption text.

3 With the text tool selected, triple-click the new caption text to select it.

4 In the Control palette click the Right-align button to align the text to the right edge of the text block.

5 In the Control palette click the Character-view button, and in the character view of the Control palette choose Myriad MM 215 Light 600 Normal from the font pop-up menu, type **7.5** points in the Size box and **12** points in the Leading box, and click the All caps button.

Now that the new caption text is formatted, you will add a soft-carriage return and a hyphen to improve the appearance of the rag.

6 With the text tool still selected, click to the left of the word *charme* in the sixth line of the caption text to establish an insertion point, hold down the Shift key (to specify a soft-carriage return), and press the Return key.

The word *charme* is positioned at the beginning of the seventh line.

7 With the text tool still selected, click between the letters i and t in the word *L'Architecture* in the eighth line of text to establish an insertion point, and type - (hyphen).

The first portion of the word *L'Architecture* moves from the eighth to the seventh line of text. When you type a regular hyphen in a word, that hyphen appears even when the word does not fall at the end of a line.

Note: Adobe PageMaker makes it possible to specify a discretionary hyphen, where a hyphen is inserted only when the word falls at the end of a line. To specify a discretionary hyphen, click to establish an insertion point, hold down the Command key (to specify a discretionary hyphen), and type - (hyphen).

8 Choose Save from the File menu.

Re-threading text blocks to modify the days of the month
Since the first day of May falls on Thursday, you will re-thread the numbers text blocks to reflect the thirty-one days of May.

1 Scroll to view the first week of the month.

2 With the pointer tool selected, hold down the Command key (to select an object within a group), click the number text 1 to select it as a text block, and drag the bottom windowshade handle to the top windowshade handle.

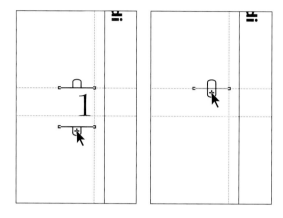

The number text 1 is displayed in the Mercredi (Wednesday) grid position.

3 Again, with the pointer tool selected, hold down the Command key (to allow you to select an object within a group), click the number text 1 to select it as a text block, and drag the bottom windowshade handle to the top windowshade handle.

The number text 1 is displayed in the Jeudi (Thursday) grid position, the correct position.

The last text block displays two lines of number text 28 and 29.

Note: As soon as you select another tool or object, the closed text block is no longer displayed.

4 With the pointer tool still selected, hold down the Command key (to allow you to select an object within a group), click the number text 28 to select it as a text block, drag the bottom windowshade handle up to display a single line of text, and click the red down arrow in the bottom windowshade handle to load the remaining text.

5 With the loaded text icon displayed, drag to define a text block that is aligned with the grid position to the right of the number text 28.

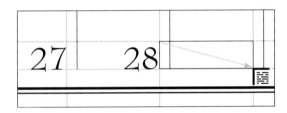

6 Again, with the number text 29 selected as a text block, click the red down arrow in the bottom windowshade handle to load the remaining text, and drag to define a text block in the next grid position.

Since the publication did not display the entire numbers story (all 31 numbers), the copy and paste operation copied and pasted the visible numbers 1-30 only. For this reason, you will add the number 31 to the pasted story.

7 With the text tool selected, click after the number 30 to establish an insertion point, press the Return key (to insert a hard-carriage return), and type **31**.

8 With the pointer tool selected, click the number text 30 to select it as a text block, and drag the bottom windowshade handle until one line of text is displayed, click the red down arrow in the bottom windowshade handle to load the remaining text, and drag to define a text block in the next grid position.

9 Choose Save from the File menu.

Note: In addition to advancing a threaded story, you can reverse this operation by selecting the first text block with the pointer tool, clicking the top windowshade handle to load the text, and dragging to define a text block that will display the first line of the story.

Locking the text and graphics elements

Now that you are finished assembling the calendar, take a moment to protect your work by locking the position of the text and graphics elements in the publication.

1 Choose View from the Layout menu and Fit in Window from the submenu to view the entire publication.

2 Click the pointer tool in the toolbox to make sure nothing is selected, and choose Select All from the Edit menu to select all text and graphics elements on the page.

3 Choose Lock Position from the Arrange menu (Command-L) to lock the selected objects, preventing you from accidentally moving them.

4 Click page icon 1 to view the first page.

5 Choose Select All from the Edit menu, and choose Lock Position from the Arrange menu.

You have completed this lesson.

6 Choose Guides and Rulers from the Layout menu and Show Guides from the submenu to hide the column, ruler, and margin guides used to assemble this calendar.

7 Choose Save from the File menu to save the *06Work* publication.

If you have determined that your service provider will perform the prepress tasks, you are ready to deliver the *06Work* file to your service provider. Be sure to include all image files that are linked to the publication.

8 Close all open publications, and choose Quit from the File menu (Command-Q) to exit the Adobe PageMaker program.

PRINTING THE CALENDAR

In addition to constructing bleeds, the prepress tasks will include specifying a custom paper size and including printer's marks (cropping marks) and page information. Whenever a publication includes bleeds, you must specify a custom paper size that is larger than the final page size of the publication to provide enough space for the printer's marks and page information. For more information on these prepress tasks, refer to the *Adobe PageMaker 6.0 User Guide* and the *Adobe Print Publishing Guide*.

Since this calendar incorporates the color black and two spot colors, your service provider must create a total of three spot-color film separations. Knowing your printer plans to print this publication with a line screen frequency of 150 lpi, your service provider will create the film separations on a imagesetter with a resolution of 2400 dpi. Once the film separations are created, you can deliver them to your printer.

Note: To achieve the best results when printing EPS images (like the images found in this publication), print to a PostScript printing device.

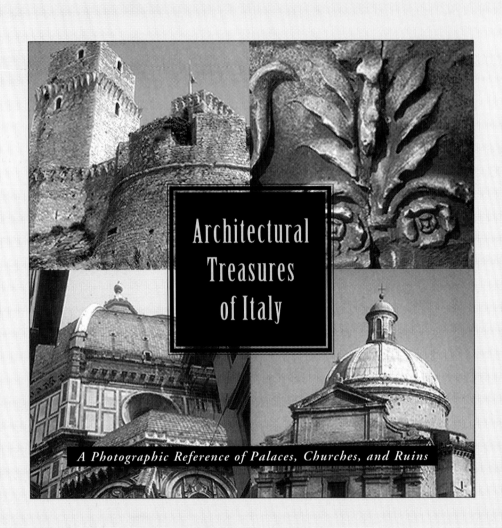

Architectural Treasures of Italy

A Photographic Reference of Palaces, Churches, and Ruins

• ITALY •

In this lesson you will create the 6-page booklet titled *The Architectural Treasures of Italy*. Featuring eight color photographs of historic Italy, the publication requirements

JEWELCASE BOOKLET

of this booklet dictate it be printed on a printing press. ■ To print color art on a commercial printing press, your service provider will separate each page containing composite art into its component colors by creating a film separation on an imagesetter for each ink-cyan, magenta, yellow, black (CMYK), and any spot colors-with each spot color requiring an individual film separation. A commercial printer uses these process color (and spot color) film separations to create the printing plates used on the press.

Designed to accompany a CD-ROM disc, this publication must be sized to fit in the front cover of a CD-ROM jewelcase. It's easy to get the right dimensions, because the Adobe PageMaker application includes a page size already established

JEWELCASE BOOKLET

for this exact purpose. Before printing this booklet on a commercial printing press, you must specify a custom paper size larger than the page size to accommodate the printer's marks (cropping marks) and page information.

This lesson covers:

• Specifying columns of unequal width

• Creating a bordered box

• Reversing text out of a box

• Adding rules to a paragraph

• Flowing text semiautomatically

• Modifying an image using the Image Control command.

BEFORE YOU BEGIN

All files and fonts needed to assemble this booklet are found on the Adobe PageMaker *Classroom in a Book* CD-ROM disc in the folders *07Lesson* and *Fonts*, respectively. In addition, the *Extras* folder on the *Classroom in a Book* CD-ROM disc includes the *07Int1* file, an interim file of artwork that you may wish to use.

It should take you approximately 90 minutes to complete this lesson.

Opening an existing document

Let's take a look at the final version of the booklet you will create in this lesson.

1 Before launching the Adobe PageMaker program, throw away the *Adobe PageMaker 6.0 Prefs* file to return all settings to their default values.

2 Make sure the fonts Adobe Garamond Regular, Adobe Garamond Semibold, Adobe Garamond Semibold Italic, and Birch are installed.

3 Double-click the *Adobe® PageMaker® 6.0* icon to launch the Adobe PageMaker program.

4 Choose Open from the File menu (Command-O), and in the Open Publication dialog box double-click the *07Final* file in the *07Lesson* folder.

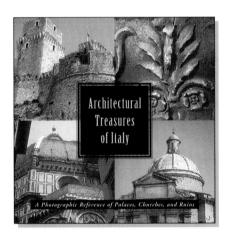

The full view of the first page displays a variety of text and graphic elements, and the page icons indicate the booklet consists of six pages.

5 Click the page icons to page through the booklet, and then click page icon 1 to display the first page.

6 Choose Guides and Rulers from the Layout menu and Show Guides from the submenu (Command-J) to display the guides used to assemble this booklet.

Talk with your printer

Designed to be printed on a commercial printing press, this booklet features images that were saved as CMYK TIFF files, making it possible to process CMYK data to a CMYK imagesetter (to create the film separations).

To reduce the demand for disk space on your system, these images were scanned at a resolution of 100 dpi. Since it is likely that your printer would recommend printing this sort of publication at a

TIP: TO OPEN THE PREFERENCES DIALOG BOX, DOUBLE-CLICK THE POINTER TOOL IN THE TOOLBOX.

line screen frequency of 150 lpi, in a real environment these images would have to be scanned at 300 dpi (double the selected line screen frequency) to meet the printing requirements of this publication.

As was discussed in an earlier lesson, any adjacent colored objects in a design will require trapping. After verifying the trapping specification, the size of the bleed, and the line screen frequency with your printer, talk with your service provider to determine who will perfom the prepress tasks and how you should deliver this publication to your service provider.

ASSEMBLING THE MASTER PAGE

For these left and right master pages, you will specify column guides, create graphics elements, and specify automatic page numbering.

Opening a new publication

After setting the options in the Document Setup dialog box, you will save and name your publication.

1 Choose New from the File menu (Command-N), and in the Document Setup dialog box choose Compact disc from the Page size pop-up menu, type **6** pages in the Number of pages box, type **.25** inch in the Inside box, **.25** inch in the Outside box, **.333** inch in the Top box, and **.333** inch in the Bottom box to set the margin guides, and click OK.

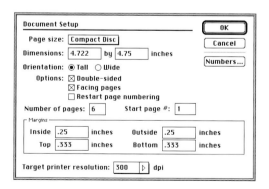

The publication window displays the first page of the untitled publication with the specified page dimensions and margin guides. Unless you specify otherwise, page number 1 of a double-sided publication is assigned to the first right page in the publication.

2 If you do not have a *Projects* folder, create one now.

3 Choose Save As from the File menu, and in the Save Publication As dialog box type **07Work** in the Name box, select the *Projects* folder, and click OK.

4 Click page icon 2/3 to view the second and third facing pages.

The zero point is aligned with the intersection of the top, inside edges of the facing pages.

Note: In previous lessons, you assembled single-sided publications, where the zero point is aligned with the upper-left corner of the page.

Establishing the measurement system

Because you use the rulers to set up your layout grid, it's a good idea to choose a measurement system before you begin laying out your pages.

1 Choose Preferences from the File menu, and in the Preferences dialog box choose Picas from the Measurements in pop-up menu and Picas from the Vertical ruler menu, and click OK.

Specifying columns of unequal width

As you have already seen, Adobe PageMaker automatically creates columns of equal width when you specify multiple columns. In this lesson you will create unequal columns, using the pointer tool to drag the column guides to the positions you want.

1 Click master-page icon L/R in the lower-left corner of the publication window.

Adobe PageMaker displays the facing master pages and highlights the master-page icon. The facing master pages also display the margin guides you specified in the Document Setup dialog box, with the zero point still aligned with the intersection of the top, inside edges of the facing pages.

2 Choose Column Guides from the Layout menu, and in the Column Guides dialog box type **2** columns in the Number of columns box, click the left and right pages separately check box (to see how you can specify different numbers of columns on the left and right pages), and click OK.

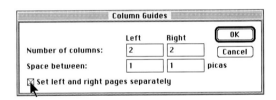

Adobe PageMaker automatically creates columns of equal widths, filling the entire image area between the margin guides.

3 With the pointer tool selected, position the cursor on the left column guide of the gutter on the right master page, hold down the mouse button, drag the column guide until it is aligned approximately with the 15p mark on the horizontal ruler (using the X indicator in the Control palette), and release the mouse button.

Note: The gutter is the vertical space between columns.

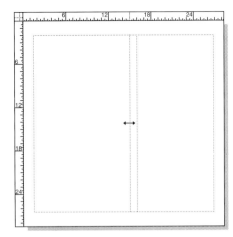

4 Drag the left column guide of the gutter on the left master page until it is aligned with the -13p6 mark on the horizontal ruler (using the X indicator in the Control palette).

Note: Since the left page is positioned to the left of the zero point, all X coordinate values for the left page are less than or equal to zero.

5 Choose Save from the File menu (Command-S).

Drawing a circle

After drawing a small circle, you will use the Control palette to resize it, and the Colors palette to fill it with the color black.

1 Magnify the lower-left portion of the left master page.

2 With the ellipse tool selected in the toolbox, hold down the Shift key (to constrain the ellipse to a circle), and drag to draw a small circle of any dimension.

3 In the Control palette make sure the Proportional-scaling button is selected, type **1p2** in the Width box (or the Height box), and press the Return key to resize the circle.

Proportional-scaling button ⌐

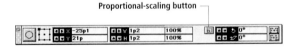

4 In the Colors palette click the Both button, and click Black to apply the color black to the line and fill of the circle.

Placed on the master pages, the circle will serve to frame the page numbers.

5 Choose Save from the File menu.

Specifying automatic numbering

To automatically number all pages in a publication, you can place page-number markers on the master pages. After specifying automatic page numbering on the left page, you will copy and paste the circle and the page-number marker to the right page, and reverse the colors.

1 With the text tool selected, drag to define a text block overlapping the black circle that is approximately 4p wide (exact height is not important), establishing an insertion point.

2 Hold down the Command and Option keys, and press the P key.

The page-number marker LM (left master) is displayed over the black circle, indicating where the page numbers will appear.

3 With the text tool selected, double-click the page-number marker LM to select it, and in the Control palette choose Adobe Garamond Semibold from the Font pop-up, type **9** points in the Size box, and click the Apply button.

4 In the Colors palette click Paper to apply the color paper to the page-number marker.

5 With the pointer tool selected, click the page-number marker LM to select it as a text block, and drag the text block to visually center the letter L in the black circle.

6 If necessary, reduce the size of the text block, by dragging a right corner handle until it is roughly aligned with the right edge of the LM text.

7 With the pointer tool selected, drag to marquee select the black circle and the page-number marker, and in the Control palette make sure the center reference point in the Proxy icon is selected, type -26p6 in the X box and **26p11** in the Y box, and press the Return key to align the center of the group with the specified coordinate position.

8 Choose Save from the File menu.

Power pasting the page-number marker

Since your publication has facing pages, you will copy and power paste the left page-number marker, and drag the pasted copy to the right master page.

1 With the pointer tool selected, drag to marquee select the black circle and the page-number marker.

2 Choose Copy from the Edit menu (Command-C), hold down the Option key (to specify a power paste), and choose Paste from the Edit menu (Command-V) to paste a copy of the group directly overlapping the original selection.

3 With the pasted selection selected, hold down the Shift key (to constrain the movement to 45°), and drag the pasted selection to the lower-right corner of the right master page.

Now that the page-number marker is positioned on a right master page, the page-number marker is automatically displayed as RM (right master).

Note: Page-number markers positioned on the pasteboard are displayed as PB (pasteboard).

TIP: TO FIND WHITE TEXT ON A WHITE BACK-GROUND, SELECT THE POINTER TOOL, CHOOSE SELECT ALL FROM THE EDIT MENU, AND DRAG THE TEXT BLOCK TO A DARK BACKGROUND.

4 With the black circle and the page-number marker still selected, in the Control palette make sure the center reference point in the Proxy icon is selected, type **26p6** in the X box and **26p11** in the Y box, and press the Return key.

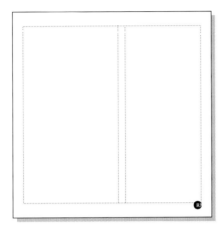

Since the circle and the page-number marker will be positioned on a black box, you will reverse the colors of both objects.

5 With the text tool selected, double-click the page-number marker RM to select it, and in the Control palette click the Reverse button to reverse the text from the color paper to the color black.

Selecting the Reverse option causes the selected text to toggle between the color paper and the color black.

6 With the pointer tool selected, click the black circle, and in the Colors palette click Paper.

7 Choose Save from the File menu.

Drawing a box

After creating the box that fills the right side of the right master page, you will fill it with the color black and adjust the stacking order to stack the black box behind the circle and the page-number marker.

1 Choose View from the Layout menu and Fit in Window from the submenu (Command-0).

2 With the rectangle tool selected in the toolbox, draw a box of any dimension on the right master page.

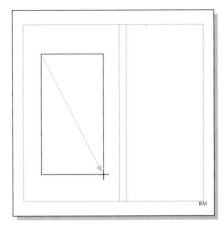

3 In the Control palette make sure a corner (or the center) reference point in the Proxy icon is selected, make sure the Proportional-scaling button is deselected, type **9p6** in the Width box and **28p6** in the Height box, and press the Return key.

4 In the Colors palette click the Both button, and click Black to apply the color black to the line and fill of the box.

5 With the pointer tool selected, drag the box to align its right edge with the outside (right) edge of the right master page, with its top and bottom edges aligned with the top and bottom edges of the right master page.

The black box overlaps the white circle and page-number marker.

6 Choose Send to Back from the Arrange menu (Command-B) to stack the black box behind the circle and the page-number marker.

The master-page design is complete, and you are ready to assemble the booklet cover.

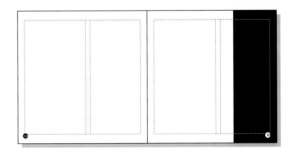

7 Choose Save from the File menu.

ASSEMBLING THE BOOKLET COVER

After hiding the display of the master-page elements on the first page (booklet cover), you will divide the page into four quadrants, place four photographs, and create the boxed text and subtitle text.

Hiding the display of master-page elements

Since it is possible to display master-page elements on a page-by-page basis, you will deselect the display of the master-page elements for the cover of the booklet.

1 Click page icon 1 to view the front cover of the booklet.

Since master-page elements are automatically displayed on each page of the publication, the first page of the publication is displayed with all master-page elements found on the right master page.

You can easily hide master-page elements on a particular page in your publication, provided it is the current page.

2 With the first page still selected, choose Display Master Items from the Layout menu to deselect it, making sure it is unchecked.

The text and graphics elements that you created are not displayed, and the nonprinting guides (margin, column, and ruler) are not affected. If you were to print this page, none of the master-page elements would be printed.

Placing and cropping a graphic

After dividing the front cover into four quadrants, you will place a photograph into each quadrant. The photographs were prepared in Adobe Photoshop by applying a single color to a grayscale TIFF image, and then sizing and saving each image in TIFF file format at a resolution of 100 dpi.

1 From the horizontal ruler, drag to create a horizontal ruler guide at approximately 14p3, and from the vertical ruler, drag to create a vertical ruler guide at approximately 14p2, dividing the booklet cover into four quadrants.

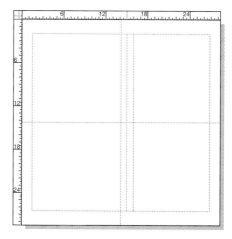

To make it a little easier to align the four photographs on the cover, you will move the zero point (the intersection of the horizontal and vertical rulers) from the upper-left corner of the page until it is aligned with the center of the page.

2 With the pointer tool selected, position the cursor on the crosshair of the zero point, and drag it until the zero point is aligned with the intersection of the ruler guides you just created.

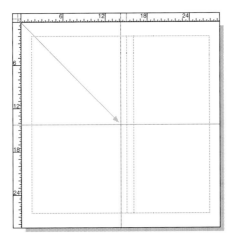

3 Choose Place from the File menu (Command-D), and in the Place Document dialog box double-click the *07GraphicA* file in the *07Lesson* folder.

4 With the graphics icon displayed, click the upper-left portion of the page to place the photograph.

Since the photographs extend to the edges of the page, each photograph was sized to allow for a bleed to overlap the edges of the page. For the sake of viewing the actual design of the cover, you will crop each photograph to be aligned with the edges of the page.

5 In the Control palette make sure the lower-right reference point in the Proxy icon is selected, type **0** in the X box and **0** in the Y box, and press the Return key to align the lower-right corner of the photograph with the zero point.

To better view the design itself, you will crop the photograph, aligning its edges with the edges of the page.

6 With the cropping tool selected in the toolbox, position the cursor over the upper-left graphics handle of the photograph, making sure the graphics handle shows through the center of the cropping tool, and hold down the mouse button until the cursor is displayed as a double-headed arrow.

7 With the mouse button still held down, drag down and right to the upper-left corner of the page, and release the mouse button, cropping the view of the photograph.

Before printing this article, you would undo the cropping, allowing for the image to overlap the edges of the page. For more information on creating a bleed, refer to the *Adobe Print Publishing Guide.*

Placing and cropping the three remaining graphics

As you place the three remaining photographs on the cover, crop each one to be aligned with the edges of the page.

1 Choose Place from the File menu, and in the Place Document dialog box double-click the *07GraphicB* file in the *07Lesson* folder.

2 With the graphics icon displayed, click the upper-right portion of the page to place the photograph; and in the Control palette make sure the lower-left reference point in the Proxy icon is selected, type **0** in the X box and **0** in the Y box, and press the Return key.

3 With the cropping tool selected, position the cursor over the upper-right graphics handle of the photograph, and drag down and left to the upper-right corner of the page to crop the view of the photograph.

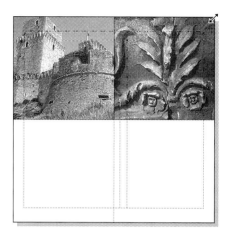

4 Choose Place from the File menu, and in the Place Document dialog box double-click the *07GraphicC* file in the *07Lesson* folder.

5 With the graphics icon displayed, click the lower-left portion of the page to place the photograph; and in the Control palette make sure the upper-right reference point in the Proxy icon is selected, type **0** in the X box and **0** in the Y box, and press the Return key.

6 With the cropping tool selected, position the cursor over the lower-left graphics handle, and drag up and right to the lower-left corner of the page.

7 Choose Place from the File menu, and in the Place Document dialog box double-click the *07GraphicD* file in the *07Lesson* folder.

8 With the graphics icon displayed, click the lower-right portion of the page to place the photograph; and in the Control palette make sure the upper-left reference point in the Proxy icon is selected, type **0** in the X box and **0** in the Y box, and press the Return key.

9 With the cropping tool selected, position the cursor over the lower-right graphics handle, and drag up and left to the lower-right corner of the page.

10 Choose Select All from the Edit menu to select the four photographs, choose Group from the Arrange menu, and then choose Lock Position from the Arrange menu to protect the alignment of the photographs.

11 Choose Save from the File menu.

Creating a bordered box for the title text

After drawing a bordered box, you will enter the text that is enclosed in the box and align the text to be centered.

1 With the rectangle tool selected in the toolbox, drag to draw a box of any dimension in the center of the page.

2 In the Control palette make sure the center reference point in the Proxy icon is selected, type **0** in the X box and **0** in the Y box, **9p7** in the Width box and **9p7** in the Height box, and press the Return key to resize and center the box.

3 In the Colors palette click Black to apply the color black to the line and fill of the box.

4 Choose Line from the Element menu and the 6-point triple line from the submenu to apply a triple line style to the line of the box, creating a border.

5 Choose Save from the File menu.

Defining process colors

You will use the Define Colors command to add two process colors to the Colors palette.

1 Choose Define Colors from the Element menu, and in the Define Colors dialog box click the Remove unused button, and when prompted, click the Yes to all button to remove all unused colors.

2 In the Define Colors dialog box click the New button, and in the Edit Color dialog box type **Sand** in the Name box, and enter the following CMYK values:

Cyan 0%
Magenta 5%
Yellow 27%
Black 7%

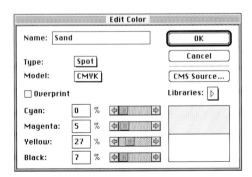

3 In the Edit Color dialog box click OK, and in the Define Colors dialog box click the New button.

4 In the Edit Color dialog box type **Dark blue** in the Name box, and enter the following CMYK values:

Cyan 45%
Magenta 20%
Yellow 0%
Black 60%

5 In the Edit Color dialog box click OK, and in the Define Colors dialog box click OK to close it.

The Colors palette displays the colors Dark blue and Sand.

6 Choose Save from the File menu.

Creating the title text

After creating the title text, you will format and color it, and center it in the bordered box.

1 With the text tool selected, click the pasteboard to establish an insertion point, type **Architectural** in uppercase and lowercase letters, press the Return key, type **Treasures**, press the Return key, and type **of Italy**.

2 With an insertion point already established, choose Select All from the Edit menu, and in the Control palette choose Birch from the Font pop-up menu, type 24 points in the Size box and .05 em space in the Kerning box, and click the Apply button.

3 With the text still selected, in the Control palette click the Paragraph-view button, and in the paragraph view of the Control palette click the Center-align button to center the text in the text block.

4 With the text still selected, in the Colors palette click Sand to apply the color to the text.

5 With the pointer tool selected, click the title text to select it as a text block, and drag a right corner handle to be roughly aligned with the text, reducing the size of the text block.

6 With the title text still selected as a text block, in the Control palette make sure the center reference point in the Proxy icon is selected, type **0** in the X box and **0** in the Y box, and press the Return key to center the text block in the black box.

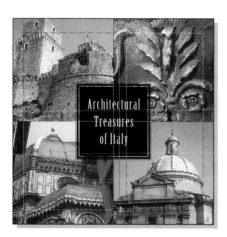

When you use the Control palette to position text objects, it may be necessary to adjust the positioning to achieve the desired results.

7 If necessary, press the arrow keys (or click the nudge buttons in the Control palette) to align the text with greater precision.

8 Choose Save from the File menu.

Reversing the subtitle text out of a box

After creating another black box to visually frame the subtitle text, you will place the text and reverse it out of the second box.

1 With the rectangle tool selected in the toolbox, drag to draw a box of any dimension below the existing black box.

2 In the Control palette make sure the center reference point in the Proxy icon is selected, type **0** in the X box, **23p8** in the Width box and **1p3** in the Height box, and press the Return key to resize the box and center it horizontally on the page.

3 In the Colors palette click the Both button, and then click Black to apply the color black to the line and fill of the box.

4 With the pointer tool selected, hold down the Shift key (to constrain the movement to 45°), and drag the black box until its bottom edge is aligned with the bottom margin guide.

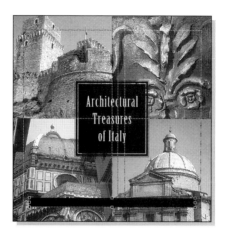

5 Choose Place from the File menu, and in the Place Document dialog box double-click the *07TextA* file in the *07Lesson* folder.

6 With the loaded text icon displayed, drag to define a text box below the black box that spans the width of the black box (exact height is not important) to place the text.

7 With the text tool selected, triple-click the subtitle text to select it, and in the Control palette click the Center-align button to center the text in the text block.

8 In the Control palette click the Character-view button, and in the character view of the Control palette choose Adobe Garamond Semibold Italic from the Font pop-up menu, type **10** points in the Size box and **.08** em space in the Kerning box, and click the Apply button.

9 In the Colors palette click Paper to apply the color paper to the subtitle text.

10 Magnify the view of the black box and the subtitle text.

11 With the pointer tool selected, click the subtitle text to select it as a text block, and press the up and down arrow keys (or click the up and down nudge buttons in the Control palette) to center the text in the black box.

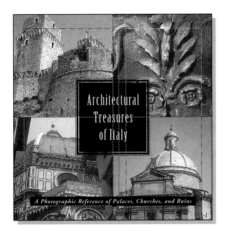

The front cover is completely assembled.

12 Choose Save from the File menu.

Note: An interim file was saved at this point. To open it, double-click the 07Int1 *file in the* Extras *folder.*

ASSEMBLING THE FIRST DOUBLE-PAGE SPREAD

In addition to placing the text and graphics elements, you will create rules above and below paragraphs, and create and apply styles.

Placing a graphic

After placing and positioning a graphic on the left page of the first double-page spread, you will apply a color to an illustration.

1 Click page icon 2/3 to view the first double-page spread.

The zero point is still aligned with the center of the right page.

2 Double-click the hairline of the zero point (in the upper-left corner of the publication window) to return it to its default position at the top, intersecting edges of the facing pages.

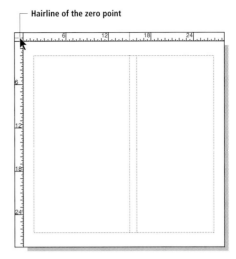

Hairline of the zero point

3 Choose Place from the File menu, and in the Place Document dialog box double-click the *07GraphicE* file in the *07Lesson* folder.

4 With the graphics icon displayed, click the upper-left corner of the left page (page 2) to place the illustration.

5 With the pointer tool selected, position the cursor on the illustration, hold down the mouse button, and quickly drag the illustration to display its bounding box.

6 With the mouse button still held down, drag the bounding box until its top edge is aligned with the top margin guide, visually centering it between the left and right edges of the page.

7 In the Colors palette make sure the Fill button is selected, and click Sand to apply the color Sand to the illustration.

8 Choose Save from the File menu.

Creating a bordered box for the table of contents text

After creating a box to frame the table of contents text, you will use the Control palette to size and position it, applying the color dark blue to the line and fill of the box.

1 With the rectangle tool selected in the toolbox, drag to draw a box of any dimension on the page.

2 In the Control palette make sure the center point of the Proxy icon is selected, type -14p2 in the X box, 14p3 in the Y box, 12p6 in the Width box, and 12p6 in the Height box, and press the Return key to resize and center the box.

3 Choose Line from the Element menu and the 5-point double line (heavy over light) from the submenu to specify a border for the box.

4 In the Colors palette make sure the Both button is selected, and click Dark blue to apply the color dark blue to the line and fill of the box.

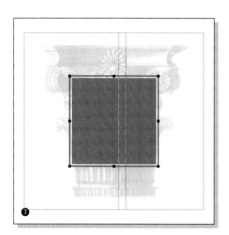

5 Choose Save from the File menu.

Placing the table of contents text

After placing the table of contents text, you will format and align the text.

1 Choose Place from the File menu, and in the Place Document dialog box double-click the *07TextB* file in the *07Lesson* folder.

2 With the loaded text icon displayed, drag to define a text block below the blue box that spans the width of the blue box (exact height is not important) to place the text.

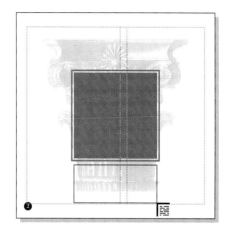

3 With the table of contents text selected as a text block, drag the bottom windowshade handle until the entire story is displayed.

4 With the text tool selected, triple-click the first line of the table of contents text to select it, and in the Control palette choose Birch from the Font pop-up menu, type **23** points in the Size box, **20** points in the Leading box, and **.1** em space in the Kerning box, and click the All caps button.

5 With the text tool still selected, drag to select the remaining lines of the table of contents text, and in the Control palette choose Birch from the Font pop-up menu, type **15** points in the Size box, **20** points in the Leading box, and **.1** em space in the Kerning box, and click the Apply button.

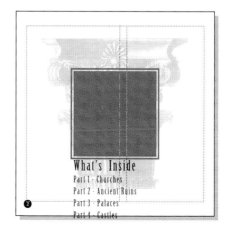

6 Click the beginning of the second line of text, and press the Return key to add a line space after the first line of text.

7 With the insertion point still established, choose Select All from the Edit menu.

8 In the Control palette click the Paragraph-view button, and in the paragraph view of the Control palette click the Center-align button to center the text in the text block.

9 With the text still selected, in the Colors palette click Paper to apply the color paper to the table of contents text.

10 With the pointer tool selected, click the table of contents text to select it as a text block, drag a windowshade handle until the entire story is displayed, hold down the Shift key (to constrain the movement to 45°), and drag the text block to be roughly centered in the dark blue box.

11 Press the up and down arrow keys (or click the up and down nudge buttons in the Control palette) to center the text block in the box.

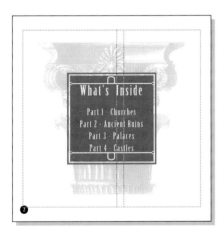

12 Choose Save from the File menu.

Creating a rule below a paragraph

Using a series of dialog boxes, you will create the double-line rule that is positioned below the first line of the table of contents text (which happens to be a single-line paragraph). Even though a rule looks like a graphic object, it is a paragraph attribute that is part of the text, moving whenever the text moves.

Time out for a movie

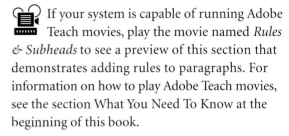 If your system is capable of running Adobe Teach movies, play the movie named *Rules & Subheads* to see a preview of this section that demonstrates adding rules to paragraphs. For information on how to play Adobe Teach movies, see the section What You Need To Know at the beginning of this book.

1 With the text tool selected, click the first line (or paragraph) of the table of contents text to establish an insertion point, and choose Paragraph from the Type menu (Command-M), and in the Paragraph Specifications dialog box click the Rules button.

2 In the Paragraph Rules dialog box click the Rule below paragraph button to establish the rule to be below the paragraph, choose the 5-point double line (heavy over light) from the Line style pop-up menu, choose Sand from the Line color pop-up menu, click the Width of text button to select it, and click the Options button.

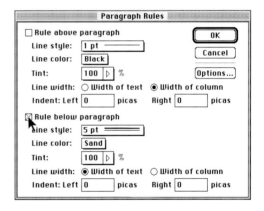

3 In the Paragraph Rule Options dialog box type **1p** in the Bottom box to position the rule lower than the default vertical position, hold down the Option key (to close the chain of dialog boxes), and click OK.

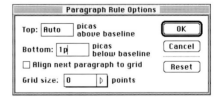

Note: Since you specified the rule to be positioned lower by 1p, the rule will increase the size of the slug of the last line of text in the paragraph. Accepting the default vertical positioning aligns the bottom edge of the rule along the bottom of the slug of the last line of text.

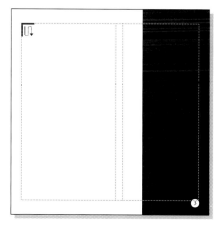

4 Choose Save from the File menu.

Flowing text semiautomatically

Since the text is meant to be positioned in specific columns in the publication, you will flow the text semiautomatically into one column at a time. Flowing text semiautomatically is very much like flowing text manually, but the text is automatically reloaded after each column of text is placed. You may recall that the Autoflow option causes text to flow into all columns in a publication.

1 Magnify the view of the right page (page 3).

2 Choose Place from the File menu, and in the Place Document dialog box double-click the *07TextC* file in the *07Lesson* folder.

3 With the loaded text icon displayed, hold down the Shift key (to specify semiautomatic flow), click in the top portion of the left column to place the text, and release the Shift key.

The cursor is displayed as a loaded text icon.

4 Click page icon 4/5 to view the second double-page spread.

5 With the loaded text icon displayed, hold down the Shift key (again, to specify semiautomatic flow), and click in the top portion of the left column on the right page (page 5) to place the text.

6 Click page icon 6 to view the final page of the booklet.

9 With the loaded text icon displayed, hold down the Shift key, and click in the top portion of the left column on the page (page 6) to place the text.

The empty bottom windowshade handle indicates the entire story is placed.

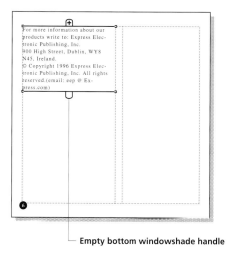

Empty bottom windowshade handle

10 Choose Save from the File menu.

Formatting the story

After using the Control palette to format the entire story you just placed, you will roughly align the text block in the left column on page 3.

1 Click page icon 2/3 to view the first double-page spread.

2 With the text tool selected, click the text on page 3 to establish an insertion point, and choose Select All from the Edit menu to select the entire story that spans multiple pages.

3 In the Control palette click the Character-view button, and in the character view of the Control palette choose Adobe Garamond Regular from the Font pop-up menu, type **8** points in the Size box and **13** points in the Leading box, and click the Apply button.

4 Magnify the view of the upper-half portion of the text on page 3.

5 With the text tool selected, triple-click the first paragraph of the text to select it.

6 In the Control palette choose Adobe Garamond Semibold Italic from the Font pop-up menu, type **9** points in the Size box and **13** points in the Leading box, and click the Apply button.

7 In the Control palette click the Paragraph-view button, and in the paragraph view of the Control palette type **2p** in the First-line indent box, and press the Return key.

First-line indent box

8 If the first line of text is not just below the top margin guide, click the text with the pointer tool to select it as a text block, and drag the top windowshade handle just above the top margin guide to display the first line of text just below the top margin guide.

9 Choose Save from the File menu.

Wrapping text around a graphic

After placing a photograph, you will use the Text Wrap command to flow text around a rectangular graphics boundary that surrounds the photograph.

1 Choose View from the Layout menu and Fit in Window from the submenu.

2 Choose Place from the File menu, and in the Place Document dialog box double-click the *07GraphicF* file in the *07Lesson* folder.

3 With the graphics icon displayed, click page 3 to place the photograph, and drag the photograph until its bottom edge is aligned with the bottom margin guide, with its left edge aligned with the left margin guide.

Since the photograph overlaps the text, you will use the Text Wrap command to define how the text will wrap around the photograph.

4 Choose Text Wrap from the Element menu, and in the Text Wrap dialog box click the rectangular graphics boundary icon (center icon) to select a Wrap option, make sure the Wrap-all-sides icon (rightmost icon) is selected for the Text flow option, type **0** in the Left box, **p9** in the Right box, **0** in the Top box, and **0** in the Bottom box to set the Standoff in picas, and click OK.

The text stands 9 points from the right edge of the photograph.

Note: To adjust any of the standoff values, choose Text Wrap from the Element menu, and enter new values in the Text Wrap dialog box.

5 With the pointer tool selected, click the text to select it as a text block, drag a windowshade handle until the entire story is displayed, and drag the text block until the baseline of the last line of text aligned with the bottom margin guide.

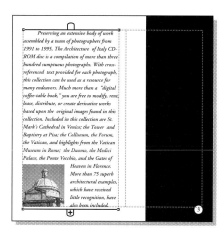

6 Choose Save from the File menu.

Placing a graphic

You will place and position another photograph in the upper-right corner of page 3.

1 Choose Place from the File menu, and in the Place Document dialog box double-click the *07GraphicG* file in the *07Lesson* folder.

2 With the graphics icon displayed, click the upper-right corner of page 3 to place the photograph, and drag it until its top edge is aligned with the top margin guide, with its left edge aligned with the right edge of the gutter.

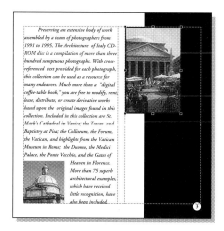

3 Choose Save from the File menu.

Placing the caption text

After placing and aligning caption text below the pantheon photograph, you will reduce the size of the caption text block.

1 Choose Place from the File menu, and in the Place Document dialog box double-click the *07TextD* file in the *07Lesson* folder.

2 With the loaded text icon displayed, click the pasteboard to the right of page 3 to place the caption text.

Since you will apply the color paper to the caption text, take a moment to position the left edge of the caption text over the black edge of the page.

3 With the caption text selected as a text block, drag it until the text overlaps the black box and the pasteboard.

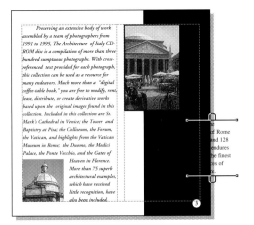

4 With the text tool selected, click the caption text to establish an insertion point, and choose Select All from the Edit menu.

5 In the Control palette click the Charater-view button, and in the character view of the Control palette choose Adobe Garamond Semibold from the Font pop-up menu, type **10** points in the Size box and **13** points in the Leading box, and click the Apply button.

6 In the Colors palette click Paper to apply the color paper to the caption text.

7 With the pointer tool selected, click the caption text to select it as a text block, and in the Control palette make sure the upper-left reference point in the Proxy icon is selected, type **7p2** in the Width box, and press the Return key.

8 With the caption text still selected as a text block, drag the bottom windowshade handle down to display the entire story.

You are ready to position the caption text under the pantheon photograph.

9 From the horizontal ruler, drag to create a horizontal ruler guide at approximately 15p6; and from the vertical ruler, drag to create a vertical ruler guide at approximately 19p8.

10 Drag the text block until the baseline of the first line of text is aligned with the 15p6 horizontal ruler guide, with the left edge of the text aligned with the 19p8 vertical ruler guide.

11 Choose Save from the File menu.

Creating a caption style

Since all captions in this publication will be formatted identically, you will save time by creating a style to be applied to each caption.

1 With the text tool selected, click the caption text you just formatted to establish an insertion point.

2 Choose Define Styles from the Type menu (Command-3), and in the Define Styles dialog box click the New button.

3 In the Edit Style dialog box type **07Caption** in the Name box, hold down the Option key (to close the chain of dialog boxes), and click OK.

The Styles palette displays the style 07Caption.

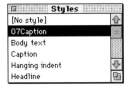

To make it possible to edit all paragraphs that reflect the style 07Caption, take a moment to apply the style 07Caption to the caption text.

4 With the insertion point still established in the caption text, in the Styles palette click 07Caption.

You have completed assembling the first double-page spread.

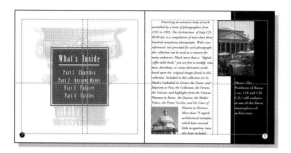

5 Choose Save from the File menu.

ASSEMBLING THE SECOND DOUBLE-PAGE SPREAD

In addition to placing and formatting more text and graphics elements on the second double-page spread, you will create a rule above a paragraph. You will also use the Image Control command to modify an image.

Creating a rule aligned with a single-line paragraph

In this lesson you will specify a dark blue rule within a paragraph, visually framing each subhead. As in earlier steps in this lesson, you will use a series of dialog boxes to set the line style and weight, color, horizontal width, and vertical positioning of rules displayed above a paragraph.

Note: Once again, rules are paragraph attributes and not independent graphic objects; they cannot be selected or edited with the pointer tool.

1 Click page icon 4/5 to view the second double-page spread.

2 Magnify the view of the top portion of the left column on the right page (page 5).

3 With the text tool selected, triple-click the subhead text (The Photographers) to select it, and in the Control palette choose Adobe Garamond Semibold from the Font pop-up menu,

type 7 points in the Size box and 13 points in the Leading box, choose Very Loose from the Tracking pop-up menu, and click the Reverse button and the All caps button.

4 With the subhead text still selected, choose Paragraph from the Type menu, and in the Paragraph Specifications dialog box type **1p2** in the Left box (to specify size of the indent), make sure Left is selected from the Alignment pop-up menu, and click the Rules button.

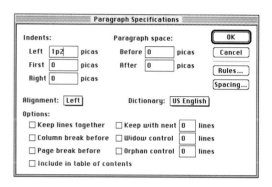

5 In the Paragraph Rules dialog box click the Rule above paragraph button, choose Custom from the Line style pop-up menu, and in the Custom Line dialog box choose the 11-point solid line from the Line weight pop-up menu, and click OK.

6 In the Paragraph Rules dialog box choose Dark Blue from the Line color pop-up menu, click the Width of column radio button to specify the Line width option, type **0** in the Left box and **4p** in the Right box (to specify a 4-pica indentation), and click the Options button.

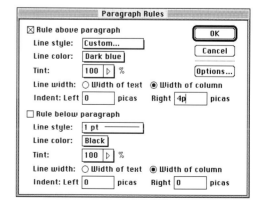

Note: The 4p indentation on the right end of the rule shortens the rule, even though you selected the Width of column option.

7 In the Paragraph Rules Options dialog box type **p8** in the Top box (to specify where the top of the rule starts above the baseline of text), hold down the Option key (to close the chain of dialog boxes), and click OK.

8 Choose Save from the File menu.

Creating and applying a subhead style

Since one more subhead must be formatted, you will save time by creating a style using the subhead text you have already formatted.

1 With the subhead text still selected, choose Define Styles from the Type menu, and in the Define Styles dialog box click the New button.

2 In the Edit Style dialog box type **07Subhead** in the Name box, hold down the Option key (to close the chain of dialog boxes), and click OK.

3 With the insertion point still established in the subhead text, in the Styles palette click 07Subhead.

You will apply the style 07Subhead to another subhead. To adjust its positioning in the rule, you will modify the paragraph specification of the second subhead.

4 With the text tool selected, click the second subhead text to establish an insertion point, choose Paragraph from the Type menu (Command-M), and in the Paragraph Specifications dialog box type **1p** in the Left box, and click OK to adjust the amount of the indentation.

5 With the pointer tool selected, click the text in the left column to select it as a text block, and drag the text block until the first line of text is just below the top margin guide, with the baseline of the last line of text aligned with the bottom margin guide.

6 If necessary, drag the bottom windowshade handle until it is just below the bottom margin guide to resize the text block.

7 Choose Save from the File menu.

Placing and cropping a graphic

After placing a photograph on the left page of the second double-page spread, you will crop the edges of the photograph to be aligned with the edges of the page.

1 Choose View from the Layout menu and Fit in Window from the submenu.

2 Choose Place from the File menu, and in the Place Document dialog box double-click the *07GraphicH* file in the *07Lesson* folder.

3 When prompted, click the No button to prevent duplicating the image data in the *07Work* publication.

To show this photograph to its best advantage, you will allow it to overlap the black circle and page-number marker in the lower-left corner of the page.

4 With the graphics icon displayed, click the upper-left corner of the left page (page 4), and drag the photograph until its right edge is aligned with the inside edge of the page, allowing the edges of the photograph to overlap the top, bottom, and outside edges of the page.

7 Choose Save from the File menu.

Placing a graphic

You will place a photograph in the lower-right corner of the right page of the second double-page spread.

1 Magnify the view of the lower-half portion of the right page (page 5).

2 From the horizontal ruler, drag to create a horizontal ruler guide at approximately 25p6.

3 Choose Place from the File menu, and in the Place Document dialog box double-click the *07GraphicI* file in the *07Lesson* folder.

4 With the graphics icon displayed, click the lower-right corner of the right page to place the photograph, and drag it until its bottom edge is aligned with the 25p6 horizontal ruler guide, with its right edge aligned with the right margin guide.

As with all graphics that extend to the edge of the page, this photograph was sized to allow for a bleed to overlap the edges of the page. Once again, you will crop the photograph to be aligned with the edges of the page, making it easier to view the design.

5 With the cropping tool selected in the toolbox, position the cursor over the upper-left graphics handle of the photograph, and drag down and right to the upper-left corner of the page, cropping the view of the photograph.

6 With the cropping tool still selected, position the cursor over the bottom-center graphics handle, and drag up to the bottom edge of the page.

5 Make sure the black border of the photograph is aligned with the guides.

6 Choose Save from the File menu.

Placing and modifying an image

The Image Control command makes it possible to alter the appearance of line art or bitmapped or grayscale images, adjusting the lightness or darkness of an entire image and adjusting the screen pattern (where you specify whether the image is composed of dots or lines). In this lesson you will use the Image Control command to change the contrast of a grayscale image, adjusting the relationship between light and dark areas within the image.

Note: You cannot use the Image Control command to alter a color TIFF image. Also, images adjusted with the Image Control command must be printed on a PostScript printing device.

1 Choose View from the Layout menu and Fit in Window from the submenu.

2 Choose Place from the File menu, and in the Place Document dialog box double-click the *07GraphicJ* file in the *07Lesson* folder.

3 With the graphics icon displayed, click in the upper-right corner of the right page (in the black box) to place the illustration.

4 With the illustration still selected, in the Control palette make sure the upper-left reference point in the Proxy icon is selected, type **20p4** in the X box and **p7** in the Y box, and press the Return key to position the illustration.

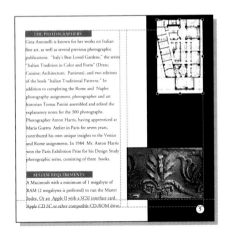

5 With the illustration still selected, choose Image from the Element menu and Image Control from the submenu.

The Image Control dialog box displays vertical slider bars that allow you to adjust lightness and contrast of an image. The four icons above the slider bars represent the four gray-level pattern options that allow you to change the image's gray levels to a selected pattern. Refer to the *Adobe PageMaker 6.0 User Guide* for more information about the Image Control command.

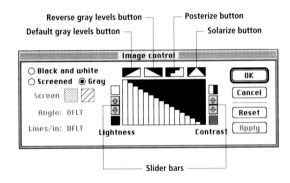

6 Drag the Image Control box so that it is possible to see a portion of the target image.

7 In the Image Control dialog box click the Reverse gray levels button (second button from the left) to reverse the image, notice how the slider bars are reversed, and click OK.

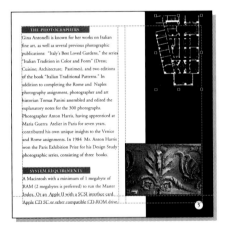

The black portions of the image are displayed white, and vice versa.

Note: Applying the color paper to the image will not serve to reverse out the image.

8 Choose Save from the File menu.

Placing caption text

After placing the caption text that accompanies the illustration and photograph on the right page, you will apply the style 07Caption and position the caption text above the photograph.

1 From the vertical ruler, drag to create a vertical ruler guide at approximately 19p6.

2 Magnify the view of the portion of the black box above the photograph in the lower-right corner of the page.

3 Choose Place from the File menu, and in the Place Document dialog box double-click the *07TextE* file in the *07Lesson* folder.

4 With the loaded text icon displayed, drag to define a text block that extends from the 19p6 vertical ruler guide to the right margin guide on the right page (exact height is not important) to place the caption text, taking note of its approximate position to be able to select it with the text tool.

Since the placed text is colored black, it cannot be viewed on the black rectangle.

5 With the text tool selected, click the caption text to establish an insertion point, choose Select All from the Edit menu, and in the Style palette click 07Caption.

6 From the horizontal ruler, drag to create a horizontal ruler guide at approximately 12p.

7 With the pointer tool selected, click the caption text to select it as a text block, hold down the Shift key (to constrain the movement to 45°), and drag the text block until the baseline of the first line of text is aligned with the 12p horizontal ruler guide.

8 With the caption text still selected as a text block, drag the bottom windowshade handle to display the entire story.

The second double-page spread is assembled.

9 Choose View from the Layout menu and Fit in Window from the submenu.

10 Choose Save from the File menu.

ASSEMBLING THE FINAL PAGE

In addition to hiding the view of master-page elements for the final page, you will place and format text and graphics elements.

Copying and pasting master-page elements to the final page

To place the master-page elements found on the right master page on this final page (a left page), you will copy the elements (black box, circle, and page-number marker) from the right master page and paste them to the final page itself.

As with the front cover of this booklet, you will hide the display of the original left master-page elements on this final page.

1 Click page icon 6 to view the final page of the booklet.

Since page 6 is a left page, the text and graphics elements found on the left master page are displayed.

2 With the final page displayed, choose Display Master Items from the Layout menu to deselect the command, removing the view of the master-page elements on this final page.

You are ready to copy right master-page elements to the final page.

3 Click master-page icon L/R in the lower-left corner of the publication window to display the left and right master pages.

4 With the pointer tool selected, drag to select the black box on the right master page, ensuring the page-number marker and circle are included in the selection, and choose Copy from the Edit menu.

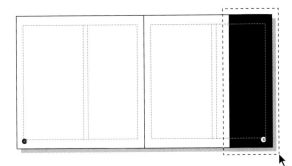

5 Click page icon 6 to view the final page.

6 Choose Paste from the Edit menu to paste the objects to the final page.

Note: Power pasting objects from a right page to a left page (or vice versa), does not align the objects on the target page.

7 With the pasted objects still selected, drag them until the black box is aligned with the top and bottom edges of the page, with its right edge aligned with the right edge of the page.

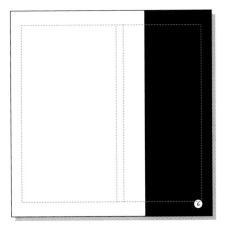

8 Choose Save from the File menu.

Placing a final graphic

Before placing the final photograph on the final page, you will align the text with the bottom margin guide.

1 With the pointer tool selected, click the text to select it as a text block, and drag it until the baseline of the last line of text is aligned with the bottom margin guide.

2 Choose Place from the File menu, and in the Place Document dialog box double-click the *07GraphicK* file in the *07Lesson* folder.

3 When prompted, click the No button to prevent duplicating the image data in the *07Work* publication.

4 With the graphics icon displayed, click the page to place the photograph, and drag the photograph until its upper-left corner is aligned with the intersection of margin guides in the upper-left corner of page 6.

You have finished assembling the booklet.

5 Choose Guides and Rulers from the Layout menu and Show Guides from the submenu to hide the guides used to assemble this booklet.

6 Choose Save from the File menu to save the *07Work* publication.

If you have determined that your service provider will perform the prepress tasks, you are ready to deliver the *07Work* file to your service provider. Be sure to include all image files that are linked to the publication.

7 Close all open publications, and choose Quit from the File menu (Command-Q) to exit the Adobe PageMaker program.

PRINTING THE BOOKLET

In addition to trapping and constructing bleeds, the prepress tasks will include specifying a custom page size and including printer's marks and page information. For more information on these prepress tasks, refer to the *Adobe PageMaker 6.0 User Guide* and the *Adobe Print Publishing Guide*.

Designed to be printed on a commercial printing press, this publication requires a total of four process color (CMYK) film separations. Knowing your printer plans to print this publication using a line screen frequency of 150 lpi, your service provider will create the four film separations on a imagesetter at a resolution of 2400 dpi. Once the film separations are prepared, you can deliver them to your printer.

•BY PAMELA BALAAT AND AMY SPITZER

TOOLS

OF THE

TRADE

The Illustrated Guide to
Carpentry and Building Contruction Tools

• SOUTH AFRICA •

In this lesson you will assemble the text and graphics elements for the front cover of the book *Tools of the Trade.* Offering a variation on our theme of architecture, this book

BOOK COVER DESIGN

cover is a full-color publication, and incorporates four studio photographs of tools commonly used in carpentry and construction work. ■ The title text features Madrone, an Adobe Originals typeface designed by Barbara Lind in 1991. Madrone was digitized from proofs of the wood type collection in the National Museum of American History in the Smithsonian Institution in Washington, D.C. A fat face roman, Madrone is typical of popular early nineteenth-century styles. Fat face types are characterized by their squatness and extreme letter width; one familiar version of this design is Bodoni Ultra Bold. Madrone is eye-catching for display uses in advertising and packaging.

The remaining text used in the design features another Adobe Originals typeface, Poplar, designed by Barbara Lind in 1990. Poplar, a Gothic condensed, was designed from photographs taken by Rob Roy Kelly of the one surviving copy of an

BOOK COVER DESIGN

1830 William Leavenworth type specimen book. Leavenworth possessed unusual artistic abilities, and his treatment of the letterform counters as narrow slits made it the only wood type of its kind displayed during the nineteenth century. Poplar is an excellent display face, its simplicity making it useful for a broad range of work.

This lesson covers:

• Compressing a TIFF image file

• Reflecting a graphic object

• Selecting graphics display options

• Pair kerning text using the Control palette

• Creating a dropshadow for text

• Setting the arrow key (and nudge button) distance

• Manually range kerning text.

BEFORE YOU BEGIN

All files and fonts needed to assemble the publication in this lesson are found on the Adobe PageMaker *Classroom in a Book* CD-ROM disc in the folders *08Lesson* and *Fonts*, respectively.

It should take you approximately 1 hour to complete this lesson.

Opening an existing publication

Let's take a look at the final version of the book cover you will assemble in this lesson.

1 Before launching the Adobe PageMaker program, throw away the *Adobe PageMaker 6.0 Prefs* file to ensure all settings are returned to their default values.

2 Make sure the fonts Madrone and Poplar are installed.

3 Double-click the *Adobe® PageMaker® 6.0* icon to launch the Adobe PageMaker program.

4 Choose Open from the File menu (Command-O), and in the Open Publication dialog box double-click the *08Final* file in the *08Lesson* folder.

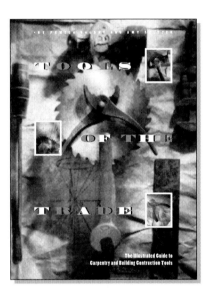

The publication window displays a single page filled with the book cover design at its highest resolution. Even though this design is meant to be incorporated into a book jacket, the scope of this lesson is limited to the cover design alone.

5 Choose Guides and Rulers from the Layout menu and Show Guides from the submenu (Command-J) to display the guides used to assemble this book cover.

Talk with your printer

To reduce the demand for disk space on your system, the images featured in this lesson were scanned at a resolution of 100 dpi. Since it is likely that your commercial printer will recommend printing this sort of publication with a line screen frequency between 150 lpi and 175 lpi, in a real environment these images would have to be scanned at 300 dpi to 350 dpi (double the selected line screen frequency) to meet the printing requirements of this publication.

Designed to be printed on a commercial printing press, the color TIFF images in this design will require four process-color film separations, with the spot color requiring a separate spot-color film separation. This means your service provider will produce a total of five film separations. If you want to reduce the cost of producing five separations, talk with your service provider about converting the spot color to a process color, reducing the film separations to four.

After verifying the trapping specification, the size of the bleed, and the line screen frequency with your printer, talk with your service provider to determine who will perfom the prepress tasks and how you should deliver this publication to your service provider.

ASSEMBLING THE BOOK COVER

After placing the four graphic elements, you will create, format, kern, and align the text for the title, byline, and subtitle.

Creating a new publication

After establishing the dimensions of the publication in the Document Setup dialog box, you will save and name your publication.

1 Choose New from the File menu (Command-N), and in the Document Setup dialog box type **6.55** inches by **9** inches in the Dimensions boxes, click the Double-sided check box to deselect it, and type **.85** inch in the Left box, **.85** inch in the Right box, **.5** inch in the Top box, and **.5** inch in the Bottom box to establish the margins, and click OK.

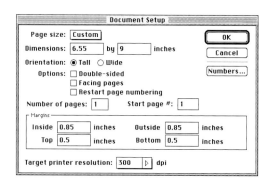

In this lesson you will use the margin guides to help you align text and graphics elements.

2 If you do not have a *Projects* folder, create one now.

3 Choose Save As from the File menu, and in the Save publication as dialog box type **08Work** in the Name box, select the *Projects* folder, and click OK.

Compressing a TIFF image file

Because TIFF (tag image file format) images sometimes require a large amount of disk space, Adobe PageMaker provides built-in TIFF compression capabilities. When you compress a TIFF image file, Adobe PageMaker compresses a copy of the image, without changing the original.

You can choose from two levels of compression: maximum and moderate. Since maximum compression is a lossy compression scheme, it may change colors and cause banding in the screen image and the printed version of the image. Where maximum compression is suited to assembling low-resolution comps (or digital proofs), it is not suited to creating film separations of high-resolution images. In this example you will apply moderate compression, a non-lossy compression scheme that preserves image data.

1 Choose Place from the File menu (Command-D), and in the Place Document dialog box *single*-click the *08GraphicA* file in the *08Lesson* folder, hold down the Command and Option keys, and without releasing the Command and Option keys, click OK to select moderate compression.

Note: To select maximum compression, hold down the Shift, Command, and Option keys, and click OK in the Place Document dialog box.

2 When the progress bar is displayed, release the Command and Option keys.

3 When prompted, click the No button to prevent duplicating the image file to the *08Work* publication.

4 With the graphics icon displayed, click the upper-left corner of the page to place the photograph.

TIP: TO SCROLL
THE PAGE, HOLD DOWN
THE OPTION KEY AND
DRAG THE PAGE IN
ANY DIRECTION.

You work with compressed TIFF images exactly as you work with uncompressed TIFF images. Even though the Adobe PageMaker program automatically decompresses TIFF images when printing a publication, printing with uncompressed TIFF images ensures optimum performance. For more information, refer to the *Adobe PageMaker 6.0 User Guide.*

Note: After scanning a Polaroid™ transfer on a flatbed scanner, this image was imported into Adobe Photoshop to be enhanced and sized.

5 With the photograph still selected, in the Control palette make sure the upper-left reference point in the Proxy icon is selected, type **-.188** inch in the X box and **-.188** inch in the Y box, and press the Return key, positioning the photograph so that its edges overlap the edges of the page.

The photograph is perfectly aligned, allowing a $3/16$-inch bleed of the image to overlap all edges of the page. Since the three remaining image files are considerably smaller, you will not compress them.

6 Choose Save from the File menu (Command-S).

Cropping a graphic

To better view the design itself, you will crop the photograph, aligning its edges with the edges of the page.

1 With the cropping tool selected in the toolbox, click the photograph to select it, position the cursor over the upper-left graphics handle of the photograph, making sure the graphics handle shows through the center of the cropping tool, and hold down the mouse button until the cursor is displayed as a double-headed arrow.

2 With the mouse button still held down, drag the graphics handle down and right to the upper-left corner of the page, and release the mouse button, cropping the view of the photograph.

3 Scroll to view the lower portion of the page.

4 With the cropping tool still selected, position the cursor over the lower-right graphics handle of the photograph, and drag up and left to the lower-right corner of the page (to the left edge of the page dropshadow), cropping more of the view of the photograph.

Even though the photograph has been cropped, the entire graphic is still available. Before printing this publication, you would undo the cropping, allowing for the image to overlap the edges of the page.

5 Choose Save from the File menu.

Placing the second graphic

After placing the pliers photograph, you will position it by entering coordinate values in the Control palette.

1 From the horizontal ruler, drag to create a horizontal ruler guide at 1 inch, and from the vertical ruler, drag to create a vertical ruler guide at 4.75 inches.

2 Magnify the view of the intersection of the ruler guides you just created.

3 Choose Place from the File menu, and in the Place Document dialog box double-click the *08GraphicB* file in the *08Lesson* folder.

4 With the graphics icon displayed, position the cursor at the intersection of the ruler guides you just created, and click to place the photograph.

5 In the Control palette make sure the upper-left reference point in the Proxy icon is selected, and make sure the X and Y values indicate 4.75 inches and 1 inch, respectively. If necessary, type one or both values in the X and Y boxes to move the photograph to the specified coordinate position.

6 Choose Save from the File menu.

Creating a keyline

The Keyline command draws a border around a selected text or graphics element. A separate object with its own handles, the keyline is automatically grouped with its target graphic when it is created.

Even though keylines can be used in traditional printing to prepare work for film separations, for this example you will create a keyline for purely decorative purposes. For more information on using the Keyline command in prepress work, refer to the *Adobe Print Publishing Guide*.

1 With the pointer tool selected, click the pliers photograph to select it.

2 Choose PageMaker Plug-ins from the Utilities menu and Keyline from the submenu, and in the Keyline dialog box type **4.5** points in the Extend outward box (to specify the keyline to extend outwards from the selected graphic), and click the Attributes button.

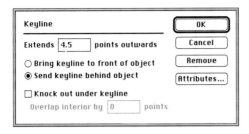

Note: By default, the Adobe PageMaker application draws keylines (and lines) inward from the selected boundary.

3 In the Fill and Line dialog box choose None from the Fill pop-up menu to specify the fill, and Custom from the Line pop-up menu (top-right portion of the dialog box).

4 In the Custom Line dialog box type **4.5** points in the Line weight box, and click OK.

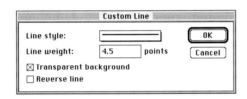

Note: If you type 0 points in the Line weight box, the keyline will be the same size as the selected object. If you enter a negative value, the keyline will be smaller than the selected object.

5 In the Fill and Line dialog box choose Paper from the Color pop-up menu (below the Line pop-up menu), click OK to close the Attributes box, and click OK again to close the Keyline box.

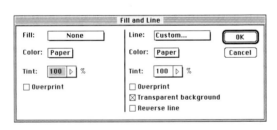

The photograph is displayed with the 4.5-point keyline (paper-colored border), with the keyline overlapping the ruler guides by 4.5 points. As was just mentioned, the keyline and the target graphic are grouped automatically into a single entity.

You will use the Control palette to move the keyline and photograph group.

6 With the group still selected, in the Control palette make sure the upper-left reference point in the Proxy icon is selected, type **4.75** inches in the X box and **1** inch in the Y box, and press the Return key to align the upper-left corner of the group with the specified coordinate position.

7 Choose Save from the File menu.

Reflecting a graphic

You will use the Control palette to reflect horizontally the display of the pliers photograph.

1 With the pointer tool selected, click the keyline and pliers photograph group to select the group.

2 In the Control palette make sure the upper-left point in the Proxy icon is selected, and click the Horizontal reflecting button (in the upper-right corner) to reflect the group from the selected reference point in the Proxy icon.

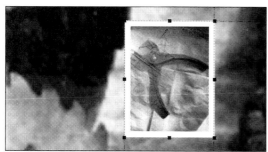

Before

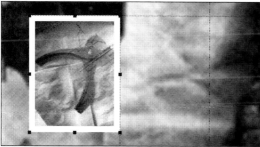

After

Since the grouped entity is reflected out of the desired position, you will undo the reflect operation, repeating the reflect operation with a different Proxy point.

Note: It is not possible to reverse a reflect operation using the Undo command in the Edit menu.

3 With the keyline and pliers group still selected, in the Control palette make sure the upper-right reference point in the Proxy is selected, and click the Horizontal reflecting button again to reverse the reflect operation.

The group regains its original alignment.

4 In the Control palette click the center reference point in the Proxy icon to select it, and click the Horizontal reflecting button.

The reflected group retains its original alignment.

5 Choose Save from the File menu.

Replacing a graphic with another graphic

It's easy to change your mind about a graphic when you use the Place command to replace it with another graphic. In this exercise you will replace the pliers photograph with the hammer photograph.

WIth the keyline and the pliers photograph already grouped into a single entity, you will select the photograph for the replace graphic operation, without ungrouping the group.

1 With the pointer tool selected, click the keyline and pliers photograph group to select the group, hold down the Command key (to select an object within a group), and click the center of the group until the graphics handles indicate the pliers photograph is selected.

2 Choose Place from the File menu, and in the Place Document dialog box *single*-click the *08GraphicC* file in the *08Lesson* folder to select it, click the Replacing entire graphic radio button to select it, and click OK.

Since the pliers photograph had been reflected, the hammer photograph is displayed as reflected as well. Having seen how to reflect an object, you will restore the hammer image to its original orientation.

3 With the hammer photograph selected, in the Control palette make sure the center reference point in the Proxy icon is selected, and click the Horizontal reflecting button.

The hammer image regains its original (un-reflected) orientation.

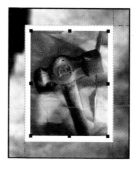

4 Choose Save from the File menu.

Copying, pasting, and replacing a graphic with another graphic

After copying and pasting the keyline and hammer photograph group, you will position the copied group, and then replace the hammer photograph with the saw photograph.

1 With the pointer tool selected, click the hammer photograph or its keyline to select the keyline and hammer photograph group.

2 Choose Copy from the Edit menu (Command-C), and then choose Paste from the Edit menu (Command-V).

A copy of the keyline and hammer photograph group is pasted slightly offset over the original group.

3 In the Control palette make sure the upper-left reference point in the Proxy icon is selected, type .85 inch in the X box and 3.5 inches in the Y box, and press the Return key to move the copy of the keyline and hammer photograph group.

4 If necessary, choose View from the Layout menu and Fit in Window from the submenu (Command-0), and magnify the view of the pasted group.

5 With the pointer tool selected, hold down the Command key (to select an object within a group), and click the center of the pasted group until the graphics handles indicate the hammer photograph is selected.

6 Choose Place from the File menu, and in the Place Document dialog box *single*-click the *08GraphicD* file in the *08Lesson* folder, and the Replacing entire graphic radio button to select it, and click OK.

The saw photograph is displayed within the keyline.

7 Choose Save from the File menu.

Pasting and replacing a graphic with another graphic

Again, pasting the keyline and hammer photograph group from the Clipboard, you will position the copied group, and then replace the hammer photograph with the pliers photograph.

1 Choose Paste from the Edit menu to paste another copy of the keyline and hammer photograph group.

A copy of the keyline and hammer photograph group is pasted overlapping the saw photograph.

TIP: TO OPEN THE PREFERENCES DIALOG BOX, DOUBLE-CLICK THE POINTER TOOL IN THE TOOLBOX.

2 In the Control palette make sure the upper-left reference point in the Proxy icon is selected, type 4.75 inches in the X box and **6** inches in the Y box, and press the Return key.

3 Choose View from the Layout menu and Fit in Window from the submenu, and magnify the view of the pasted group.

4 With the pointer tool selected, hold down the Command key (to select an object within a group), and click the center of the final pasted group until the graphics handles indicate the hammer photograph is selected.

5 Choose Place from the File menu, and in the Place Document dialog box *single*-click the *08GraphicB* file in the *08Lesson* folder, and the Replacing entire graphic radio button to select it, and click OK.

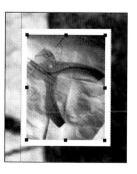

The pliers photograph is displayed within the keyline.

6 Choose Save from the File menu.

Displaying grayed-out graphics

Since the graphics elements are placed and positioned, you can select a graphics display option that will help you work more efficiently. For the fastest screen display, you will use the Preferences dialog box to gray-out the graphics.

1 Choose View from the Layout menu and Fit in Window from the submenu.

2 Choose Preferences from the File menu, and in the Preferences dialog box click the Gray out radio button to select a Graphics display option, and click OK.

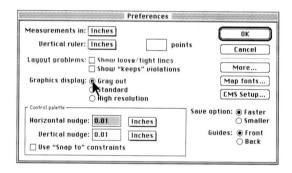

The publication is displayed with gray boxes in place of graphics.

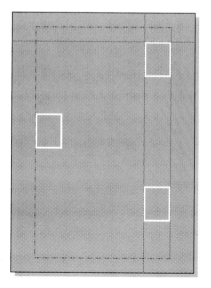

Creating the first line of the title text

You will enter, format, and align the title text TOOLS OF THE TRADE.

1 With the text tool selected, click the upper-left portion of the page to establish an insertion point, and type **tools**.

2 Double-click the text to select it, and in the Control palette choose Madrone from the Font pop-up menu, type **24** points in the Size box and **28** points in the Leading box, and click the All caps button and the Reverse button.

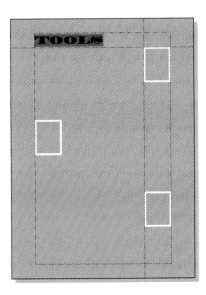

In this example, selecting the Reverse button in the Control palette created a paper-colored text on a colored background.

Reverse button ┘   └ All caps button

3 From the horizontal ruler, drag to create a horizontal ruler guide at 1.75 inches.

4 With the pointer tool selected, click the text to select it as a text block, and drag it until the baseline of the text is aligned with the 1.75-inch horizontal ruler guide, with the left edge of the text aligned with the left margin guide.

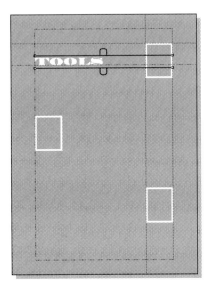

5 From the vertical ruler, drag to create a vertical ruler guide at 4.25 inches.

6 With the text still selected as a text block, drag a right corner handle until it is aligned with the 4.25-inch vertical ruler guide, reducing the width of the text block.

7 Choose Save from the File menu.

Creating the second line of title text

After copying and pasting the TOOLS text, you will replace it with more text, saving you the effort of formatting the pasted line of text.

1 From the horizontal ruler, drag to create a horizontal ruler guide at 4.25 inches.

2 With the pointer tool selected, click the title text to select it as a text block, choose Copy from the Edit menu, and then choose Paste from the Edit menu.

The title text is pasted from the Clipboard.

3 With the pasted text selected as a text block, drag it until the baseline of the text is aligned with the 4.25-inch horizontal ruler guide, with the right corner handles of the text block aligned with the right margin guide.

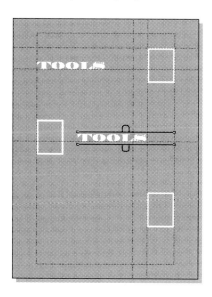

4 With the text tool selected, double-click the pasted title text to select it.

5 In the Control palette click the Paragraph-view button, and in the paragraph view of the Control palette click the Right-align button to align the text with the right edge of the text block.

Right-align button

6 With the pasted text still selected, type **of the** to replace the pasted text.

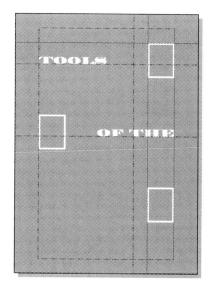

The replaced text reflects the selected type and paragraph specifications of the original text.

7 Choose Save from the File menu.

Creating the third line of title text

After pasting the contents of the Clipboard to create the third line of the title text, you will align the pasted text and replace it with more text.

1 From the horizontal ruler, drag to create a horizontal ruler guide at 6.75 inches.

2 With the text tool selected, click near the 6.75-inch horizontal ruler guide to establish an insertion point, and choose Paste from the Edit menu.

The title text is pasted from the Clipboard.

3 With the pointer tool selected, click the pasted text to select it as a text block, and drag it until the baseline of the text is aligned with the 6.75-inch horizontal ruler guide, with the left edge of the text aligned with the left margin guide.

TIP: TO TOGGLE
BETWEEN DISPLAY SIZES
FIT IN WINDOW AND
ACTUAL SIZE, HOLD
DOWN THE COMMAND
AND OPTION KEYS,
AND CLICK THE PAGE OR
THE PASTEBOARD.

4 With the text tool selected, double-click the
pasted text to select it.

5 Type **trade** to replace the pasted text.

6 With the pointer tool selected, click the text
TRADE to select it as a text block, and drag a
right corner handle until it is roughly aligned
with the right edge of the text, reducing the size
of the text block.

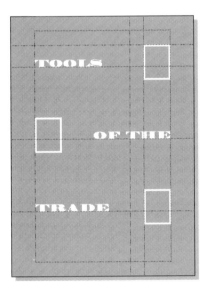

7 Choose Save from the File menu.

Adjusting the stacking order for a selection of multiple objects

After selecting the three text blocks, you will bring
them all to the top of the stack and group them
together. It will be much easier to create the title
text dropshadow when the text blocks share the
same stacking position.

1 If the entire page is not displayed, choose View
from the Layout menu and Fit in Window from
the submenu.

2 With the pointer tool selected, hold down the
Shift key (to select multiple objects), and click
each of the three lines of title text to select them
all as text blocks.

3 Choose Bring to Front from the Arrange menu
(Command-F) to position the selected text blocks
at the top of the stack.

4 Choose Group from the Arrange menu (Command-G) to group selected text blocks into a
single entity.

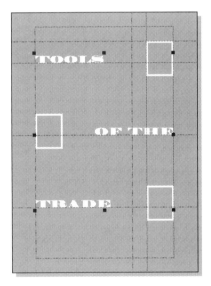

To better organize your work space, grouping
the text blocks into a single entity helps you
avoid accidentally modifying one of them.

5 Choose Save from the File menu.

Pair kerning the title text using the Control palette

Since each line of title text has different widths,
you will assign a different kerning value to each
line of title text. After kerning the title text, you
will pair kern the text, where the letter spacing
between specific letters is adjusted.

1 With the text tool selected, double-click the
text TOOLS to select it.

2 In the Control palette click the Character-view button, and in the character view of the Control palette type 1 em space in the Kerning box in the upper-right corner, and click the Apply button.

Kerning box

3 With the text tool still selected, triple-click the text OF THE to select it, and in the Control palette type .27 em space in the Kerning box in the upper-right corner, and click the Apply button.

4 Double-click the text TRADE to select it, and in the Control palette type .59 em space in the Kerning box in the upper-right corner, and click the Apply button.

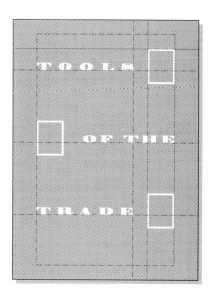

The letter spacing on either side of the letter A in the text TRADE appears to be uneven.

5 With the text tool still selected, click between the letters R and A in the text TRADE to establish an insertion point.

6 In the Control palette click the right Kerning button two times to expand the letter spacing between the selected letters.

Kerning buttons

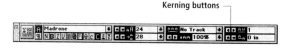

The Kerning box displays .61 em space, since .01 em space is added each time you press the right Kerning button.

7 Press the right arrow key to position the insertion point between the letters A and D in the text TRADE.

8 In the Control palette click the left Kerning button two times to reduce the letter spacing between the selected letters.

The Kerning box displays .57 em space, since .01 em space is subtracted each time you press the left Kerning button.

9 Choose Save from the File menu.

Power pasting the title text to create a dropshadow

After copying and pasting the title text, you will reverse the color of the pasted title text from paper to black.

1 With the pointer tool selected, click any portion of the title text to select the title group.

2 Choose Copy from the Edit menu, hold down the Option key (to specify a power paste), and then choose Paste from the Edit menu.

A pasted title text group is precisely aligned over the original copy of the title text group.

To apply color to text, you must select the target text with the text tool.

3 With the text tool selected, double-click the pasted text TOOLS to select it, and in the Control palette click the Reverse button to reverse the color of the text to black.

4 Triple-click the pasted text OF THE to select it, and in the Control palette click the Reverse button.

5 With the text tool still selected, double-click the pasted text TRADE to select it, and in the Control palette click the Reverse button.

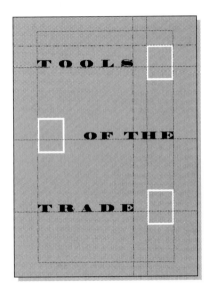

6 Choose Save from the File menu.

Setting the arrow key and nudge button distance

After moving the dropshadow text 2 points to the right of the paper-colored text, you will use the Send Backward command to position the black (dropshadow) text behind the paper-colored text.

Since we want to nudge the black title text in 1-point increments, it is necessary to specify the distance a selected object moves each time you press an arrow key (or click a nudge button in the Control palette) to equal one point (p1).

1 Choose Preferences from the File menu, and in the Preferences dialog box type **p1** in the Horizontal nudge box and **p1** in the Vertical nudge box, and click OK.

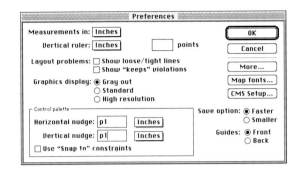

2 With the pointer tool selected, click any portion of black title text to select the black title group.

3 Press the right arrow key (or click the right horizontal nudge button in the Control palette) two times to move the group 2 points (p2) to the right.

4 Choose Send Backward from the Arrange menu (Command-9) to adjust the stacking order, so that the paper-colored text overlaps the black text.

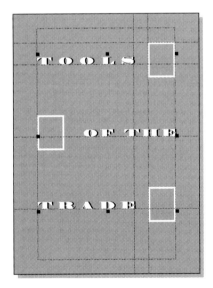

5 Choose Save from the File menu.

Displaying graphics as low-resolution images

To get a better view of your publication, you can use the Preferences dialog box to display graphics as low-resolution screen images. Low-resolution images allow faster screen display than high-resolution images.

1 If necessary, choose View from the Layout menu and Fit in Window from the submenu.

2 Choose Preferences from the File menu, and in the Preferences dialog box click the Standard radio button to select a Graphics display option, and click OK.

Adobe PageMaker displays a low-resolution, pixelated PICT preview of the graphic.

Manually range kerning the byline text

After entering and formatting the byline text, you will range kern it until it spans the image area (between the left and right margin guides), and then align it at the top portion of the page.

1 Magnify the view of the entire page above the first line of title text.

2 With the text tool selected, click above the top margin guide to establish an insertion point.

Note: Rather than press the spacebar to create a word space between the bullet and the byline text, you will pair kern the space between the bullet and the character to expand it.

3 Hold down the Option key, and press the 8 key to specify a bullet; and then type **BY PAMELA BALANT AND AMY SPITZER** in uppercase letters.

4 With an insertion point still established in the byline text, choose Select All from the Edit menu to select the byline text.

5 In the Control palette choose Poplar from the Font pop-up menu, type **9** points in the Size box, and click the Reverse button.

Even though it is possible to enter a precise value in the Kerning box, you will click the kerning nudge buttons in the Control palette to manually kern the text until it spans the image area.

6 With the byline text still selected, hold down the Command key (to specify the .1 em space power nudge), and in the Control palette click the right kerning nudge button 8 times, causing the byline text to span the image area.

The value in the Kerning box equals .8 em space, and the spacing is adjusted between all character pairs in the selection. To further demonstrate how you can adjust the kerning of text, you will reduce the kerning value by .01 em space, the default nudge distance.

7 With the byline text still selected, in the Control palette click the left kerning nudge button once to reduce the kerning value by .01 em space.

The value in the Kerning box equals .79 em space.

8 With the pointer tool selected, click the byline text to select it as a text block, and drag it until the baseline of the text is aligned with the top margin guide, with the bullet aligned with the left margin guide.

9 Choose Save from the File menu.

Creating the subtitle text

After entering, formatting, and kerning the subtitle text, you will align it in the lower-right portion of the page.

1 Choose View from the Layout menu and Fit in Window from the submenu, and magnify the view of the entire page below the third line of title text.

2 With the text tool selected, click above the bottom margin guide to establish an insertion point.

3 Type **The Illustrated Guide to**, hold down the Shift key (to specify a soft-carriage return) press the Return key, and type **Carpentry and Building Construction Tools** in uppercase and lowercase letters.

4 With the insertion point still established in the subtitle text, choose Select All from the Edit menu.

5 In the Control palette choose Poplar from the Font pop-up menu, type **15** points in the Size box, **18** points in the Leading box, and **.05** em space in the Kerning box, and click the Reverse button.

6 With the text still selected, in the Control palette click the Paragraph-view button, and in the paragraph view of the Control palette click the Right-align button to align the text with the right edge of the text block.

7 With the pointer tool selected, click the subtitle text to select it as a text block, and drag it until the baseline of the second line of text is aligned with the bottom margin guide, with the right edge of the text aligned with the right margin guide.

8 Choose Save from the File menu.

Applying color to the title text

As a finishing touch, you will apply the color red to every other letter in the title text TOOLS OF THE TRADE.

1 Choose View from the Layout menu and Fit in Window from the submenu.

2 With the text tool selected, drag to select the second letter (the first O) in the word TOOLS, and in the Colors palette click Red.

3 Drag to select the letter L in the word TOOLS, and in the Colors palette click Red.

4 Drag to select the letter O in the word OF, and in the Colors palette click Red.

5 Drag to select the letter T in the word THE, and in the Colors palette click Red.

6 Continue selecting alternate letters and applying the red color, the letter D being the final letter you color red.

7 Choose Save from the File menu.

Displaying graphics at full resolution

Now that you have completed assembling the book cover, hide the view of the rulers, and use the Preferences dialog box to display the graphics at their full resolution.

1 Choose Guides and Rulers from the Layout menu and Show Guides from the submenu to hide the guides used to assemble this book cover.

2 Choose Preferences from the File menu, and in the Preferences dialog box click the High resolution radio button to select a Graphics display option, and click OK.

The Adobe PageMaker program displays the images in the publication is at full resolution.

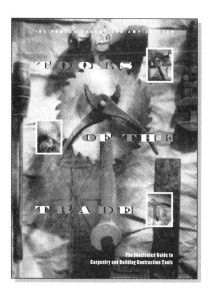

Note: To temporarily display graphics at full resolution, hold down the Control key as you click to the magnifying glass in the toolbox, or as you select a display size command.

3 Choose Save from the File menu to save the *08Work* publication.

If you have determined that your service provider will perform the prepress tasks, you are ready to deliver the *08Work* file to your service provider. Be sure to include all image files that are linked to the publication.

4 Close all open publications, and choose Quit from the File menu (Command-Q) to exit the Adobe PageMaker application.

PRINTING THE BOOK COVER

In addition to trapping and constructing bleeds, the prepress tasks will include specifying a custom paper size and including printer's marks and page information. For more information on these prepress tasks, refer to the *Adobe PageMaker 6.0 User Guide* and the *Adobe Print Publishing Guide.*

Note: Since this book cover design will eventually be incorporated into a book jacket, there is no need to allow for a bleed along the left and right edges of the page.

Knowing your printer plans to print with a line screen frequency between150 lpi and 175 lpi, your service provider will create the film separations on a imagesetter with a resolution of 2400 dpi to 3200 dpi. Once the film separations are created, you can deliver them to your printer.

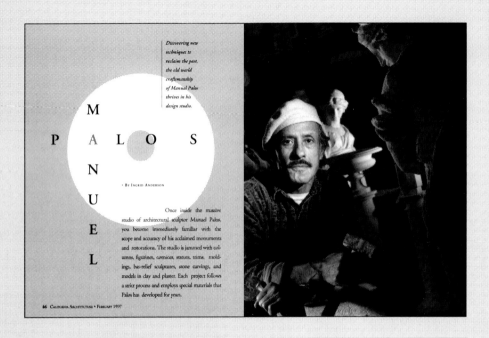

M
PALOS
MANUEL

Discovering new techniques to reclaim the past, the old world craftsmanship of Manuel Palos thrives in his design studio.

• BY INGRID ANDERSON

Once inside the massive studio of architectural sculptor Manuel Palos, you become immediately familiar with the scope and accuracy of his acclaimed monuments and restorations. The studio is jammed with columns, figurines, cornices, statues, trims, moldings, bas-relief sculptures, stone carvings, and models in clay and plaster. Each project follows a strict process and employs special materials that Palos has developed for years.

Whether a project involves a restoration or an original design, Palos begins by crafting a scaled-down model of the figure. After making a fiberglass mold and using an enlarging machine to dramatically increase the size, Palos fills the mold with one of his customized materials, depending on the job. "Very few work like this outside of Italy," explains Palos, referring to the old world techniques he uses today.

The son of a shoemaker, Palos began his career in Mexico, receiving a Bachelor of Arts degree in Sculpture from the University of Zacatecas. "Of

course I helped my father. I had to. Along the way I saved enough money to come to San Francisco to work in the studios and workshops like here." Encouraged by teachers insisting he

study in Europe, he traveled to Italy and Spain, enabling himself to train with some of the finest craftspeople in the world. "If you're talking about who is the best at representing natural beauty, it's the Italians. They're the best." He still visits Italy annually to teach and collect marble. "Shipping the marble across the ocean means, well, I suppose I don't sleep so well until it arrives."

Monumental projects

In addition to marble, the Palos portfolio includes works in bronze, stone, plaster, terra cotta, and various fiberglass-based materials. His experience in the restoration of historic details includes some of San Francisco's most prominent architectural ornamentation, arches, ceilings, doorways, medallions, columns, cornices, and fountains. These projects include of the City of Paris in the Neiman Marcus Building, and the figures at the Palace of the Legion of Honor, the Art Deco Rotunda of the Western Merchandise Mart's Center for Design, and the interior of the Crocker Bank Headquarters.

The Palos studio may be best known for the restoration of the Eagles atop the newly restored Pacific Telephone Building. Created from drawings of the granite originals that once adorned the building, each thirteen-foot Eagle towers twenty-seven stories

fire breathing dragon

EVEN THOUGH PALOS ENJOYS INTERNATIONAL recognition as a pioneer in the renovation business, he most enjoys assignments where he's creating original designs. Perhaps the most striking and memorable piece in the Palos portfolio is the Limestone Dragon fireplace he designed and carved for actor Nicholas Cage's Pacific Heights home in 1993. Flipping through albums of photographs, Palos finally recalls the entire process, "It was a pleasure every minute. I really loved it."

Borrowing inspiration from a children's book about dragons, Palos sketched the design that features a huge dragon that reaches from the floor to the ceiling (thirteen-feet-tall-by-ten-feet-wide) with the mouth of the dragon as the opening of the fireplace. Palos points out a photograph that shows a child hiding in the dragon's mouth. "I'm still excited to talk about this project."

In order to obtain enough black limestone for the project, Palos moved his studio to Mexico, where he labored over the sculpture for nearly five months. After matching and assembling thirteen pieces of stone, Palos chiseled the twists and bends of the beast, using pneumatic tools to finish the scales that coat its sinewy coils. "If any part of the face broke, I would have to start over." With the completed sculpture loaded on a truck, Palos drove it back to San Francisco himself.

In the mean time, the foundation and the walls of Cage's Victorian home were reinforced to hold the weight of the four-and-a-half ton dragon fireplace. The three week installation involved using a crane to hoist pieces of the fireplace from the street to the house. Palos and four assistants reassembled it using a special system of scaffolds and pulleys, securing the pieces with stainless steel pins and epoxy. "Most people figure that carving the dragon was the most demanding part of the project. It turned out that installing it was much more work than carving it," he added, shaking his head.

above the city. Cast in fiberglass and weighing a mere fifteen-hundred pounds, these enormous creatures were returned to the skyline of San Francisco in 1984.

Another much-noted project involved replacing the six nine-foot-tall statues atop San Francisco's Palace of the Legion of Honor. Originally patterned after nineteenth-century statues found in Paris, the statues of Homer,

Diana, Medusa, Neptune, Mars, and Venus had begun to fall apart after having been in place since 1924.

Over the course of his thirty-year career, Palos has designed many fireplaces for businesses and private residences. Two are in San Francisco hotels, including the eight-foot-by-eight-foot Art Nouveau style fireplace with undulating curves in The Galleria Park and the fireplace in the Villa Florence

that has a traditional European design with medallions, brackets, and an egg and dart cornice on top.

Today Palos's designs are widely available, allowing customers to purchase his original designs; including columns, bas reliefs, fountains, furniture, and capitals. In addition, Palos has fabricated a line of pre-cast fireplace facades and mantels that are also available for recasting.

• UNITED STATES •

Magazine Article

Adobe PageMaker 6.0 now provides the ability to assemble multi-page publications using multiple master pages, where each publication can have a virtually unlimited number of master pages. To demonstrate the use of this feature, you will assemble a four-page magazine article for the ficticious quarterly publication *California Architecture*, incorporating the use of two master pages. ■ Since both master pages share design attributes, you will create the first master page from scratch, and then you will duplicate and edit it to create the second master page. In addition to basing a new master page on an existing master page, you can base a new master page on an existing publication page.

In addition to incorporating the use of two master pages, this magazine article also includes the use of three colors: black, PANTONE 367 CVC, and PANTONE Warm Red CVC. After building the template that contains the styles, colors, and

MAGAZINE ARTICLE

master pages for a biography-type article featured in every issue of the magazine, you will assemble the magazine article.

This lesson covers:

• Creating, duplicating, revising, and assigning multiple master pages within a single publication

• Copying colors from one publication to another

• Establishing a publication default link option

• Using the Expert Tracking command.

BEFORE YOU BEGIN

All files and fonts needed to assemble this magazine article are found on the Adobe PageMaker *Classroom in a Book* CD-ROM disc in the folders *09Lesson* and *Fonts*, respectively. In addition, the *Extras* folder on the *Classroom in a Book* CD-ROM disc includes files *09Int1* and *09Int2*, interim files of artwork that you may wish to use.

It should take you approximately 2 hours to complete this lesson.

Opening an existing document

Let's take a moment to look at the final version of the magazine article you will assemble.

1 Before launching the Adobe PageMaker program, throw away the *Adobe PageMaker 6.0 Prefs* file to ensure all settings are returned to their default values.

2 Make sure the fonts Adobe Garamond, Adobe Garamond Bold, and Adobe Garamond Semibold are installed.

3 Double-click the *Adobe® PageMaker® 6.0* icon to launch the Adobe PageMaker program.

4 Choose Open from the File menu (Command-O), and in the Open Publication dialog box double-click the *09Final* file in the *09Lesson* folder to view the magazine article you will create.

The full view of the publication displays a variety of text and graphic elements. The page icons in the lower-left corner indicate the article consists of four pages.

5 Click page icon 48/49 to view the second spread, and then click page icon 46/47 to return to the first spread.

6 Choose Guides and Rulers from the Layout menu and Show Guides from the submenu (Command-J) to display the guides used to assemble this magazine article.

Talk with your printer

To reduce the demand for disk space on your system, the images featured in this lesson were scanned at a resolution of 100 dpi. Since its likely that your printer will recommend printing this sort of publication with a line screen frequency between 175 lpi and 300 lpi, in a real environment these images would have to be scanned at 350 dpi to 600 dpi (double the selected line screen frequency) to meet the printing requirements of this publication.

After verifying the trapping specification, the size of the bleed, and the line screen frequency with your printer, talk with your service provider to determine who will perfom the prepress tasks and how you should deliver this publication to your service provider.

CREATING A CUSTOM TEMPLATE

In addition to establishing a strong identity for this magazine, developing a template can save time and effort in the future. For this reason, you will create the four-page template that contains the colors, styles, and two master pages for this featured article.

Opening a new publication

To create the template, begin by opening, naming, saving a new publication.

1 Choose New from the File menu (Command-N), and in the Document Setup dialog box choose Magazine from the Page size pop-up menu, type **4** pages in the Number of pages box and **46** in the Start page # box, and click OK.

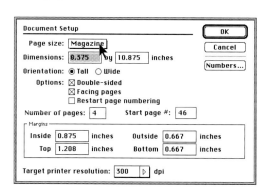

By definition, the untitled publication is 8.375 inches wide by 10.875 inches high. The default margins are displayed, and the page icons in the lower-left corner indicate the publication consists of four pages, starting at page number 46 as you specified.

2 If you do not have a *Projects* folder, create one now.

3 Choose Save As from the File menu, and in the Save publication as dialog box select the *Projects* folder, type **09Template** in the Name box, click the Template radio button to save this file as a template, and click OK.

Creating the first master page spread

The master page you will create for the first double-page magazine spread includes automatic page numbering and repeating text elements.

1 Choose Master Pages from the Window menu (Command-H) to open the Master Pages palette.

The Master Pages palette provides the ability to create, organize, and apply one or more master pages. The bracketed master pages [None] and [Document Master] in the Master Pages palette cannot be removed.

Note: The master page Document Master is applied automatically to the pages in each new publication, with the options specified in the Document Setup dialog box determining the margins and orientation of the master page. To create publications pages without basing them on master pages, apply the master page None.

2 In the Master Pages palette choose New Master from the Master Pages palette pop-up menu (arrow in the upper-right corner).

Master Pages palette pop-up menu

TIP: TO OPEN THE
CREATE MASTER PAGE
DIALOG BOX, HOLD
DOWN THE COMMAND
KEY, AND CLICK
NONE IN THE MASTER
PAGES PALETTE.

3 In the Create New Master Page dialog box type **Opening Spread** in the Name box, make sure both Columns boxes indicate 1 column, and click the Create button.

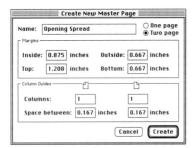

The right and left master pages are displayed with the default margins guides. The Master Pages dialog box displays the newly created master page Opening Spread.

4 Choose Save from the File menu (Command-S).

Specifying automatic page numbering and repeating text

To automatically number all pages in a publication, place page-number markers on the left and right pages of a master page.

1 Magnify the view of the lower-left corner of the left master page.

2 With the text tool selected, click the left master page just above the bottom margin guide (between the left and right margin guides) to establish an insertion point.

The insertion point is aligned with the left margin guide.

3 Hold down the Command and Option keys, and press the P key.

The page-number marker LM (left master) is displayed, indicating where the page number will appear.

4 With the insertion point still established to the right of the LM page-number marker, press the spacebar three times, and in uppercase and lowercase letters type **California Architecture**, press the spacebar, hold down the Option key and press the 8 key (to create a bullet), press the spacebar, and type **February 1997**.

5 With the text tool selected, triple-click the newly created text to select it, and in the Control palette choose Adobe Garamond from the Font pop-up menu, and click the Small caps button.

Small caps button

Bold button

6 With the text tool still selected, drag to select the LM page-number marker, and in the Control palette click the Bold button.

Note: Provided the bold typeface for a font is installed on your system, your publication will print using the actual bold typeface. If the bold typeface is not installed, Adobe PageMaker will embolden (add weight to) the roman version of that font.

7 From the horizontal ruler, drag to create a horizontal ruler guide at 10.625 inches.

8 With the pointer tool selected, click the formatted text to select it as a text block, hold down the Shift key (to constrain the movement to 45°), and drag the text block until the baseline of the text is aligned with the 10.625-inch horizontal ruler guide.

9 With the text still selected as a text block, drag a right corner handle until it is roughly aligned with the right edge of the text, better organizing your work space.

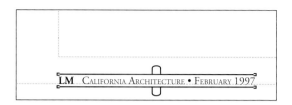

10 Choose Save from the File menu.

Cutting, pasting, and editing text

After cutting and pasting the page-number marker and repeating text from the left master page to the right master page, you will edit the pasted text so that it mirrors the text on the left master page.

1 With the text tool selected, triple-click the formatted text to select it, and choose Copy from the Edit menu (Command-C).

2 Scroll to the bottom portion of the right master page, click the right master page above the bottom margin guide (between the left and right margin guides) to establish an insertion point, and choose Paste from the Edit menu (Command-V).

The LM page-number marker is displayed as a RM (right master) page-number marker.

3 With the text tool still selected, drag to select the RM page-number marker, choose Cut from the Edit menu (Command-X), click just to the right of the text to establish an insertion point, press the spacebar three times, and choose Paste from the Edit menu.

Now that the RM page-number marker is correctly positioned in respect to the repeating text, you can retype the repeating text so that it mirrors the text on the facing master page.

4 With the text tool still selected, drag to select the text, without selecting the RM page-number marker.

5 In uppercase and lowercase letters type **February 1997**, press the spacebar, hold down the Option key and press the 8 key (to create a bullet), press the spacebar, and type **California Architecture.**

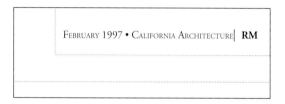

Since the repeating text and page-number marker are left-aligned on the left master page, you will align them to the right on the right master page.

6 With an insertion point still established in the text, in the Control palette click the Paragraph-view button, and in the paragraph view of the Control palette click the Right-align button.

7 With the pointer tool selected, click the formatted text to select it as a text block, and drag a left corner handle to the left edge of the text to better organize your work space.

8 With the text still selected as a text block, hold down the Shift key (to constrain the movement to 45º), and drag it until the baseline of the text is aligned with the 10.625-inch horizontal ruler guide.

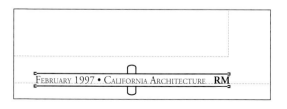

9 Choose View from the Layout menu and Fit in Window from the submenu (Command-0) to view the left and right master pages.

The first master page spread is complete. After you finish assembling the second master page spread, you will assign the two master pages to the four pages in your template-in-progress.

10 Choose Save from the File menu.

Duplicating and revising a master page

The second master page is identical to the first master page, except it has three columns per page instead of two columns per page. Rather than copying and pasting master-page elements from the Opening Spread to the second master page, you will duplicate the first master page, and then revise the second master page to include three columns per page.

1 In the Master Pages palette choose Duplicate from the palette pop-up menu.

2 In the Duplicate Master Page dialog box type **Jump Spread** in the Name of new Master box, and click the Duplicate button.

The page-number marker and repeating text have the same position on the master page Jump Spread as on master page Opening Spread, and the Master Pages dialog box displays the newly created master page Jump Spread. You are ready to revise the master page to specify three columns per page.

3 In the Master Pages palette choose Setup from the Master Pages palette pop-up menu, and in the Master Page Setup dialog box type **3** columns in both column boxes and **.208** inch in both Space Between boxes, and click OK.

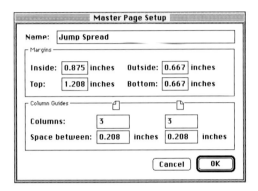

The second master page is assembled.

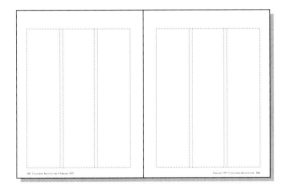

4 Choose Save from the File menu.

Applying master pages

Now that the two master pages are assembled, you are ready to assign them to specific pages in your template-in-progress.

1 Click page icon 46/47 to view the first spread.

The master page Document Master is assigned to the first spread, and Document Master is highlighted in the Master Pages dialog box. By default, the master page Document Master is assigned to each spread in the publication.

TIP: TO APPLY A MASTER PAGE, POSITION THE CURSOR ON THE PAGE ICON CORRESPONDING TO THE TARGET PAGE, HOLD DOWN THE MOUSE BUTTON, AND CHOOSE A MASTER PAGE FROM THE POP-UP MENU.

2 In the Master Pages palette click Opening Spread to assign master page Opening Spread to pages 46 and 47.

Pages 46 and 47 are displayed with the Opening Spread master-page elements.

3 Click page icon 48/49 to view the second spread.

Again, the default master page Document Master is highlighted in the Master Pages palette, with the publication window displaying the master page Document Master.

4 In the Master Pages palette click Jump Spread to assign master page Jump Spread to pages 48 and 49.

Pages 48 and 49 are displayed with the Jump Spread master-page elements.

5 Click the Master Page palette close box to close it, and choose Save from the File menu.

Copying styles from one publication to another

After removing the existing styles in the Styles palette of the *09Template* document to better organize the palette, you will copy styles from the Styles palette of the *09Final* publication to the template.

1 Choose Styles from the Window menu (Command-Y) to open the Styles palette for the *09Template* publication.

2 Choose Define Styles from the Type menu (Command-3), and in the Define Styles dialog box click the first style below [Selection], and click the Remove button.

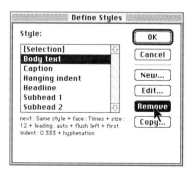

3 With the following style already selected in the list of styles, click the Remove button until all styles have been removed, and click the Copy button.

Note: It is not possible to remove the style [Selection].

4 In the Copy Styles dialog box double-click the *09Final* file in the *09Lesson* folder.

5 In the Define Styles dialog box notice how the copied styles are displayed, and click OK.

The Styles palette displays the copied styles.

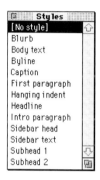

6 Choose Save from the File menu.

Copying colors from one publication to another

Just as you copied styles from one publication to another, you can copy colors from the Colors palette in the *09Final* publication to the template.

1 Choose Colors from the Window menu (Command-K) to open the Colors palette for the *09Template* publication.

2 Choose Define Colors from the Element menu.

Since you will not use the colors Red, Green, and Blue in this lesson, take a moment to remove them.

3 In the Define Colors dialog box click Blue to select it, and click the Remove button.

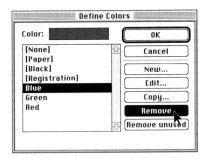

4 Repeat this step two more times, selecting and removing the colors Green and Red, without closing the dialog box.

Note: The four bracketed colors cannot be removed from the list.

5 In the Define Colors dialog box click the Copy button, and in the Copy Colors dialog box double-click the *09Final* file in the *09Lesson* folder.

6 In the Define Colors dialog box notice how the copied colors are displayed, and click OK.

The Colors palette displays the copied colors PANTONE 367 CVC and PANTONE Warm Red CVC.

The template is completely assembled, and you are ready to assemble the magazine article.

6 Choose Save from the File menu.

ASSEMBLING THE FIRST SPREAD

After opening a copy of the template you just assembled, you will place and align text to assemble the first spread of the magazine article, creating the title of the article that features the name Manuel Palos.

Opening a copy of the template

After opening a copy of the custom template you just created, you will place some text on the pasteboard.

1 Click the close box in the title bar of *Template09* to close the template you just created.

2 Choose Open from the File menu, and in the Open Publication dialog box double-click the *09Template* file in the *Projects* folder to open an untitled copy of the template.

3 Click page icon 46/47 to view the first spread.

4 With the magnifying glass selected in the toolbox, drag to marquee select the entire left page.

5 Choose Place from the File menu (Command-D), and in the Place Document dialog box double-click the *09TextA* file in the *09Lesson* folder.

6 Click the pasteboard approximately 3 inches to the left of the left page to place the text.

7 Choose Save As from the File menu, and in the Save publication as dialog box type **09Work** in the Name box, select the *Projects* folder, and click OK.

Formatting and positioning the vertical title text

After cutting and pasting a portion of the placed text, you will format it and arrange the vertical text MANUEL.

1 With the text tool selected, triple-click the first line of placed text to select it.

2 In the Control palette click the Character-view button, and in the character view of the Control palette choose Adobe Garamond Semibold from the Font pop-up menu, type **40** points in the Size box and **80** points in the Leading box, and click the All caps button.

└─ **All caps button**

3 With the text still selected, choose Cut from the Edit menu.

4 Choose View from the Layout menu and Fit in Window from the submenu.

5 Click near the upper-left corner of the page, and choose Paste from the Edit menu.

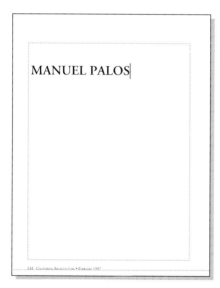

MANUEL PALOS|

6 With the text tool selected, click between the first two letters M and A in the text Manuel, and press the Return key to insert a hard-carriage return.

7 Continue inserting hard-carriage returns after the next four letters in the first line of text, without adding a hard-carriage return after the last letter L.

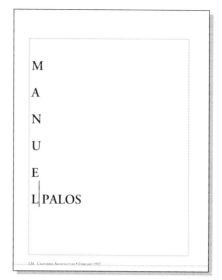

M
A
N
U
E
L PALOS

8 With the text tool selected, drag to select the vertical text MANUEL, without selecting the text PALOS, and choose Cut from the Edit menu.

9 Click near the upper-left intersection of margin guides to establish an insertion point, and choose Paste from the Edit menu.

10 With the pointer tool selected, click the vertical text MANUEL to select it as a text block, hold down the Shift key (to constrain the movement to 45º), and drag a right corner handle until it is roughly aligned with the text to reduce the size of the text block.

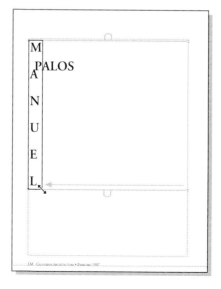

M
A PALOS
N
U
E
L

11 With the text tool selected, drag to select the vertical text MANUEL.

12 In the Control palette click the Paragraph-view button, and in the paragraph view of the Control palette click the Center-align button.

13 From the horizontal ruler, drag to create a horizontal ruler guide at 4.562 inches; and from the vertical ruler, drag to create a vertical ruler guide at –5.969 inches.

14 With the pointer tool selected, click the vertical text MANUEL to select it as a text block, and drag the text block until the baseline of the letter A is aligned with the 4.562-inch horizontal ruler guide, with the left edge of the letter A aligned with the -5.969-inch vertical ruler guide.

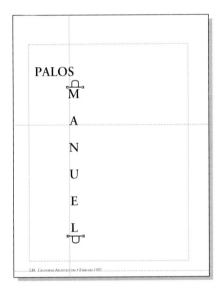

15 With the text tool selected, drag to select the letter A in the vertical text MANUEL, and in the Colors palette click PANTONE Warm Red CVC to apply the spot color to the letter A.

16 Choose Save from the File menu.

Formatting and positioning the horizontal title text

You are ready to position the horizontal title text PALOS.

1 With the text tool selected, click between the first two letters P and A in the text PALOS to establish an insertion point, and press the space-bar eight times.

2 With the pointer tool selected, click the text PALOS to select it as a text block, and drag the text block until the letter A in the text block is precisely aligned over the red letter A in the vertical text MANUEL.

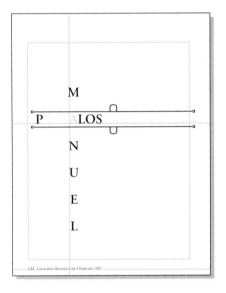

3 With the mouse button still held down, notice how the letter A in the text block is displayed as blue (white on a black and white monitor) when it is precisely aligned over the red letter A, and release the mouse button.

You may recall that Adobe PageMaker maintains the stacking order. In this case, the vertical text MANUEL is at the top of the stack since it was pasted most recently. And so, the red letter A in MANUEL is displayed over the letter A in PALOS.

TIP: TO SELECT A SIN-GLE LETTER, POSITION THE I-BEAM CURSOR NEXT TO THE TARGET LETTER, HOLD DOWN THE SHIFT KEY, AND PRESS THE ARROW KEY THAT MOVES THE I-BEAM CURSOR TO THE OTHER SIDE OF THE TARGET LETTER.

4 With the text PALOS still selected, choose Bring to Front from the Arrange menu (Command-F) to bring the text PALOS to the top of the stack.

5 With the text tool selected, drag to select the letter A in the text PALOS, and press the Delete key.

Since you just deleted the letter A, the letter L in the text PLOS overlaps the red letter A in MANUEL.

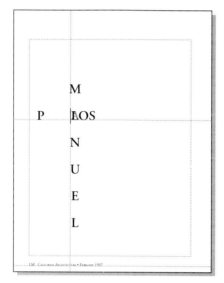

6 With the insertion point established just before the letter L in PLOS, press the spacebar seven times.

7 Press the right arrow key to position the insertion point before the letter O in the text PLOS, and press the spacebar six times.

8 Press the right arrow key to position the insertion point before the letter S in the text PLOS, and press the spacebar nine times.

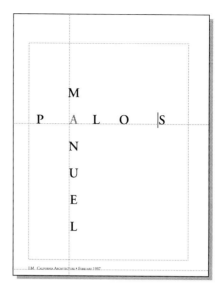

9 Choose Save from the File menu.

Positioning the byline text

You will continue assembling the left page of the first spread by formatting and positioning the byline text.

1 Scroll to the pasteboard to the left of the left page, and magnify the view of the remaining placed text on the pasteboard (to the left of the left page).

2 With the text tool selected, triple-click the first line of the remaining placed text to select it, and choose Cut from the Edit menu.

3 Choose View from the Layout menu and Fit in Window from the submenu.

4 With the text tool still selected, drag to define a text block approximately 3 inches wide (exact height is not important) below the letter L in the text PALOS, and choose Paste from the Edit menu.

5 With the text tool still selected, click the pasted line of text to establish an insertion point, and in the Styles palette click Byline to apply a style.

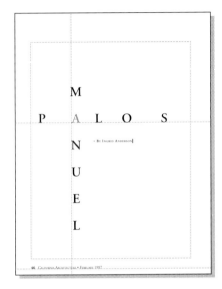

6 With the pointer tool selected, click the byline text to select it as a text block, and drag a right corner handle until it is roughly aligned with the text, reducing the size of the text block.

7 Drag the existing 4.562-inch horizontal ruler guide to be aligned with the 6.125-inch mark on the vertical ruler, and then drag the existing –5.969-inch vertical ruler guide to be aligned with the –4.688-inch mark on the horizontal ruler.

8 With the pointer tool selected, click the byline text to select it as a text block, and drag it until the baseline of the text is aligned with the 6.125-inch horizontal ruler guide, with the left edge of the bullet character aligned with the -4.688-inch vertical ruler guide.

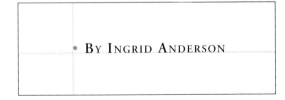

9 With the text tool selected, drag to select the bullet at the beginning of the byline text to select it, and in the Colors palette click PANTONE Warm Red CVC.

10 Choose Save from the File menu.

Formatting and positioning the blurb text

After formatting the blurb text, you will position it in the upper-right portion of the left page.

1 Choose View from the Layout menu and Fit in Window from the submenu, and scroll to view the remaining placed text on the pasteboard.

2 With the text tool selected, click the remaining placed text on the pasteboard to establish an insertion point, and in the Styles palette click Blurb.

3 From the vertical ruler, drag to create a vertical ruler guide at -3 inches.

4 With the pointer tool selected, click the remaining placed text on the pasteboard to select it as a text block, and drag it until the baseline of the second line of text is aligned with the top margin guide, with the left edge of the text aligned with the -3-inch vertical ruler guide.

5 Magnify the view of the blurb text.

6 From the vertical ruler, drag to create a vertical ruler guide at –1.438-inches.

7 With the pointer tool selected, click the blurb text to select it as a text block, and drag a right corner handle until it is roughly aligned with the –1.438-inch vertical ruler guide to reduce the size of the text block.

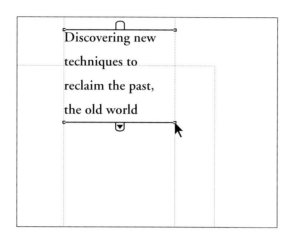

8 With the text tool selected, triple-click the blurb text, and in the Control palette click the Character-view button, and in the character view of the Control palette click the Italic button.

Italic button

Note: Provided the italic typeface for a font is installed on your system, your publication will print using the actual italic typeface. If the italic typeface is not installed, Adobe PageMaker will oblique the roman version of that font.

9 With the pointer tool selected, click the blurb text to select it as a text block, and drag the bottom windowshade handle down until the entire story is displayed.

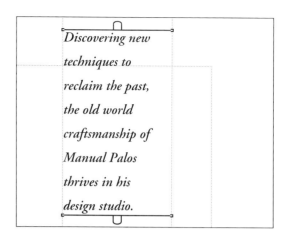

10 Choose Save from the File menu.

Correcting an uneven rag

To correct the uneven rag along the right edge of the blurb text, you will insert a soft-carriage return. Since a hard-carriage return indicates the end of a paragraph, insert a soft-carriage return when you want to force a line to break within a selected range of text, without splitting a paragraph into two paragraphs.

Note: To prevent a line from breaking, select the words you want to keep on one line with the text tool, choose Type Specs from the Type menu, and in the Type Specifications dialog box check the No break radio button, and click OK.

1 With the text tool selected, click before the last word (of) in the fifth line of text to establish an insertion point, hold down the Shift key (to specify a soft-carriage return), and press the Return key to force the word to the sixth line of text.

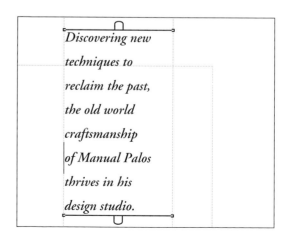

The rag appears to be more balanced.

You are ready to draw a vertical line that will serve to anchor the blurb text visually.

2 With the constrained-line tool selected in the toolbox, position the cursor at the top of the blurb text, approximately .125 inch to the left of the text, and drag down to the baseline of the last line of text to draw a vertical line .

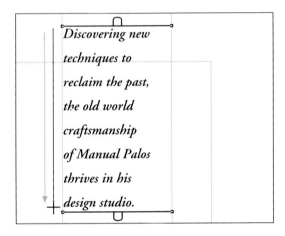

3 Choose Line from the Element menu and the .5-point solid line from the submenu to apply a line style and weight.

4 Choose Save from the File menu.

Setting a publication default link option

In previous lessons when you imported image files that were 256K or larger, you prevented duplication of the file to your publication to control the size of your Adobe PageMaker file. In this example, you will establish a publication default link option that will automatically prevent duplicating all image files to the *09Work* publication.

1 Choose Link Options from the Element menu, and in the Link Options: Defaults dialog box click the *second* Store copy in publication check box to deselect the Graphics option, and click OK.

You are ready to import the image files of any size without duplicating image data to the *09Work* publication.

Placing and cropping a graphic

The photograph you are about to place was sized to allow for a 3/16-inch bleed to overlap the top, bottom, and right edges of the page. Since the photograph extends to the edge of the page, the bleeds will ensure that when the printed paper is trimmed during the finishing process, the ink coverage will extend to the very edge of the paper.

1 Choose View from the Layout menu and Fit in Window from the submenu.

2 Choose Place from the File menu, and in the Place Document dialog box double-click the *09GraphicA* file in the *09Lesson* folder.

3 With the graphics icon displayed, position the cursor near the upper-left corner of the right page, and click to place the graphic.

In addition to positioning the photograph, you will use the Control palette to crop the photograph by entering the precise dimensions of the page.

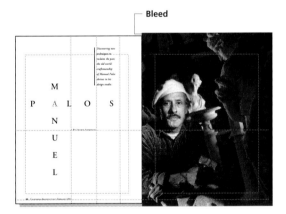

Bleed

4 With the photograph selected, in the Control palette make sure the upper-left reference point in the Proxy icon is selected, type **0** inches in the X box and **0** inches in the Y box, click the Cropping button to select it, type **8.375** inches in the Width box and **10.875** inches in the Height box, and press the Return key.

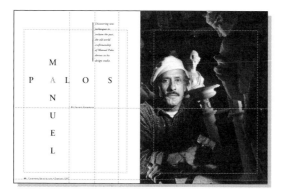

5 Choose Save from the File menu.

Placing and formatting the body text

Even though the first spread is not completely assembled, you will place the body text on the second spread, so that you can cut the first paragraph and paste it to the first spread.

1 Click page icon 48/49 to display the second spread.

2 Choose Autoflow from the Layout menu to select it, making sure it is checked.

3 Choose Place from the File menu, and in the Place Document dialog box double-click the *09TextB* file in the *09Lesson* folder.

4 Position the loaded text icon in the top portion of the left column on the left page (page 48), and click to place the text.

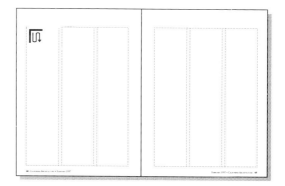

The right page (page 49) displays the last lines of the body text story.

5 With the text tool selected, click the flowed text to establish an insertion point, choose Select All from the Edit menu (Command-A), and click Body text in the Styles palette.

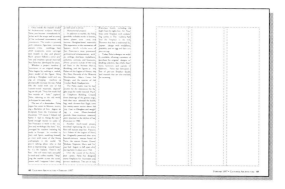

6 Choose Save from the File menu.

Cutting, pasting, and formatting the intro paragraph text

After cutting the first paragraph of the feature text on the second spread, you will paste it to the first spread and format it.

1 Magnify the view of the upper-left corner of the left page.

2 With the text tool selected, triple-click the first paragraph in the left column to select it, and choose Cut from the Edit menu.

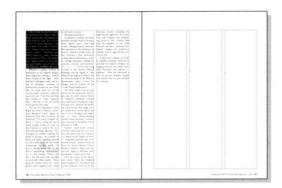

3 Click page icon 46/47 to display the first spread.

4 With the text tool still selected, drag to define a text block approximately 4 inches wide (exact height is not important), below the byline text in the middle of the left page (page 46), and choose Paste from the Edit menu.

5 With the text tool still selected, click the pasted text to establish an insertion point, and click Intro paragraph in the Styles palette to apply a custom style.

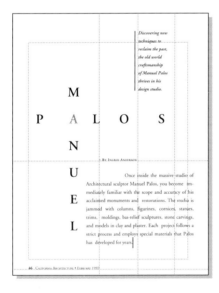

6 With the magnifying glass selected in the toolbox, drag to marquee select the entire intro paragraph text.

7 With the pointer tool selected, click the intro paragraph text to select it as a text block, drag a left corner handle until it is aligned with the –4.688-inch vertical ruler guide, and drag a right corner handle to be aligned with the right margin guide, resizing the text block.

8 With the intro paragraph text still selected as a text block, drag the bottom windowshade until the entire story is displayed, and drag the text block until the baseline of the last line of text is aligned with the bottom margin guide.

9 Choose Save from the File menu.

Fine-tuning the intro paragraph text

You will use the Expert Tracking command to adjust algorithmically the space between letters and words (tracking) in the intro paragraph text. To further adjust the letter spacing, you will add a soft-carriage return to force text to the next line, without creating two paragraphs.

1 With the text tool selected, triple-click the intro paragraph text to select it.

2 Choose Expert Tracking from the Type menu and Normal from the submenu.

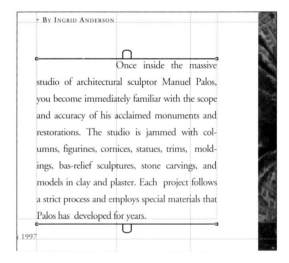

Because Normal tracking reduces letter spacing for this point size (of this typeface), the tightened tracking has reduced the number of lines by one.

Note: For small point sizes (of typeface), Normal tracking increases the letter spacing between letters and words.

3 If necessary, click the intro paragraph text with the pointer tool to select it as a text block, hold down the Shift key (to constrain the movement to 45°), and drag the text block until the last line of text is aligned with the bottom margin guide.

Notice how the letter spacing in the third line of text seems a little tight in comparison to the letter spacing in the fifth line of text.

5 With the text tool selected, click before the last word (scope) in the third line of text to establish an insertion point, hold down the Shift key (to specify a soft-carriage return), and press the Return key.

The overall letter spacing throughout the intro paragraph text seems more balanced.

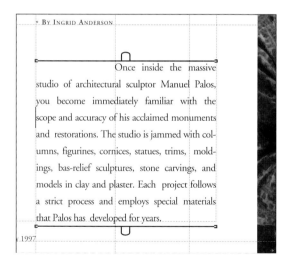

5 Choose Save from the File menu.

Creating the spot-color background

After drawing a box that outlines the entire right page, you will apply a spot color to the box.

1 Choose View from the Layout menu and Fit in Window from the submenu.

2 With the rectangle tool selected in the toolbox, draw a box outlining the entire left page (page 46).

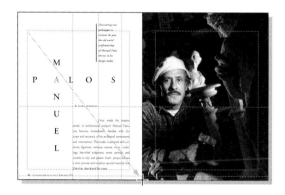

3 To verify the dimensions of the box equal the dimensions of the magazine, make sure the Control palette indicates the width equals 8.375 inches and the height equals 10.875 inches.

Note: If necessary, type one or both of these values into the Width and Height boxes in the Control palette, and press the Return key.

4 Make sure the box is still selected; and in the Colors palette make sure the Both button is selected, click PANTONE 367 CVC, and choose 90% from the Tint pop-up menu.

As with the photograph on the right page of this spread, you would create a ³⁄₁₆-inch bleed of this spot-color background to overlap the top, bottom, and left edges of the page before printing this article.

5 Choose Save from the File menu.

Placing and positioning the display letter O

After placing and positioning the display letter O, you will group it with the spot-color background you just created, and then adjust the stacking order to allow all remaining elements on the page to overlap the letter O and the spot color. The letter O graphic was created in Adobe Illustrator and saved as an EPS file.

1 Choose Place from the File menu, and in the Place Document dialog box double-click the *09GraphicB* file in the *09Lesson* folder.

2 With the graphics icon displayed, click anywhere on the left page to place the letter O graphic.

The letter O graphic overlaps the background (the 90% tint of PANTONE 367 CVC).

3 In the Control palette make sure the upper-left point in the Proxy icon is selected, type **-6.76** inches in the X box and **1.939** inches in the Y box, and press the Return key to move the letter O graphic.

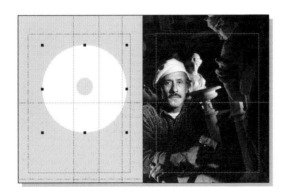

4 With the letter O graphic still selected, hold down the Shift key (to select multiple objects), and click the spot-color background to select it, too.

5 Choose Group from the Arrange menu (Command-G) to group the two graphics elements together.

6 Choose Send to Back from the Arrange menu (Command-B) to send the grouped objects to the bottom of the stack.

7 Choose View from the Layout menu and Fit in Window from the submenu.

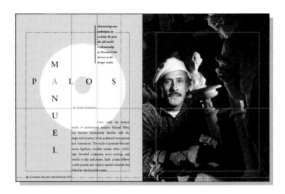

You have completed assembling the first spread.

8 Choose Save from the File menu.

Note: An interim file was saved at this point. To open it, double-click the 09Int1 *file in the* Extras *folder.*

ASSEMBLING THE SECOND SPREAD

You are ready to assemble the second spread of the magazine article. In previous steps you assigned the master page Jump spread to this spread.

Placing a graphic and applying a text wrap

You will place the photograph that is positioned in the lower-left corner of the left page on the second spread. Scanned on a flatbed scanner, this graphic was sized in Adobe Photoshop, and saved in TIFF file format at a resolution of 100 dpi.

1 Click page icon 48/49 to view the second spread.

2 Choose View from the Layout menu and Fit in Window from the submenu.

3 Choose Place from the File menu, and in the Place Document dialog box double-click the *09GraphicC* file in the *09Lesson* folder.

4 Click anywhere on the left page to place the graphic.

5 With the photograph still selected, drag to align the bottom edge of the photograph with the bottom margin guide, with the left edge of the photograph aligned with the left margin guide.

6 Magnify the view of the photograph, and make sure it's aligned with the margin guides.

7 With the pointer tool selected, click the photograph to select it, and choose Text Wrap from the Element menu, and in the Text Wrap dialog box

click the rectangular graphics boundary icon (middle icon) to select a Wrap option, click the Column-break icon (left icon) to select a Text flow option, and click OK.

Selecting the Column-break icon stops the text flow above the graphic and then continues the flow at the start of the next column.

Notice how the space above the photograph and below the text seems to be too big. Even though it is possible to adjust the standoff using the Text Wrap dialog box, you will adjust it manually.

9 From the horizontal ruler, drag to create a horizontal ruler guide at 4.312 inches.

10 With the pointer tool selected, position the cursor on the graphics boundary (dotted line) above the photograph, and drag the standoff guide down until it is aligned with the 4.312-inch horizontal ruler guide.

Standoff guide

Adjusting the graphics boundary allows another line of text to be displayed above the photograph.

11 Choose Save from the File menu.

Placing another graphic

You will place the photograph that is positioned in the upper-right corner of the left page, applying a text wrap. Like the previous graphic, this graphic was scanned on a flatbed scanner, sized in Adobe Photoshop, and saved in TIFF file format at a resolution of 100 dpi.

1 Choose View from the Layout menu and Fit in Window from the submenu.

2 Choose Place from the File menu, and in the Place Document dialog box double-click the *09GraphicD* file in the *09Lesson* folder.

3 Click the left page, and drag to align the top edge of the photograph aligned with the top margin guide, with the right edge of the photograph with the right margin guide.

4 Magnify the view of the column photograph, and make sure it's aligned with the margin guides.

5 With the pointer tool selected, click the photograph to select it.

6 Choose Text Wrap from the Element menu, and in the Text Wrap dialog box click the rectangular graphics boundary icon (middle icon) to select a Wrap option, type .1 in the Bottom box to set the Standoff in inches, and click OK.

7 Choose Save from the File menu.

Applying styles to remove indentations

To comply with the established publication style, you will apply a style that will remove the indentation in the first paragraph in the left column, and the indentation in the paragraph that follows a subhead.

1 Scroll to the upper-left column on the left page.

2 With the text tool selected, click the first paragraph text in the left column to establish an insertion point, and in the Styles palette click First paragraph.

Whether a project involves a restoration or an original design, Palos begins by crafting a scaled-down model of the figure. After making a fiberglass mold and using an enlarging machine to dramatically increase the size, Palos fills the mold with one of his custom-mixed materials, depending on the job. "Very few work like this outside of Italy," explains Palos, referring the old world techniques he uses today.

Sculpture from the Zacatecas. "Of cour father. I had to. A

The son of a shoemaker, Palos

The selected paragraph is no longer indented.

3 Scroll to the right column on the left page.

4 With the text tool selected, click the first paragraph text in the right column that follows the subhead text (Monumental Projects) to establish an insertion point, and in the Styles palette click First paragraph.

sleep so well until it arrives."
Monumental projects
In addition to marble, the Palos portfolio includes works in bronze, stone, plaster, terra cotta, and various fiberglass-based materials. His experience in the restoration of historic details includes some of San Francisco's most prominent architectural ornamentation, arches, ceilings, doorways, medallions, columns, cornices, and fountains. These projects include of the City of Paris in the Neiman Marcus Building, and the figures at the Palace of the Legion of Honor, the Art Deco Rotunda of the Western Merchandise Mart's Center for Design, and the interior of the Crocker Bank Headquarters.
The Palos studio may be best

You will apply a style to the subhead text.

5 With the text tool still selected, click the subhead text Monumental Projects (above the paragraph you just formatted) to establish an insertion point, and in the Styles palette click Subhead 1.

sleep so well until it arrives."

Monumental projects
In addition to marble, the Palos portfolio includes works in bronze, stone, plaster, terra cotta, and

6 Choose Save from the File menu.

Creating a drop cap

Now that the text is formatted, you will create two drop caps on the left page.

1 Choose View from the Layout menu and Fit in Window from the submenu, and magnify the view of the upper-left portion of the left page.

2 With the text tool selected, drag to select the first letter W in the first paragraph in the left column to select it.

Note: Even though it is possible to create a drop cap with the first letter of a paragraph by simply establishing an insertion point in the target paragraph, you have selected the specific letter because you will be applying a color to it.

3 Choose PageMaker Plug-ins from the Utilities menu and Drop Cap from the submenu, and in the Drop Cap dialog box type **3** lines in the Size box, and click OK.

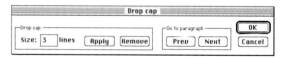

4 Click the zoom box in the upper-right corner of the publication window to force the screen to be redrawn.

5 With the drop cap still selected, in the Colors palette click PANTONE Warm Red CVC.

Whether a project involves a restoration or an original design, Palos begins by crafting a scaled-down model of the figure. After making a fiberglass mold

6 Scroll to view the right column.

7 With the text tool selected, drag to select the first letter in the paragraph that follows the subhead text (Monumental Projects) to select it.

8 Choose PageMaker Plug-ins from the Utilities menu and Drop Cap from the submenu, and in the Drop Cap dialog box type **3** lines in the Size box, and click OK.

9 With the drop cap still selected, in the Colors palette click PANTONE Warm Red CVC.

10 Click the zoom box in the upper-right corner of the publication window to force the screen to be redrawn.

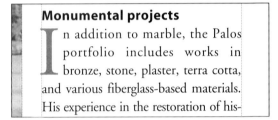

11 Choose Save from the File menu.

Creating the sidebar box

After drawing a sidebar box on the right page, establishing standoff, and applying color to the box, you will flow the remaining body text below the box.

1 With the rectangle tool selected in the toolbox, drag to draw a box of any dimension on the right page (page 49).

2 In the Control palette make sure the upper-left point in the Proxy icon is selected, type **.875** inch in the X box, **1.208** inches in the Y box, **6.833** inches in the Width box, and **6.792** inches in the Height box, and press the Return key to move and resize the box.

The box is displayed with the desired dimensions and positioning.

3 With the box still selected, in the Colors palette make sure the Both button is selected, click PANTONE 367 CVC, and choose 20% from the Tint pop-up menu.

A 20% tint of PANTONE 367 CVC is applied to the line and fill of the box.

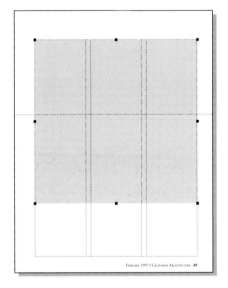

4 Choose Save from the File menu.

Flowing the body text semiautomatically

Now that the sidebar box is positioned, you will flow the remaining text semiautomatically from the left page to the right page.

1 Magnify the view of the right column of the left page (page 48).

2 With the pointer tool selected, click the text in the right column on the left page to select it as a text block, drag the bottom windowshade handle until the text fills the entire column, and drag the text block until the baseline of the last line of text in the is aligned with the bottom margin guide, (with the first line of text approximately one line space below the photograph).

3 Choose View from the Layout menu and Fit in Window from the submenu.

4 With the text in the right column still selected as a text block, click the red arrow in the bottom windowshade handle to load the remaining text.

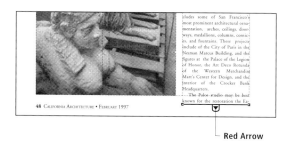

— Red Arrow

5 Choose Autoflow from the Layout menu to deselect it, making sure it is unchecked.

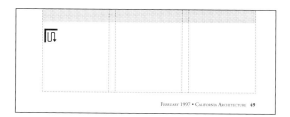

6 With the loaded text icon displayed, hold down the Shift key (to specify semiautomatic text flow), and click just below the sidebar box in the left column on the right page to flow the text into the left column.

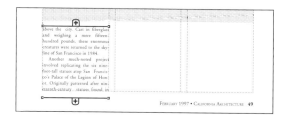

7 With the loaded text icon displayed, hold down the Shift key (to specify semiautomatic text flow), and click just below the sidebar box in the middle column to flow the text into the right column.

8 With the loaded text icon displayed, click just below the sidebar box in the right column to flow the text into the right column.

You are ready to align the text blocks in each of the columns.

9 Magnify the view of the text in the lower portion of the right page.

10 With the pointer tool selected, click the text in the left column of the right page to select it as a text block, hold down the Shift key (to constrain the movement to 45°), and drag the text block until the baseline of the first line of text is approximately one line space below the sidebar box, with the last line of text aligned with the bottom margin guide.

11 Repeat this step for the text blocks in the middle and right columns, aligning the last line of text in both text blocks with the bottom margin guide.

The text block in the right column displays a red down arrow in the bottom windowshade handle, indicating the entire story is not displayed. In the following instructions, you will address this issue.

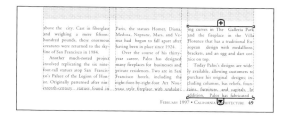

12 Choose Save from the File menu.

Adjusting the tracking

Now that the text is formatted and positioned, you will use the Expert Tracking command to adjust algorithmically the letter space between letters and words (tracking) in the feature text.

Since no tracking has been set for the feature text, tightening the tracking may allow all text to fit within the two pages.

1 With the text tool selected, click the feature text to establish an insertion point, and choose Select All from the Edit menu to select all feature text.

2 Choose Expert Tracking from the Type menu and Normal from the submenu.

Because Normal tracking reduces letter spacing for this point size (of this typeface), the tightened tracking allows all text to fit within the two pages.

3 Choose Save from the File menu.

Creating different numbers of columns on a single page

With the three columns of feature text positioned in the lower portion of the page, you can establish the page to be divided into two columns without affecting the text in the three columns.

1 Choose View from the Layout menu and Fit in Window from the submenu.

2 Choose Column Guides from the Layout menu, and in the Column Guides dialog box make sure 3 columns is displayed in the Number of columns box for the Left page, type 2 columns in the Number of columns box for the Right page, make sure the Set left & right pages separately check box is selected, and click OK.

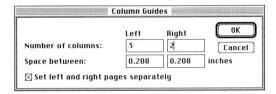

The column guides indicate the image area is divided into two columns, and the text in the lower portion of the page remains in three separate columns. Once a text block is defined and positioned, removing column guides has no effect on the dimensions and positioning of a text block.

Adobe PageMaker makes it possible to manually override the position of column guides.

3 With the pointer tool selected, use the X indicator in the Control palette to align the left column guide of the left column with the 1.156-inch mark on the horizontal ruler, and then align the right column guide of the right column with the 7.438-inch mark on the horizontal ruler.

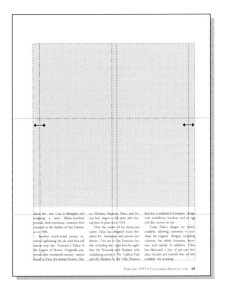

4 Choose Save from the File menu.

Placing and aligning the sidebar text and headline

After placing and aligning text into the first of two columns in the sidebar box, you will cut the headline text from the placed text and paste it at the top of the sidebar box.

1 From the horizontal ruler, drag to create two horizontal ruler guides at 2.094 inches and 7.656 inches.

2 Choose Autoflow from the Layout menu to select it, making sure it is checked.

3 Choose Place from the File menu, and in the Place Document dialog box double-click the *09TextC* file in the *09Lesson* folder.

4 With the loaded text icon displayed, click in the left column, above the 2.094-inch horizontal ruler guide to flow the text into the two columns automatically.

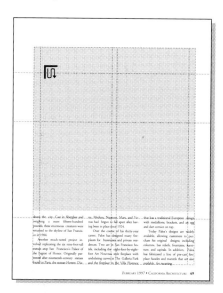

Both text blocks are displayed to be selected as text blocks.

5 Hold down the Shift key (to deselect an object), and click the text block in the right column.

6 Magnify the view of the top portion of the left column in the sidebar box.

7 With the pointer tool selected, drag the text block in the left column until the baseline of the first line of text is aligned with the 2.094-inch horizontal ruler guide.

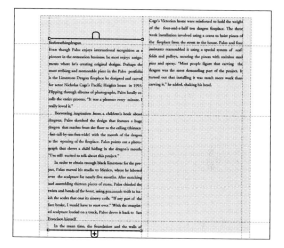

8 Scroll to view the lower portion of the left column.

9 With the text block still selected, drag the bottom windowshade handle until it is aligned with the 7.656-inch horizontal ruler guide.

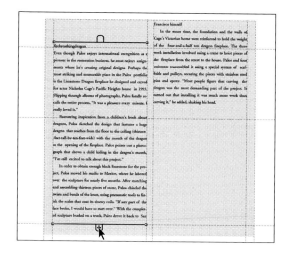

10 Scroll to view the upper portion of the right column of the sidebar box.

11 With the pointer tool selected, click the text in the right column to select it as a text block, hold down the Shift key (to constrain the movement to 45°), and drag the text block until the baseline of the first line of text is aligned with the 2.094-inch horizontal ruler guide.

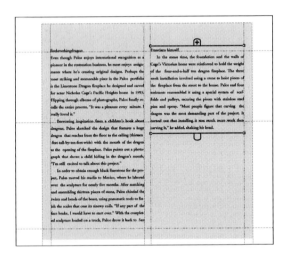

12 Choose Save from the File menu.

Creating the sidebar headline

After cutting the first line of text from the sidebar text, you will drag to define a text block that spans the two columns to establish an insertion point and the dimensions of the sidebar headline text block.

1 Scroll to view the upper portion of the left column.

2 With the text tool selected, triple-click the first line of text in the left column of the sidebar text to select it, and choose Cut from the Edit menu.

3 Drag to define a text box above the sidebar text, spanning the width of the two columns (exact height is not important), and choose Paste from the Edit menu.

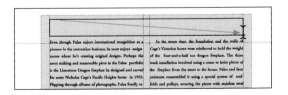

4 With the text tool selected, click the sidebar headline text to establish an insertion point, and in the Styles palette click Sidebar head.

5 With the text tool still selected, click the sidebar headline text between the first two words fire and breathing; and in the Control palette type .7 em space in the Kerning box, and click the Apply button to expand the letterspacing between the characters.

6 Again, click the sidebar headline text between the two words breathing and dragon to establish an insertion point; and in the Control palette type .7 em space in the Kerning box, and click the Apply button.

7 With the insertion point still established in the headline, choose Select All from the Edit menu, and in the Colors palette click PANTONE Warm Red CVC.

8 From the horizontal ruler, drag to create a horizontal ruler guide at 1.656 inches.

9 With the pointer tool selected, click the sidebar headline text to select it as a text block, hold down the Shift key (to constrain the movement to 45°), and drag the text block until the baseline of the text is aligned with the 1.656-inch horizontal ruler guide.

10 Choose Save from the File menu.

Overriding a style

Even though the sidebar text was correctly formatted before being imported into Adobe PageMaker, you will override the applied style to capitalize the first five words in the first paragraph of the sidebar text.

1 With the text tool selected, drag to select the first five words in the first paragraph in the sidebar, and in the Control palette click the All caps button.

2 Choose Save from the File menu.

Placing and positioning a graphic

After placing and positioning the dragon photograph, you will create a custom graphics boundary around the dragon, allowing the text to wrap around the dragon photograph. This photograph of a model was scanned on a flatbed scanner, sized in Adobe Photoshop, and saved as an EPS file at a resolution of 100 dpi.

Note: Since this image file includes a clipping path, it was saved as an EPS file.

1 Choose View from the Layout menu and Fit in Window from the submenu.

2 Click the pointer tool in the toolbox to make sure no insertion point is established in existing text.

3 Choose Place from the File menu, and in the Place Document dialog box double-click the *09GraphicE* file in the *09Lesson* folder.

4 With the graphics icon displayed, click the sidebar box to place the photograph.

The dragon photograph overlaps the text in the sidebar box.

5 In the Control palette make sure the center reference point in the Proxy icon is selected, type **4.285** inches in the X box and **4.69** inches in the Y box, and press the Return key.

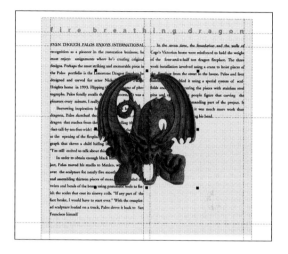

6 Choose Save from the File menu.

Note: An interim file was saved at this point. To open it, double-click the 09Int2 *file in the* Extras *folder.*

Creating a custom text wrap

You will create a custom text wrap that will allow the text to wrap around the bounds of the dragon photograph.

Time out for a movie

If your system is capable of running Adobe Teach movies, play the movie named *Text Wraps* to see a preview of creating a custom text wrap that is covered in this section. For information on how to play Adobe Teach movies, see the section What You Need To Know at the beginning of this book.

1 With the pointer tool selected, click the dragon photograph to select it, choose Text Wrap from the Element menu, and in the Text Wrap dialog box click the rectangular graphics boundary icon (middle icon) to select the Wrap option, type .05 inch in the Left box, .05 inch in the Right box, **0** inches in the Top box, and **0** inches in the Bottom box to set the Standoff in inches, and click OK.

Note: After customizing a graphics boundary, the rightmost Wrap option icon in the Text Wrap dialog box is highlighted.

To make it easier to follow the instructions for customizing the graphics boundary, you will move the zero point (the intersection of the vertical and horizontal rulers) from the upper-left corner of the page to a new location, so the ruler measures the working area of the graphics boundary.

2 With the magnifying tool selected in the toolbox, drag to marquee select the entire dragon photograph.

3 With the pointer tool selected, click the dragon photograph to view the graphics boundary.

4 With the pointer tool still selected, position the cursor on the crosshair of the zero point, and drag it until the zero point is aligned with the upper-left corner of the graphics boundary of the dragon photograph.

5 With the pointer tool still selected, position the cursor on the top edge of the graphics boundary of the dragon, aligned with the 2.75-inch mark on the horizontal ruler, and click to create a handle.

6 Position the cursor on the upper-right corner handle of the graphics boundary, hold down the Shift key (to constrain the movement to 45º), and drag to the right edge of the graphics boundary, aligning it with the 1.25-inch mark on the vertical ruler, using the X value in the Control palette if necessary.

7 Click to create three handles on the right edge of the graphics boundary, aligned with the vertical ruler at 2.25 inches, 2.5 inches, and 2.75 inches.

8 Drag the middle 2.5-inch handle on the right edge of the graphics boundary until the Control palette indicates the X and Y coordinates equal 2.75 inches and 2.438 inches, respectively.

9 To drag the graphics boundary itself (as opposed to dragging a handle), position the cursor on the right edge of the graphics boundary, between the 2.75-inch handle on the graphics boundary and the lower-right corner handle, and hold down the mouse button.

10 Drag the right edge of the graphics boundary toward the dragon photograph until it is aligned with the 3.141-inch mark on the horizontal ruler, and release the mouse button.

11 Click to create three handles on the left edge of the graphics boundary, aligned with the vertical ruler at 2 inches, 2.5 inches, and 3 inches.

12 Drag the middle 2.5-inch handle on the left edge of the graphics boundary until the Control palette indicates the X and Y coordinates equal .485 inch and 3 inches, respectively.

13 To drag the graphics boundary itself, position the cursor on the left edge of the graphics boundary, between the 3-inch handle on the graphics boundary and the lower-left corner handle, and hold down the mouse button.

14 Drag the left edge of the graphics boundary toward the dragon photograph until it is aligned with the .5-inch mark on the horizontal ruler, and release the mouse button.

15 Click to create a handle on the top edge of the graphics boundary, aligned with the .625-inch mark on the horizontal ruler.

16 Drag the upper-left corner handle of the graphics boundary to the left edge of the graphics boundary, aligning it with the 1-inch mark on the vertical ruler.

The custom graphics boundary is complete, and you are finished assembling the magazine article.

Saving the file

Before closing the 09Work file, take a moment to view your work.

1 Choose View from the Layout menu and Fit in Window from the submenu.

2 Choose Guides and Rulers from the Layout menu and Show Guides from the submenu to hide the guides.

3 Choose Save from the File menu to save the *09Work* publication.

If you have determined that your service provider will perform the prepress tasks, you are ready to deliver the *09Work* file to your service provider. Be sure to include all image files that are linked to the publication.

4 Close all open files, and choose Quit from the File menu (Command-Q) to exit the Adobe PageMaker application.

PRINTING THE MAGAZINE ARTICLE

In addition to trapping and constructing bleeds, the prepress tasks will include specifying a custom paper size and including printer's marks and page information. For more information on these prepress tasks, refer to the *Adobe PageMaker 6.0 User Guide* and the *Adobe Print Publishing Guide.*

Designed to be printed on a commercial printing press, this magazine publication incorporates the color black and two spot colors, requiring a total of three spot-color film separations. Knowing your printer plans to print this publication with a line screen frequency between175 lpi and 300 lpi, your service provider will create three film separations on a imagesetter with a resolution of 3200 dpi. Once the film separations are created, you can deliver them to your printer.

Struktur

Winter 1999

•GERMANY•

10

In this lesson you will assemble the elements for a full-color, seven-page catalog. This publication is developed and distributed biannually by Struktur, a German concern offer-

MULTIMEDIA CATALOG

ing professional supplies used by designers and architects. In addition to being printed, this lesson discusses some of the issues involved with distributing on-screen publications using Adobe PageMaker with Adobe Acrobat® Version 2. Adobe Acrobat enables you to take any document from Macintosh, Windows®, DOS®, or UNIX® platforms and convert it to Portable Document Format (PDF) as easily as you print it. The PDF file retains the page layout, color, graphics, and typography of the original document and can be viewed on-screen or printed using Acrobat Reader™ or Acrobat Exchange™.

Where Acrobat Reader allows you to open, view, and print PDF files, Acrobat Exchange offers additional enhancements for PDF files. In addition to Acrobat Reader and Acrobat Exchange, Adobe Acrobat includes a third component, Acrobat

MULTIMEDIA CATALOG

Distiller™. The Distiller takes PostScript language files and converts them to PDF files, allowing for great flexibility in producing PDF files. Once an Adobe PageMaker file has been converted to a PDF file, your client, members of your work group, or anyone else who needs to review the file can do so, provided Acrobat Reader is installed on their system.

This lesson covers:
• Overriding tabs established in another application

• Placing an inline graphic

• Inserting an en space

• Creating a print style

• Creating a PDF file from an Adobe PageMaker file.

BEFORE YOU BEGIN

All files and fonts needed to complete this lesson are found on the Adobe PageMaker *Classroom in a Book* CD-ROM disc in the folders *10Lesson* and *Fonts*, respectively. In addition, the *Extras* folder on the *Classroom in a Book* CD-ROM disc includes the *10Int1* file, an interim file of artwork that you may wish to use.

It should take you approximately 90 minutes to complete this lesson.

1 Make sure Acrobat Reader, Acrobat Distiller, and the Acrobat Distiller PPD are installed on your system.

Note: In addition to the Acrobat Reader and Acrobat Distiller applications, the Acrobat Distiller PPD (in the Xtras folder in the Distiller folder) is on the Adobe PageMaker 6.0 Deluxe CD-ROM disc.

Acrobat Exchange is not included with the Adobe PageMaker 6.0 application, but is available in the retail version of Adobe Acrobat. For information on how to install the Reader and the Distiller, refer to the Adobe PageMaker 6.0 Getting Started *booklet.*

2 If you want to follow the steps to create the PDF file (at the end of this lesson), and you do not have at least 24 megabytes of RAM on your computer, choose Control Panels from the Apple menu, double-click the *Memory* file, and in the Memory Control Panel activate the Virtual Memory option.

Note: If you do not plan to create the PDF file at the end of this lesson, you do not need to allocate more RAM.

Opening the PDF file format version of the catalog

Before viewing the final version of the catalog you will assemble in Adobe PageMaker, take a moment to view the electronic version of the catalog with Adobe Acrobat.

3 To launch Acrobat Reader and open the electronic version of the catalog, double-click the *10Final.PDF* file in the *10Lesson* folder.

The front cover (first page) of the catalog is displayed in standard-screen mode.

4 Choose Full Screen from the View menu (Command and Shift keys-L) to view the document in full-screen mode.

5 Press the right arrow key on the keyboard to page forward in the catalog.

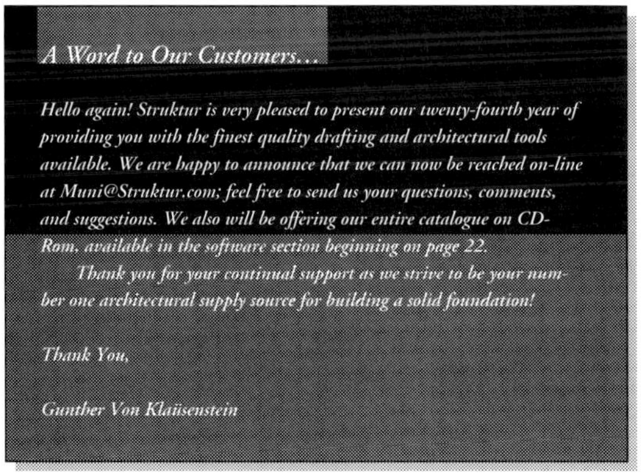
A Word to Our Customers...
Hello again! Struktur is very pleased to present our twenty-fourth year of providing you with the finest quality drafting and architectural tools available. We are happy to announce that we can now be reached on-line at Muni@Struktur.com; feel free to send us your questions, comments, and suggestions. We also will be offering our entire catalogue on CD-Rom, available in the software section beginning on page 22.
Thank you for your continual support as we strive to be your number one architectural supply source for building a solid foundation!
Thank You,
Gunther Von Klaüsenstein

The inside cover (second page) is displayed.

6 Again, press the right arrow key to page forward in the catalog.

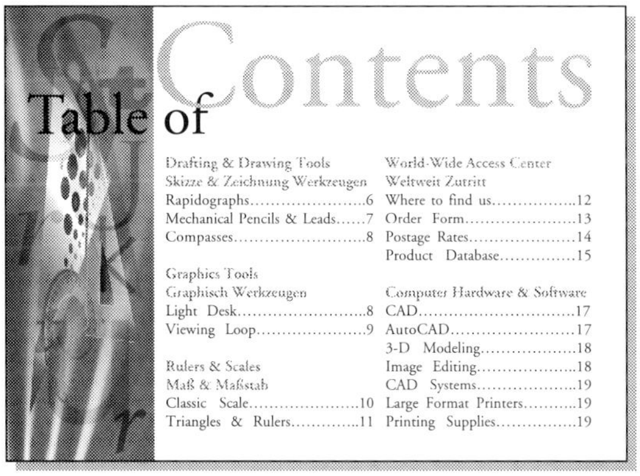
Table of Contents
Drafting & Drawing Tools
Skizze & Zeichnung Werkzeugen
Rapidographs....6
Mechanical Pencils & Leads....7
Compasses....8
Graphics Tools
Graphisch Werkzeugen
Light Desk....8
Viewing Loop....9
Rulers & Scales
Maß & Maßstab
Classic Scale....10
Triangles & Rulers....11
World-Wide Access Center
Weltweit Zutritt
Where to find us....12
Order Form....13
Postage Rates....14
Product Database....15
Computer Hardware & Software
CAD....17
AutoCAD....17
3-D Modeling....18
Image Editing....18
CAD Systems....19
Large Format Printers....19
Printing Supplies....19

The table of contents (third page) is displayed. Some of the headings in the table of contents have been established as "hot spots," or hypertext links to other pages in the catalog.

7 Scroll to the third page, and click the headings Drafting & Drawing tools or Graphics tools to page through the catalog.

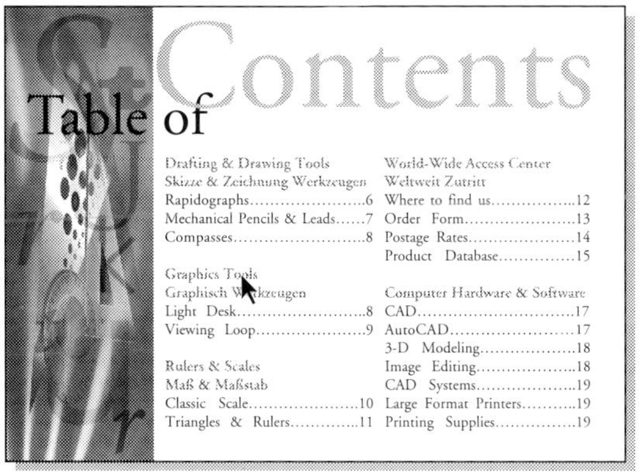
Table of Contents
Drafting & Drawing Tools
Skizze & Zeichnung Werkzeugen
Rapidographs....6
Mechanical Pencils & Leads....7
Compasses....8
Graphics Tools
Light Desk....8
Viewing Loop....9
Rulers & Scales
Maß & Maßstab
Classic Scale....10
Triangles & Rulers....11
World-Wide Access Center
Weltweit Zutritt
Where to find us....12
Order Form....13
Postage Rates....14
Product Database....15
Computer Hardware & Software
CAD....17
AutoCAD....17
3-D Modeling....18
Image Editing....18
CAD Systems....19
Large Format Printers....19
Printing Supplies....19

8 To redisplay the table of contents, click the left double arrows button in the toolbox to navigate to the front of the file.

9 When you are finished browsing through the catalog, hold down the Command key, and press period (.) to display the document in standard-screen mode.

10 Hold down the Command key, and press Q to exit the program.

Opening an existing publication

Let's take a look at the final version of the catalog in Adobe PageMaker.

1 Before launching the Adobe PageMaker program, throw away the *Adobe PageMaker 6.0 Prefs* file to ensure all settings are returned to their default values.

2 Make sure the fonts Adobe Garamond and Adobe Garamond Italic are installed.

3 Double-click the *Adobe® PageMaker® 6.0* icon to launch the Adobe PageMaker program.

4 Choose Open from the File menu (Command-O), and in the Open Publication dialog box double-click the *10Final* file in the *10Lesson* folder.

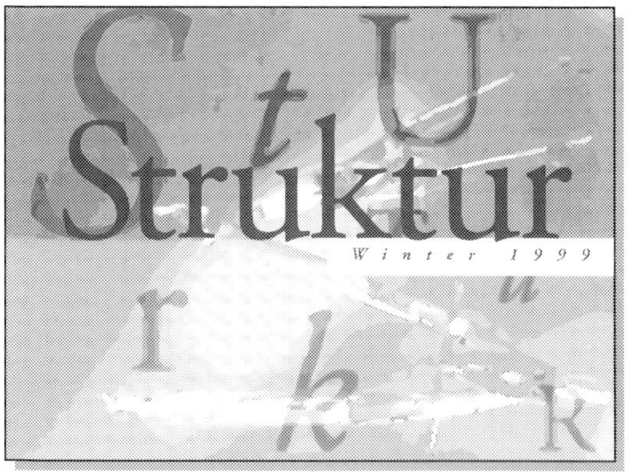
Struktur
Winter 1999

The publication window displays the front cover of the catalog.

TIP: TO REPAINT THE
SCREEN, CLICK THE
ZOOM BOX IN THE
UPPER-RIGHT CORNER
OF THE PUBLICATION
WINDOW ONCE
OR TWICE.

5 Page through the publication to view a variety of text and graphics elements.

6 Choose Guides and Rulers from the Layout menu and Show Guides from the submenu (Command-J) to display the guides used to assemble this catalog.

Talk with your printer

To reduce the demand for disk space on your system, the images featured in this lesson were scanned at a resolution of 100 dpi. Since it is likely that your printer will recommend printing this sort of publication with a line screen frequency of 150 lpi, in a real environment these images would have to be scanned at 300 dpi (double the selected line screen frequency) to meet the printing requirements of this publication.

After verifying the trapping specification, the size of the bleed, and the line screen frequency with your printer, talk with your service provider to determine who will perfom the prepress tasks and how you should deliver this publication to your service provider.

Opening a copy of a template

Since this catalog represents the latest issue in a series of catalogs, many of the styles, text, and graphics have already been provided. With these design and style elements established, the Struktur catalog maintains a high level of recognition in the design world, and minimizes the time and effort needed to assemble each issue.

1 Choose Open from the File menu, and in the Open Publication dialog box double-click the *10Template* file in the *10Lesson* folder.

The untitled copy of the template displays the completed front cover of the catalog. The Colors palette and the Styles palette include the custom colors and styles already established for this catalog. With the front cover design already established for this catalog, you will assemble three double-page spreads.

2 Click page icon 2/3 to view the first double-page spread.

Because the illustrations are positioned on the pasteboard, they are displayed whenever the publication is open, making the pasteboard a good place to organize miscellaneous elements that are established for a publication.

3 Click the L/R master-page icon to view the master page elements, and notice the page-number marker in the lower-right corner of the right master page.

The page-number marker is positioned on the right master page to number all odd-numbered pages.

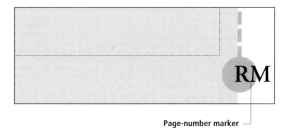

Page-number marker

4 If you do not have a *Projects* folder, create one now.

5 Choose Save As from the File menu, and in the Save publication as dialog box type **10Work** in the Name box, select the *Projects* folder, and click OK.

Replacing the letter text

The front cover is already assembled, so you will begin by using the Place command to replace the letter text on page 2 with new letter text.

6 With the loaded text icon displayed, align the top of the cursor with the 2.14-inch horizontal ruler guide in the right column, and click to place the text.

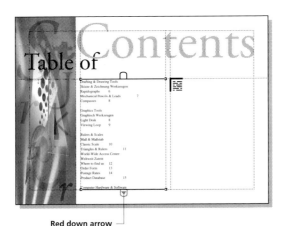

Red down arrow

7 With the text tool selected, click the text on the right page to establish an insertion point, and choose Select All from the Edit menu, and in the Styles palette click 10TOC.

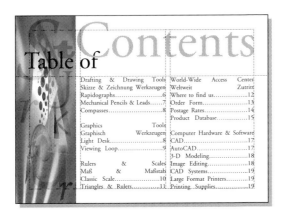

8 Choose Save from the File menu.

Formatting the subhead text

After selecting the subhead text, you will apply a style.

1 With the text tool still selected, drag to select the two lines of the first subhead text, and in the Styles palette click 10Subhead.

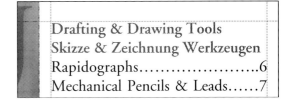

2 Continue selecting the remaining subheads on the right page of the first spread (page 3), applying the style 10Subhead to each subhead.

3 If either text block is not aligned with the bottom margin guide, click the text in either column with the pointer tool, and drag the text block until the baseline of the last line of text is aligned with the bottom margin guide.

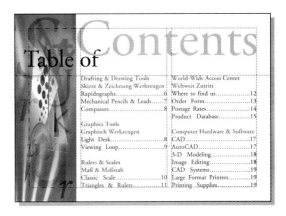

The right page of the first spread is complete.

4 Choose Save from the File menu.

ASSEMBLING THE SECOND SPREAD

After placing a photograph on the left page, you will place and customize the text on the second double-page spread.

Placing, aligning, and cropping a graphic

After scanning this still-life photograph, it was sized in Adobe Photoshop and saved in TIFF file format with a resolution of 100 dpi.

1 Click page icon 4/5 to view the second double-page spread.

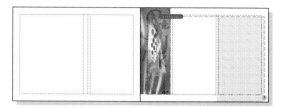

2 Click the pointer tool in the toolbox to deselect all objects in the publication.

3 Choose Place from the File menu, and in the Place Document dialog box double-click the *10GraphicA* file in the *10Lesson* folder.

4 When prompted, click the No button to prevent duplicating the image data to the *10Work* publication.

5 With the graphics icon displayed, click near the upper-left corner of the left page of the second spread (page 4) to place the photograph.

6 With the pointer tool selected, drag the photograph until its right edge is aligned with the right edge of the left column, with its remaining edges overlapping the edges of the page.

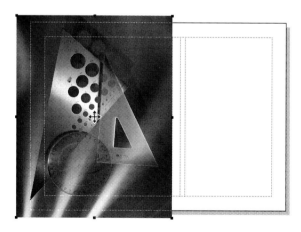

7 With the cropping tool selected in the toolbox, position the center of the cropping tool on the upper-left graphics handle of the photograph, and drag until it is aligned with the upper-left corner of the page.

8 Position the center of the cropping tool on the lower-middle graphics handle of the photograph, and drag until it is aligned with the bottom edge of the page.

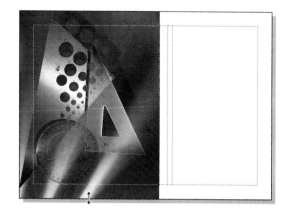

9 Choose Save from the File menu.

Placing and formatting text

You will place, format, and align the text on the right page of the second spread.

1 Choose Place from the File menu, and in the Place Document dialog box double-click the *10TextC* file in the *10Lesson* folder.

2 With the loaded text icon displayed, click in the left column of the right page (page 5), just below the word Struktur to place the text.

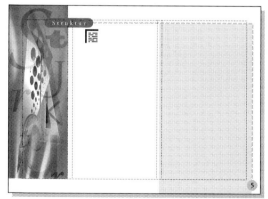

TIP: TO SCROLL THE
VIEW, HOLD DOWN
THE OPTION KEY,
AND DRAG THE PAGE
IN ANY DIRECTION.

3 With the pointer tool selected, click the red down arrow in the bottom windowshade handle to load the remaining text.

4 With the loaded text icon displayed, click in the top portion of the right column on the right page to place the text.

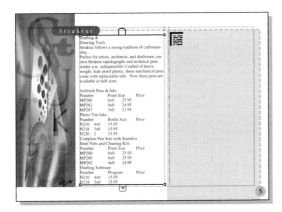

5 Choose Save from the File menu.

Cutting and pasting text

After cutting a portion of the text from the right page of the second spread, and pasting it to the left page, you will apply a style to the text and align it.

1 Magnify the view of the first lines of placed text in the left column of the right page (page 5).

2 With the text tool selected, drag to select the first two lines of text in the left column, and choose Cut from the Edit menu (Command-X).

3 Scroll to the left page (page 4), click the photograph to establish an insertion point, and choose Paste from the Edit menu (Command-V).

4 With an insertion point still established, choose Select All from the Edit menu, and in the Styles palette click 10Title.

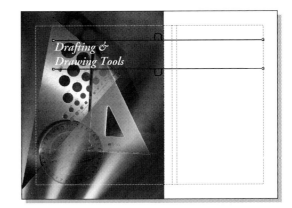

5 Choose View from the Layout menu and Actual Size from the submenu.

6 With the text selected as a text block, drag a right corner handle until it is roughly aligned with the right edge of the text, better organizing your work space.

7 From the horizontal ruler, drag to create a horizontal ruler guide at approximately .8 inch.

8 With the pointer tool selected, click the pasted text on the left page to select it as a text block, and drag it until the baseline of the first line of text is aligned with the .8-inch horizontal ruler guide, with the left edge of the text aligned with the left margin guide.

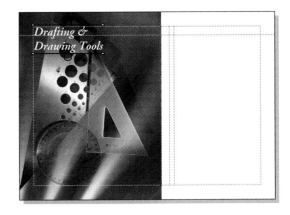

9 Scroll to the right page of the second spread (page 5).

10 With the text tool selected, drag to select the first nine lines of text in the left column (up to and including the text "available in half sizes"), and choose Cut from the Edit menu.

11 Scroll to the left page of the second spread (page 4).

12 Click in the top portion of the right column on the left page to establish an insertion point, and choose Paste from the Edit menu.

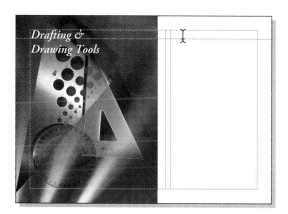

13 With the text tool selected, click the first line of the pasted text to establish an insertion point, and in the Styles palette click 10IntroPhrase.

14 With the text tool selected, click the text below the first line of pasted text in the right column to establish an insertion point, and in the Styles palette click 10ChapterIntro.

15 With the pointer tool selected, click the pasted text in the right column of the left page to select it as a text block, drag the bottom windowshade handle until the entire story is displayed, and drag the text block until the baseline of the last line of text is aligned with the bottom margin guide.

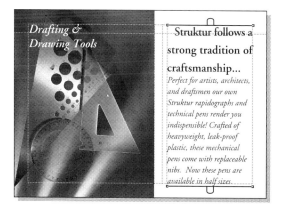

The left page of the second spread is complete.

16 Choose Save from the File menu.

Formatting and aligning text

After applying a style to the text, you will align it on the right page of the second spread.

1 Scroll to the right page of the second spread (page 5).

2 With the text tool selected, click the text in either column on the right page to establish an insertion point, choose Select All from the Edit menu, and in the Styles palette click 10BodyText.

3 From the horizontal ruler, drag to create a horizontal ruler guide at approximately 1.4 inches.

4 With the pointer tool selected, click the text in the left column to select it as a text block, drag it until the baseline of the first line of text is aligned with the 1.4-inch horizontal ruler guide, and drag the bottom windowshade handle until the last line of text is just above the bottom margin guide.

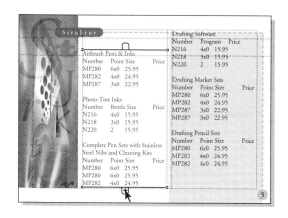

5 With the pointer tool selected, click the text in the right column to select it as a text block, and drag it until the baseline of the first line of text is aligned with the 1.4-inch horizontal ruler guide.

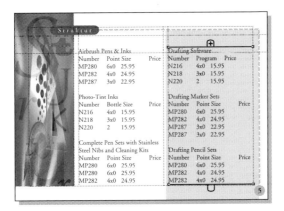

Since some of the text is out of alignment, you will override the existing tab settings.

6 Choose Save from the File menu.

Overriding existing tabs

As you can see, the text is not properly aligned. When tabs are included in another text-processing application, it may be necessary to customize the tabs in Adobe PageMaker.

Time out for a movie

If your system is capable of running Adobe Teach movies, play the movie named *Using Tabs* to see a preview of how to use the Indents/tabs dialog box that is covered in this section. For information on how to play Adobe Teach movies, see the section What You Need To Know at the beginning of this book.

1 Click the text in either column on the right page to establish an insertion point, and choose Select All from the Edit menu.

2 Choose Indents/tabs from the Type menu (Command-I), and in the Indents/tabs dialog box click the Left-align button in the upper-left corner of the dialog box.

The ruler at the bottom of the dialog box has a right indent marker (black arrow), indicating the width of the column.

3 Position the cursor on the ruler, hold down the mouse button, drag until the Position value indicates 1.25 inches, and release the mouse button to place a tab stop (small black arrow) on the ruler.

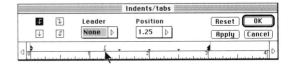

4 Once again, position the cursor on the ruler, hold down the mouse button, drag until the Position value indicates 2.25 inches, release the mouse button to place a second tab stop, and click the Apply button in the Indents/tabs dialog box to preview the results.

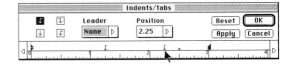

Previewing the results before you close the dialog box makes it possible to make any adjustments to the tabs and indents, without reopening the Indents/tabs dialog box.

5 Click OK to close the Indents/tabs dialog box.

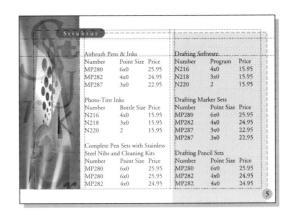

6 Choose Save from the File menu.

Formatting the subhead text

You will apply a style to the subheads on the right page of the second spread.

1 With the text tool selected, click the first subhead to establish an insertion point, and in the Styles palette click 10Subhead.

2 Continue selecting each of the remaining subheads on the right page, applying the style 10Subhead to each one.

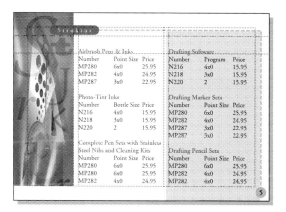

3 Choose Save from the File menu.

Placing inline graphics

When you want a graphic element to remain with specific text, you can place or paste the graphic as an inline graphic. Any graphic that you can use as an independent graphic, you can also use as an inline graphic.

1 Scroll to view the graphics on the pasteboard above the right page.

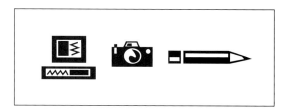

2 With the pointer tool selected, click the camera graphic (middle illustration) on the pasteboard to select it, and choose Copy from the Edit menu (Command-C).

3 With the text tool selected, click just to the left of the second subhead in the left column to establish an insertion point.

4 Choose Paste from the Edit menu, hold down the Command and Shift keys, and press N to insert an en space between the inline graphic and the subhead.

An en space is half the width of an em space.

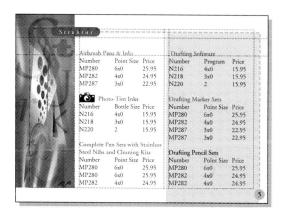

5 With the pointer tool selected, click the computer graphic (left illustration) on the pasteboard to select it, and choose Copy from the Edit menu.

6 With the text tool selected, click just to the left of the first subhead in the right column to establish an insertion point.

7 Choose Paste from the Edit menu, hold down the Command and Shift keys, and press N to insert an en space.

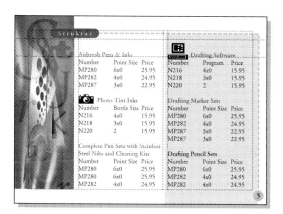

8 If the baseline of the first line of text in the left column is not aligned with the 1.4-inch horizontal ruler guide, click the text with the pointer tool, drag the bottom windowshade handle to display the entire story, and drag the text block until it is aligned.

9 With the pointer tool selected, click the pencil graphic (right illustration) on the pasteboard to select it, and choose Copy from the Edit menu.

10 With the text tool selected, click just to the left of the third subhead in the right column to establish an insertion point at the beginning of the subhead text.

11 Choose Paste from the Edit menu, and hold down the Command and Shift keys, and press N to insert an en space.

12 If the baseline of the first line of text in the right column is not aligned with the 1.4-inch horizontal ruler guide, click the text with the pointer tool, and drag the text block until it is aligned.

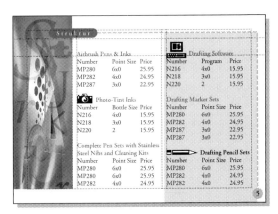

The right page of the second spread is complete.

13 Choose Save from the File menu.

Note: An interim file was saved at this point. To open it, double-click the 10Int1 *file in the* Extras *folder.*

ASSEMBLING THE THIRD SPREAD

The steps to assembling the third double-page spread are virtually identical to the steps you used to assemble the previous double-page spread.

Like the photograph you placed in the second spread, this photograph was scanned, sized in Adobe Photoshop, and saved in TIFF file format with a resolution of 100 dpi.

1 Click page icon 6/7 to view the third double-page spread.

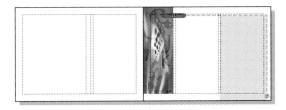

2 Choose Place from the File menu, and in the Place Document dialog box double-click the *10GraphicB* file in the *10Lesson* folder.

3 When prompted, click the No button to prevent duplicating image data to the *10Work* publication.

4 With the graphics icon displayed, click near the upper-left corner of the left page of the third spread (page 6) to place the photograph.

5 With the pointer tool selected, drag the photograph until its right edge is aligned with the right edge of the left column, with its remaining edges overlapping the edges of the page.

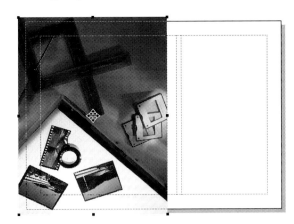

6 With the cropping tool selected in the toolbox, position the center of the cropping tool on the upper-left graphics handle of the photograph, and drag until it is aligned with the upper-left corner of the page.

7 Position the center of the cropping tool on the lower-middle graphics handle of the photograph, and drag until it is aligned with the bottom edge of the page.

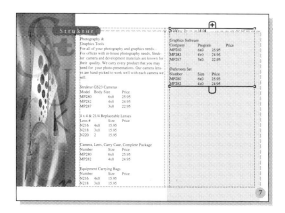

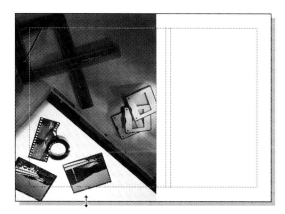

8 Choose Save from the File menu.

Placing text and applying a style

You will place, format, and align the text on the right page of the second spread.

1 Choose Place from the File menu, and in the Place Document dialog box double-click the *10TextD* file in the *10Lesson* folder.

2 With the loaded text icon displayed, click in the left column of the right page (page 7), just below the word Struktur to place the text.

3 With the pointer tool selected, click the red down arrow in the bottom windowshade handle to load the remaining text.

4 With the loaded text icon displayed, click in the top portion of the right column of the right page to place the remaining text.

5 Choose Save from the File menu.

Cutting and pasting text

After cutting a portion of the text from the right page of the third spread, and pasting it to the left page, you will apply a style to the text and align it.

1 Magnify the view of the first lines of placed text in the left column of the right page (page 7).

2 With the text tool selected, drag to select the first two lines of text in the left column, and choose Cut from the Edit menu.

3 Scroll to the left page (page 6), click the photograph to establish an insertion point, and choose Paste from the Edit menu.

4 With an insertion point still established in the text, choose Select All from the Edit menu, and in the Styles palette click 10Title.

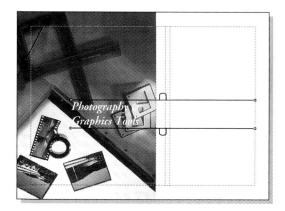

5 With the pointer tool selected, click the text to select it as a text block, and drag a right corner handle until it is roughly aligned with the text, better organizing your work space.

6 From the horizontal ruler, drag to create a horizontal ruler guide at .8 inch.

7 With the pointer tool selected, click the pasted text on the left page to select it as a text block, and drag it until the baseline of the first line of text is aligned with the .8-inch horizontal ruler guide, with the left edge of the text aligned with the left margin guide.

8 Scroll to the right page of the third spread (page 7).

9 With the text tool selected, drag to select the first six lines of text in the left column, and choose Cut from the Edit menu.

10 Scroll to the left page of the second spread (page 6).

11 Click in the top portion of the right column of the left page to establish an insertion point, and choose Paste from the Edit menu.

12 With the text tool selected, click the first line of pasted text in the right column to establish an insertion point, and in the Styles palette click 10IntroPhrase.

13 With the text tool selected, click the text below the first line of pasted text in the right column to establish an insertion point, and in the Styles palette click 10ChapterIntro.

14 With the pointer tool selected, click the pasted text in the right column of the left page to select it as a text block, drag the bottom windowshade handle until the entire story is displayed, and drag the text block until the baseline of the last line of text is aligned with the bottom margin guide.

The left page of the third spread is complete.

15 Choose Save from the File menu.

Formatting and aligning text

After applying a style to the text, you will align it on the right page of the third spread.

1 Scroll to the right page of the third spread (page 7).

2 From the horizontal ruler, drag to create a horizontal ruler guide at approximately 1.4 inches.

3 With the text tool selected, click the text in either column on the right page to establish an insertion point, choose Select All from the Edit menu, and in the Styles palette click 10BodyText.

4 With the pointer tool selected, click the text in the left column to select it as a text block, drag it until the baseline of the first line of text is aligned with the 1.4-inch horizontal ruler guide, and drag the bottom windowshade handle until the last line of text is just above the bottom margin guide.

5 With the pointer tool selected, click the text in the right column to select it as a text block, and drag it until the baseline of the first line of text is aligned with the 1.4-inch horizontal ruler guide.

Again, since the text is out of alignment, you will override the existing tab settings.

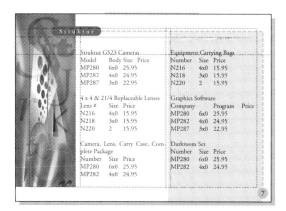

6 Choose Save from the File menu.

Overriding existing tabs

As you have already seen, when tabs are included in another text-processing application, it may be necessary to customize the tabs in Adobe PageMaker.

1 With the text tool selected, click the text in either column to establish an insertion point, and choose Select All from the Edit menu.

2 Choose Indents/tabs from the Type menu, and in the Indents/tabs dialog box click the Left-align button in the upper-left corner of the dialog box.

3 Position the cursor on the ruler, hold down the mouse button, and drag until the Position value indicates 1.25 inches, and release the mouse button to place a tab stop (small black arrow) on the ruler.

4 Once again, position the cursor on the ruler, hold down the mouse button, drag until the Position value indicates 2.25 inches, release the mouse button to place a second tab stop, and click the Apply button in the Indents/tabs dialog box to preview the results.

5 Click OK to close the Indents/tabs dialog box.

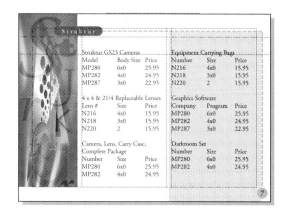

6 Choose Save from the File menu.

Formatting the subhead text

You will apply a custom style to the subheads on the right page of the third spread.

1 With the text tool selected, click the first subhead text to establish an insertion point, and in the Styles palette click 10Subhead.

2 Continue selecting each of the remaining subheads on the right page, applying the style 10Subhead to each one.

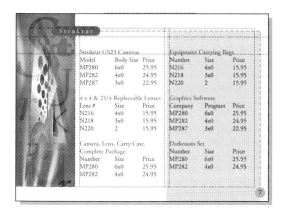

3 Choose Save from the File menu.

Placing inline graphics

As before, you will copy and paste an illustration to be an inline graphic.

1 Scroll to view the graphics on the pasteboard above the right page.

2 With the pointer tool selected, click the camera graphic (middle illustration) on the pasteboard to select it, and choose Copy from the Edit menu.

3 With the text tool selected, click just to the left of the first subhead in the left column to establish an insertion point.

4 Choose Paste from the Edit menu, hold down the Command and Shift keys, and press N to insert an en space between the inline graphic and the subhead.

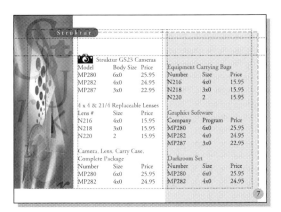

5 With the pointer tool selected, click the text in the left column to select it as a text block, and drag it until the baseline of the first line of text is aligned with the 1.4-inch horizontal ruler guide.

6 With the pointer tool selected, click the computer graphic (left illustration) on the pasteboard to select it, and choose Copy from the Edit menu.

7 With the text tool selected, click just to the left of the second subhead in the right column to establish an insertion point.

8 Choose Paste from the Edit menu, hold down the Command and Shift keys, and press N to insert an en space.

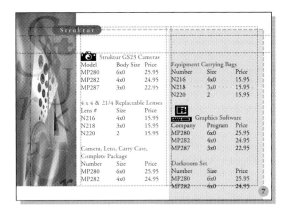

9 With the pointer tool selected, click the text in the right column to select it as a text block, and drag it until the baseline of the first line of text is aligned with the 1.4-inch horizontal ruler guide.

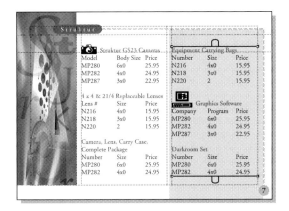

The right page of the third spread is complete, and you have finished assembling the entire publication.

10 Choose View from the Layout menu and Fit in Window from the submenu (Command-O).

11 Choose Guides and Rulers from the Layout menu and Show Guides from the submenu to hide the guides used to assemble this catalog.

12 Choose Save from the File menu to save the *10Work* publication.

If you have determined that your service provider will perform the prepress tasks, you are ready to deliver the *10Work* file to your service provider. Be sure to include all image files that are linked to the publication.

PRINTING THE CATALOG

In addition to trapping and constructing bleeds, the prepress tasks will include specifying a custom paper size and including printer's marks and page information. For more information on these prepress tasks, refer to the *Adobe PageMaker 6.0 User Guide* and the *Adobe Print Publishing Guide*.

Designed to be printed on a commercial printing press, this catalog publication will require four process-color film separations. Knowing your printer plans to print this publication with a line screen frequency of 150 lpi, your service provider will create the film separations on a imagesetter with a resolution of 2400 dpi. Once the film separations are created, you can deliver them to your printer.

CREATING A PDF FILE

As was stated at the beginning of this lesson, Adobe PageMaker 6.0 enables you to take any document and convert it to PDF (Portable Document Format), which retains the page layout, color, graphics, and typography of the original publication, and can be viewed on-screen using Acrobat Reader.

Preparing an Adobe PageMaker file for PDF requires adjusting the production process to take the requirements of electronic distribution into account. Some of these issues include reconciling the page numbering system, combining multiple Adobe PageMaker files into one PDF file, keeping index and table of contents links up-to-date, set-

ting up fonts, and setting Adobe PageMaker print options. Once you have addressed these issues, you are ready to create an Adobe PDF file. For a complete description of these production issues, refer to the *Adobe PageMaker 6.0 User Guide*.

Establishing a printer style

A printer style allows you to save a profile of print dialog box settings, eliminating the need to configure the print settings each time your print with frequently used settings. Since this document is a non-standard page size and orientation (wider than it is tall), it is necessary to set up a special printer style to make it possible to convert Adobe PageMaker files to a PDF files.

1 Choose Printer Styles from the File menu and Define from the submenu, and in the Define Printer Styles dialog box click the New button.

2 In the Name Printer Style dialog box type **Catalog PDF** (to name the new style), and click OK.

3 In the Define Printer Styles dialog box click the Edit button, in the Print Document dialog box choose Acrobat Distiller (PPD) from the PPD pop-up menu, make sure the Tall orientation button is selected (reverse-highlighted), and click the Paper button.

Note: Use Tall orientation when you select a Custom paper size.

4 In the Print Paper dialog box choose Custom from the Size pop-up menu, and in the Custom Paper Size dialog box make sure the Width box indicates a value of 9 inches and Height box indicates a value of 6.5 inches, and click OK.

5 In the Print Paper dialog box click OK, and then in the Define Printer Styles dialog box click OK.

Using the Create Adobe PDF command

You are ready to use the Create Adobe PDF command to convert the *10Work* file to be a PDF file.

Note: If you do not have 24 megabytes of RAM, choose Control Panels from the Apple menu, double-click the Memory file, and in the Memory Control Panel activate the Virtual Memory option.

1 Choose Create Adobe PDF from the File menu, and if prompted, click the Yes button to save the original Adobe PageMaker file.

2 In the Create Adobe PDF dialog box make sure the Distill Now radio button is selected, click the View PDF File Using check box to select it, make sure that Acrobat Reader is selected in the corresponding pop-up menu (to open the PDF file in Acrobat Reader after it has been created).

3 Click the Include downloadable fonts check box to select it (to embed the fonts into the PDF document and to ensure that the type will display correctly), select Catalog PDF from the PageMaker Printer style pop-up menu, make sure the All radio button is selected (to ensure all pages will be printed), and click the Create button.

Distilling is the process of converting a document from its application format (in this case, Adobe PageMaker) to PostScript, and then from PostScript to PDF. For information about additional options (such as file compression, font subsets, and automatic links), refer to the *Adobe PageMaker 6.0 User Guide*.

4 When prompted, type **10Final1.PDF** in the Save As PDF box, select the *Projects* folder, and click the Save button.

A page status dialog box appears and PostScript is generated for the file. Next, Acrobat Distiller converts the PostScript to a PDF file. Once the process is complete, the Acrobat Reader application opens and displays the PDF file on your screen.

Browsing a PDF File

The Acrobat Reader allows you to view and print PDF files. To view your documents, you will use the buttons in the tool bar at the top of your file.

1 Click the right and left triangle arrows to page forward and backward through the document.

You can now distribute this file to anyone that needs to review it by attaching it to an electronic mail message. As long as the recipient has Acrobat Reader installed, they will be able to open, view and print the file.

2 After you have browsed through the file, close all open files, and choose Quit from the File menu (Command-Q) to exit the Acrobat Reader and Adobe PageMaker applications.

INDEX

COLOPHON

DOCUMENTATION

Author: Robin Krueger

Project Designers: Andrew Faulkner, Sharon Anderson

Art Director: Sharon Anderson

Technical Illustrator: Jeffrey Schaaf

Book Production: Jeffrey Schaaf

Book Production Assistant: Necia Doughty

Book Production Management: Jim Rzegocki

Publication Management: Kisa Harris

Photographers: Scott Peterson, Winthrop Faulkner, Robin Krueger

Illustrator: Sandra Kelch

Architectural Design Materials: *Winthrop Faulkner & Partners*

Cover Design: Sharon Anderson

CD Cover Design: Sandra Kelch

Adobe Teach Movies: Andrew Faulkner

Video Consulting: Paul McKerrow

Film Production: Cheryl Elder, Karen Winguth

Adobe Press: Patrick Ames

Special thanks to: Patrice Anderson, David Cohen, Kay Diamond, Necia Doughty, Carita Klevickis

ALPHA TEST TEACH PARTICIPANTS:

Sharon Anderson, *Sharon Anderson Design*

Juliet Butler, *Adobe Customer Service*

David Cohen, *Adobe Technical Support*

Andrew Faulkner, *Andrew Faulkner Design*

Jim Holland, *Adobe Customer Services*

Robin Krueger, *Adobe Educational Services*

Kirsten Moore, *President, Electronic Presentations*

Jim Rzegocki, *Adobe Educational Services*

Katherine Tirone

Tom Tirone

BETA TEST TEACH PARTICIPANTS:

Patrice Anderson, *Adobe Educational Services*

Olaf Besgen, *Adobe Customer Services*

Dean Bernheim, *Manager, Adobe Technical Support*

Greg Birkett, *Vice President, Research and Development, U.S./Grant Materials Technology*

Jessica Burghart, *Adobe Customer Support*

David Cohen, *Adobe Technical Support*

Kisa Harris, *Adobe Educational Services*

Ted Helminski, *Producer, Performing Arts Video*

Susan Hopwood, *Life Coach Training Services*

Robin Krueger, *Adobe Educational Services*

Jim Meehan, *Adobe Production Imaging Products*

Joel Meyers, *Adobe Customer Support*

Michael Nolan, *Editor-in-Chief of Design Books, Macmillan Computer Publishing*

John Roll, *Prepress Technician*

Jim Rzegocki, *Adobe Educational Services*

Roberta Woolf, *Computer Customer Support, The Douglas Stewart Company*

PRODUCTION NOTES

This book was created electronically using Adobe PageMaker on the Macintosh Quadra 800. Art was produced using Adobe Illustrator, Adobe Photoshop, and SnapJot on the Quadra 800. Working film was produced with the PostScript language on an Agfa 5000 Imagesetter. The Minion and Frutiger families of typefaces are used throughout this book.